Exploring Gender: Questions and Implications for English Language Education

Other titles in this series include

BYGATE, Martin, TONKYN, Alan and WILLIAMS, Eddie (eds)
Grammar and the language teacher

NEWMARK, Peter
Approaches to translation

NUNAN, David
Language teaching methodology: A textbook for teachers

ROBINSON, Pauline
ESP Today: A practitioner's guide

WEIR, Cyril
Communicative language testing

WENDEN, Anita and RUBIN, Joan
Learner strategies in language learning

WENDEN, Anita
Learner strategies and learner autonomy

Exploring Gender:
Questions and Implications
for English Language Education

Edited by Jane Sunderland
Lancaster University

Prentice Hall
New York   London   Toronto   Sydney   Tokyo   Singapore

PRENTICE HALL INTERNATIONAL ENGLISH LANGUAGE TEACHING

To Edward, Deborah, Shân, Janet, Julie, Robert, David, Johanna, Christine, Margaret, Jill, Kathryn, Jenny, Catherine, Annemarie, Lilie, David, Rebecca, Fran, William, Katie, Madeline, Ingrid and Judy.

First published 1994 by
Prentice Hall International (UK) Ltd
Campus 400, Maylands Avenue
Hemel Hempstead
Hertfordshire HP2 7EZ
A division of
Simon & Schuster International Group

Typeset in 10/12pt Times
by York House Typographic Ltd, London W13

Printed and bound in Great Britain by
Redwood Books, Trowbridge, Wiltshire

Library of Congress Cataloging-in-Publication Data

Exploring gender : questions and implications for
English language education / edited by Jane
Sunderland.
    p.   cm.
Includes bibliographical references.
1. English language——Study and
teaching——Social aspects. 2. English
language——Sex differences. 3. Sex differences in
education. 4. Nonsexist language. 5. Sexism in
language.
I. Sunderland, Jane.
PE1066.E95   1994
428′.007——dc20   93-41826

British Library Cataloguing in Publication Data

A catalogue record for this book is available from
the British Library

ISBN 0-13-042524-9

1 2 3 4 5 98 97 96 95 94

Contents

Acknowledgements

The extract from Julian Barnes' *Talking It Over*, which appears on page 23, is reproduced by kind permission of Jonathan Cape; the Doonesbury cartoon on page 155 by permission of Universal Press Syndicate and the 'Her story' cartoon from Charles and Jill Hadfield's *Writing Games* on page 65 by permission of Thomas Nelson and Sons Ltd. I am grateful to all the above.

I would also like to thank Chris Candlin, Isobel Fletcher de Téllez, Simon Gieve, Sara Mills, Amos Paran, Jenny Pugsley and Mary Talbot for reading different parts of the text and for their constructive criticism, Dick Allwright and Marilyn Martin-Jones for their intellectual stimulation, and John McGovern for his trust and professional support.

Most of all, I would like to thank the Language and Gender in the Classroom (LAGIC) research group at Lancaster University for their continuing enthusiasm for and commitment to LAGIC-related issues, and Graham for his patience and understanding.

List of Contributors

William Burns	*General English Education Program, Sogang University, Korea*
Fran Byrnes	*National Centre for ELT and Research, Macquarie University, Australia*
Deborah Cameron	*Programme in Literary Linguistics, Strathclyde University, UK*
David Carroll	*The British Council, Cairo, Egypt*
Lilie Chouliaraki	*Linguistics Department, Lancaster University, UK*
Bessie Dendrinos	*English Department, University of Athens, Greece*
Madeleine du Vivier	*Freelance author and teacher trainer*
Jill Florent	*Heinemann Publishers, Oxford, UK*
Ingrid Freebairn	*Freelance author*
Kathryn Fuller	*Hampstead Garden Suburb Institute, EFL Department, UK*
Judy Garton-Sprenger	*Freelance author and teacher trainer*
David Haines	*Prentice Hall International, Hemel Hempstead, UK*
Margaret Hennessy	*National Centre for ELT and Research, Macquarie University, Australia*
Janet Holmes	*Department of Linguistics, Victoria University of Wellington, New Zealand*
Julie Kerekes	*ESL Department, University of Hawaii, USA*
Johanna Kowitz	*RETO, United States Information Service, Tunis, Tunisia*
Christine Mannheim	*London School of English, UK*
Robert O'Neill	*Author, teacher and academic consultant (English Language Centre, Hove, UK)*
Rebecca Oxford	*College of Education, University of Alabama, USA*
Katie Plumb	*English Department and Department of Education, Oula University, Finland*
Jenny Pugsley	*English Language Division, The British Council, UK*
Jane Sunderland	*Linguistics Department, Lancaster University, UK*
Catherine Walter	*Freelance author and teacher trainer*
Shân Wareing	*Department of English, Roehampton Institute, UK*
Edward G. Woods	*Institute for English Language Education, Lancaster University, UK*
Annemarie Young	*Cambridge University Press, Cambridge, UK*

General Introduction

JANE SUNDERLAND

Imagine a school attended by both boys and girls. In the staffroom, a teacher is complaining 'If I hear anyone else telling me that he or she's seen someone chewing, I'll scream. I don't want to know. I just wish they'd keep quiet and let me get on with the lesson.' In the Craft, Design and Technology class, Mr Watson is trying to help a girl construct a bird box out of wood. She is using a hammer, a saw and a drill. He still finds this a little strange – girls never did woodwork when he was at school – but he is trying to encourage her, and give her as much attention as the boys, if not more. She is unresponsive. After the class the girl complains to her friends: 'That Mr Watson. I was trying to finish my bird box and he kept interfering.'

These two small events illustrate the two senses in which gender is used in the title of this book. The first sense is the linguistic, 'grammatical category' sense, as in 'Is gender in the English language purely natural?' This use of gender extends to so-called masculine and feminine 'equivalents', such as *master* and *mistress*. It also extends to linguistic variation in third person singular pronoun usage when referring to a person whose sex is unknown or unspecified: 'generic' *he*, *he or she*, *she or he*, *s/he*, 'singular' *they* or 'generic' *she*. As the first event reminds us, someone nowadays may use *he or she*, but not always consistently: in this case the speaker followed it up with 'singular' *they*, even though *he or she* and *they* shared the same referent, *anyone*. Even in an individual, use of such gender words is not fixed.

Gender can also mean human gender, which can be defined as 'a culturally-shaped group of attributes and behaviours given to the female or to the male' (Maggie Humm, 1989: 84). Learners have gender, teachers have gender, and characters in textbook dialogues, reading comprehension texts, exercises and even test items have gender. The second event described above reminds us that human gender, like linguistic gender, is not fixed. Neither is human gender understood in the same way by everyone. Mr Watson may have been trying his best to help, yet the girl feels she is being patronised; feels that because she is a girl Mr Watson does not trust her to finish the bird box unaided, though she has every confidence she can. Her own 'gender identity' does not correspond neatly to Mr Watson's attitudes and understanding of gender.

Gender can be distinguished from sex. Most people are born either biologically female, with XX chromosomes, or male, with XY chromosomes. This is our sex. It determines aspects of our anatomy, physiology and neurology and may also have a role in shaping our behavioural, cognitive and affective characteristics. Eleanor

Maccoby and Carol Jacklin, in a 1974 survey of studies, concluded that aggression, and certain aspects of spatial and verbal ability, were related to biological sex as well as to social factors, males being in some ways innately more aggressive, and in some ways spatially superior, females in some ways verbally superior. It remains impossible, however, to ascertain the relative importance of biology and 'culturally-shaping' influences on these and other attributes. Sex and cultural factors are likely to interact, cultural factors building on innate sex differences.

Gender is both a cultural and an individual concept. A society's or group's culture shapes, or 'genders', the people within it according to their biological sex (or, occasionally, perceived sex, for example when a baby is thought to be a girl but in fact is a boy). The resultant concepts of gender associated with males are called 'masculine' and those with females 'feminine'. A culture includes beliefs, social practices and institutions, such as child-rearing practices, family, school, economic structures and employment structures. In that these vary, different cultures shape biological males in different ways, and biological females in different ways. Different cultures accordingly espouse different concepts of gender.

From the concept of gender comes the concept of gender relations: relations between males and females, females and females, males and males. Gender relations exist at all levels, from the intimate and personal (for example, ways of behaving with a member of the opposite sex to whom one is attracted), through to the structural (for example, the relative position of male and female practitioners in a religious hierarchy).

Human gender characteristics are thus not just given, but rather socially constructed.[1] Institutions and practices can be described as gendering.[2] Gendering shapes gender roles: what men and women, boys and girls do, occupationally and socially. To the extent that this social construction of gender continues to 'masculinise' biological males and 'feminise' biological females, gender, in terms of roles and relations, is not static, but can be continually reproduced, from one generation to another. This is a two-way process: institutions, practices and beliefs shape gender, but gender roles and relations in their turn shape beliefs, practices and institutions.

The reproduction of gender does not, however, mean reproduction of identical gender roles and relations. Society's ideas of gender shift with time – as Mr Watson is aware. Riding a bicycle used to be considered 'unfeminine' for young women in Britain. Not only does this now no longer apply; in some contexts riding a bicycle may be seen as appropriately 'feminine' in contrast with, say, riding a motor bike. Bicycle-riding might of course be considered unmasculine by a young man, who may therefore ride a motor bike instead. His girlfriend may also be able to ride a motor bike – but when she is with him, may always ride pillion. Such can be the effects of gender roles and relations.

Because cultures are not homogeneous, within any culture and even subculture there will be many 'masculinities' and many 'femininities' – in the underlying beliefs of societies and in the minds of individuals. This can be crudely exemplified by the idea of 'two sorts' of women, say 'madonnas'/'virgins' and 'whores' (see e.g. Sheila

Ruth, 1980), which features in some sexist discourses (see Introduction to Quadrant I). Included in the range of masculinities and femininities will be some sort of popular 'ideal', such as masculinity connoting a well-developed musculature and femininity lacy flowery frocks.

Gender, unlike sex, cannot be an absolute category. A group of girls may all demonstrate characteristics associated by a culture with that culture's concept of femininity, of what girls and women are 'like', but will probably do so in different ways. Alternatively, a minority may not correspond with the culture's concept of femininity at all. If fifteen out of the twenty girls in a mixed-sex history class behave in a certain way, for example presenting their written work very tidily, and most of the boys do not, then in that class tidy presentation can validly be said to have something to do with gender. Not all the girls need to have high standards of presentation before such a claim can be made. Gender is a matter of tendency and degree.

As indicated, cultural shaping, the social construction of gender, does not operate in a monolithic, universal way. As well as being born into a particular culture, a female or male also has an age, perhaps a particular class background, and perhaps some disability. Each of these may have particular associations with gender, and thus may play their own role in gendering. When we add to this the fact that each individual may also be innately different, we can see that each woman and girl will be differently gendered, as will each man and boy. It is thus not possible to see women or girls (or men or boys) as a homogeneous group. To do so would be to be guilty of 'essentialism'. To do so even within a class or ethnic background would be to run the risk of stereotyping: to have a preconceived idea about, say 'Moslem women' or 'upper class white girls', an idea which may have some truth in reality, or may have little more than a grain. And stereotyping can itself play a role in the social construction of gender. Inge Broverman *et al.* (1972: 76) claim that 'sex-role stereotypes continue to be held by large and relatively varied samples of the population'. To the extent that this is still true (as it may be, though the stereotypes in question may have changed), it is potentially limiting for the males and females who are stereotyped, and for the ideas of those doing the stereotyping.

In addition to being a social concept, gender is an individual concept in the sense that it is also something people feel about themselves. They have gender identities: 'their identities as women or men' (Mary Talbot, 1992: 174). Each woman has a sense of her own femininity; each man of his own masculinity. Gender identities vary from woman to woman, man to man, and any individual's sense of masculinity or femininity may or may not coincide with a popular societal notion of masculinity or femininity. Part of an individual's gender identity will be her or his sexuality. A gay woman and a heterosexual woman will both have a feminine gender identity, but these feminine identities will be rather different.

A person's gender identity may include characteristics commonly associated by other members of her/his society with the opposite sex. A man, who may be heterosexual, may for example enjoy wearing women's clothes.[3] Conversely, other individuals have a fear of being considered 'unfeminine' or 'unmasculine', and will go to great lengths to accord with their society's understanding of gender roles and relations.

Just as in any one society there have been, are and will be many concepts of masculinity and femininity, an individual's gender identity may also be both fragmentary and continually shifting. Perhaps the best contemporary illustration of a woman or girl's non-unitary and shifting feminine identity is the superstar Madonna's many and varied media images of herself – but there are less extreme manifestations. A teenage girl may at times see herself as a quiet, serious schoolgirl, but at other times as a girl who just wants to have fun (Pam Nilan, 1991). Different social and textual practices contribute in shaping these identities. The girl in the Craft, Design and Technology class may at times see her nineties femininity dovetailing with the ability to make a bird box as competently as her male peer: the syllabus and her teachers may all have helped position her in this way. At other times, her femininity may lie in being solely an object of desire, in line with the way she is 'positioned' by the front cover of *Playboy* or *Men Only*. A further feminine identity may be that of a clever consumer, this identity having been shaped by articles and advertisements in magazines such as *Cosmopolitan* or *Jackie* (see Mary Talbot, 1992).

The social construction of gender is neither deterministic nor unproblematic. Constructing forces are often resisted, or 'contested': one teenage girl may not wish to go along with those shifting and widening boundaries of femininity within which girls making bird boxes is not questioned; another may reject magazine articles telling her to appear interested in her boyfriend's sporting interests, even when she is not.

Importantly, gender is not just an effect of different social practices, but also an effect (and potential reproducer) of power and structural inequality. That women are not decision makers at high levels can be seen in one televised public event after another, and in most countries the pay differential for full-time work between male and female employees is still salient: in the United Kingdom women still only earn on average 77% of what men do (EOC, 1991), despite the Equal Pay and Sex Discrimination Acts of 1975. These socially and politically constructed gender differences in fact on the whole operate in the interests of men.

The term 'gender', then, is in this book used as a kind of shorthand for 'socially constructed gender roles, relations and identities'. If gender is said to be relevant in a given context, this means that something is happening in this context which is a function of the fact that biological females are socially constructed differently from biological males. Gender does not automatically refer to an effect of conscious discrimination, unintended differential treatment, or bias in people's thinking – though it may, and often does. Neither does it have to refer to something going on within a mixed-sex group of people: gender effects are perhaps most salient within single-sex groups.

The concepts of sex and gender are often fudged. (Which, for example, do advocates of *Vive la différence!* have in mind?) Of the two, sex is popularly seen as having primacy. Deborah Cameron argues that

. . . sex differences are taken for granted, naturalised. We are programmed to look for them, and also, when we find them, to treat women as 'the sex', the ones who are different.

Conversely, we are not sensitised to the possibility of sociocultural differences between the sexes, because they seem to share a culture and a history in common, living as they do in close proximity. . . . These two tendencies – looking for natural difference and failing to see cultural difference – reinforce one another, causing men to be studied and women to be stereotyped. (1992a: 58)

The inevitable result of 'looking for natural difference and failing to see cultural difference' is frequently sexism, one meaning of which is discrimination, actual or verbal, against or in favour of a member or members of one sex because of their sex. Thus when someone says 'Women are good at X' or 'Men are bad at Y', this sort of claim not only denies the huge range in abilities within women, and within men, and the extent to which women's and men's abilities overlap, but also denies the existence of gendering and gendered social practices, and the possibilities for change. Yet even progressive forces do not always concede the constructed nature of gender. In the 1992 debate in the UK over the ordination of women in the Church of England, essentialism was both implicit and explicit on both sides, some proponents of women priests arguing that the Church should make full use of 'women's special skills' and 'men's special skills'.

A less liberal meaning of sexism is the practice of discrimination against women by men – or 'a social relationship in which males denigrate females' (Humm, 1989: 202). This meaning is best (indeed, only) understood in the context of 'patriarchy', patriarchy being a whole system of male authority which 'oppresses women through its social, political and economic institutions' (Humm, 1989: 159). Used in this way, 'sexism' does not mean that men cannot be discriminated against as men; it does mean that discrimination against men is of a different order from that against women since, by and large, and by definition, men have the forces of patriarchy on their side and women have the forces of patriarchy against them. This makes discrimination against men a different phenomenon from discrimination against women, and one which requires a different label.

An amendment to this second definition is that sexism can indeed only operate against women, but can also be perpetuated *by* women. In the 'Ordination of Women' debate, many opponents were women, many of these being members of WAOW ('Women Against the Ordination of Women').

Sexism persists because it is in certain groups' and individuals' economic, social, psychological or sexual interests (or perceived interests) that it does so. Most domestic work is done by women, and a woman whose housework includes maintaining her partner in terms of keeping him clothed, fed and content is conveniently helping his employers by releasing them from any need to do this. Still in the domestic context, demanding his 'rights' may lend a sexual dimension of power to an economically powerful man, as well as to an economically powerless one. Because women doing most if not all of the housework (often in addition to working outside the home), and men being dominant in sexual matters, may seem 'normal' or 'natural', however, sexism often goes unrecognised.

To return to the social construction of gender, the institutions and practices which 'construct' include a whole range of societal organisations and social practices, from child-rearing to employment practices. They also include language. Language can be seen both as a social practice in its own right, and as the means by which knowledge of other social practices, such as work and schooling, is transmitted. Having been shaped in part by language, people's own gender identities may be in part realised in different linguistic practices. One man may feel discussing women's feelings surrounding abortion is not appropriate for him as a man; another, who perhaps sees himself as a 'new man', may welcome opportunities to do so. A young woman who views herself positively as 'feminine' (in the 'popular' sense of the term) may use non-sexist alternatives to 'generic' *he* with a different frequency from one who views 'being feminine' and lacy flowery frocks as something she wants to distance herself from at all costs. And the women in an English language class (or indeed any class) may feel more uncomfortable about interrupting the teacher to ask a question than the men do. As social practices themselves, these linguistic realisations of gender identity are themselves social practices which can further shape and reproduce gender. The relationship between social practices (including linguistic practices) and gender roles, relations and identities is a dialectical one, an ongoing two-way process.

To return to education, any school or other educational establishment must play some role in the construction of its learners' gender. In a patriarchal society (and all societies are, arguably, patriarchal in some way), patriarchal values will be brought into the classroom by learners and teachers, through (perhaps unrecognised) gendered practices, and gender roles, relations and identities. This is true even for single-sex boarding schools where all staff are the same sex as the students. In the classroom, gender can then be reproduced. This role of the school may be seen as undesirable by some parents and teachers; it may be seen as desirable by others, especially if they view the school as an instrument for the perpetuation of dominant values of society.

Learner gender is not only shaped by but may also shape the classroom. Learner gender may shape learning opportunities: for example, if the teacher regularly asks boys harder questions than girls. *Exploring Gender* examines the role of the English language classroom in this two-way process. The focus is on English as a Foreign Language (EFL), though several contributions look at the teaching of English as a Second Language (ESL), and several pertain to English for Specific Purposes (ESP). What is relevant to human gender in the English language classroom is also likely to be relevant to the French, Japanese or any other classroom in which a language which is not the learners' mother tongue is taught – and, conversely, research from other foreign/second language classrooms is likely to be relevant to the English language classroom. Readers are therefore invited to substitute another foreign/second language for English (or, occasionally, English for another foreign/second language) where they feel this is appropriate.

The English language classroom may play a particular role in the social construction and reproduction of gender. Firstly, this is because of the subject itself.

English (like other languages) is gendered linguistically in its 'code', which means that learning English is (among other things) learning to conceptualise the world in a gendered way. (To the extent that this is also true of the first language, learning English is in a sense relearning this.) English is also gendered in the human sense in discourse, i.e. use of the code, in that in many contexts women and men use the resources of English rather differently, for example in the length of their utterances, and the amount and quality of the feedback they provide. This variation by gender may be transmitted by the teacher, or may be reflected in classroom materials – authentic texts and perhaps specially created ones. Learning English, productively and receptively, can thus be learning (or, again, relearning) a gendered discourse role.

A second reason concerns English language teaching methodology. Studies of classroom interaction in mixed-sex classes in a range of subjects taught through the first language have repeatedly come up with the findings that female students receive less teacher attention than males, and that male students talk more than females. Much language teaching methodology is now communicative, in that there is an increasing acceptance of learner-centredness, pairwork, groupwork, and co-operative projectwork, and oral skills are now widely recognised as important. If the practices of classrooms where the first language is used transfer to the foreign/second language classroom, and in particular to the use of the target language, this would potentially expose all learners in mixed-sex classes to an asymmetry of gender roles in discourse, and leave women and girls at a disadvantage as far as language practice opportunities are concerned, in ways which did not occur prior to the advent of communicative language teaching.

A third reason concerns verbal ability. Parents often credit their daughters with superior verbal ability to their sons when as little girls they are learning their first language, and Eleanor Maccoby and Carol Jacklin (1974) suggest girls' verbal ability may be innately superior to boys' in certain respects. If this superior verbal ability does exist, it may also transfer to or be otherwise manifested in the learning of a subsequent language. In a study of the learning of French, with some 17,000 pupils in British schools, from age eight in primary school to the fifth year in secondary school, Clare Burstall *et al.* (1974) found that at all stages girls' French results on different tests were on the whole higher than the boys', often significantly (see also Burstall, 1975). Certainly superior proficiency is often attributed by teachers to older girls learning a subsequent language; girls worldwide tend to select languages more than boys do, and more than they select 'technical' subjects; and in Burstall *et al.*'s study significantly more girls than boys liked learning French after five years' study (1974: 160) (see also Robert Powell and Julia Batters, 1985).

Burstall *et al.* write that their findings 'should not be interpreted as an indication that girls are, in some mysterious way, better endowed than boys to reach a high level of achievement when they attempt to learn a foreign language' (1974: 30). They identify two alternative likely contributory factors. The first is early socialisation and differential first language acquisition opportunities for girls and boys, with the resultant possibility that foreign language learning is more a 'girls' world' than a 'boys' world'. If girls do get more early exposure to language, they may indeed do better in learning a subsequent one, which is of course learning language through language. Secondly, the girls in their study were more highly motivated to achieve success – something which is likely to be related to the first factor (see also Powell and Batters, 1985). These factors would make the foreign language learning process, at least in the classroom, gendered in a very profound way. They do not, however, rule out the possibility of an innate superiority in some aspects of girls' (and women's) ability to learn languages in general.

Exploring Gender: Questions and Implications for English Language Education has a teacher education rather than training function. It is not a book of suggestions for classroom activities focussing on gender – though there is clearly room for such a book. Rather, the book is intended to help trainee and practising language teachers, including very experienced teachers, look at their work through gendered eyes. For unless all participants have spent all their lives in a same-sex environment, gender roles, identities and relations can never be absent from the language classroom or indeed any classroom: because of the variety of socially constructing practices, learners are gendered, teachers are gendered, and whether the participants in the class in question are all female, all male, or male and female, gender is there just as is, say, class background. Participants in a classroom usually speak; and discourse, as much research and several contributions in this book show, is gendered. Some participants may not speak; but silence can be gendered too. Classroom materials – textbooks, readers, teacher-produced worksheets, grammars and dictionaries, teacher's guides – are peopled by specially created (or sometimes real) characters who are recognisably women or men, girls or boys. All these factors can impact on learning opportunities and hence language acquisition.

Exploring Gender is thus in tune with contemporary thinking about language education – that it is not only a question of teaching about the subject matter and methodology, linguistics and pedagogy, what to teach and how best to teach it. It is also a matter of learning, and of the individual learner, whose gender, as well as her age, class, ethnic background and personality, can all have a bearing on her learning processes, the roles she plays, her interpretation of classroom texts, and the relations she has with other participants in the classroom.

This does not aim to be a consistently feminist book. It does contain several explicitly anti-sexist contributions. Several contributions indicate that, despite their real or apparent psycholinguistic advantages, in many areas of language learning and teaching women and girls are, or can easily be, disadvantaged and disempowered. *Exploring Gender*'s intention is to encourage teachers to look at this situation critically, to be willing to recognise gendered and gendering beliefs and practices, to see these as socially constructed – hence neither natural nor invariate – and, where appropriate, to challenge these beliefs and practices. To this end, it intends to promote discussion about gender and put gender firmly on the agenda throughout the whole of English language education, lifting it out of separate compartments such as 'sexist language' and 'textbook stereotypes'. If 'Gender on the Agenda' helps empower female language learners in areas which disempowered them, male language learners in areas which disempowered *them* (teachers' expectations?), and helps teachers to facilitate this empowerment, the book will be doing its work.

Characteristics of that indefinable concept, 'postmodernism', would seem to include nothing being fixed or having one meaning only; anything and everything being capable of being seen from an infinite number of perspectives; anything and everything being open to criticism (not least the criticism); rational thought not being a path to truth or understanding; nothing being straightforwardly causal of anything else; and there being no absolute truths anyway. Some English teachers and learners live in less postmodern worlds than others, worlds where the perspectives from which something can be seen may be prescribed (and may not include gender), where what (and who) is open to criticism may be proscribed ('there used to be a problem with X, but we solved it'), and where what causes what has been established. For these teachers and learners, the idea of 'empowering' or 'becoming empowered' may seem alien, irrelevant or threatening. Yet these processes can happen slowly, in small ways, perhaps below the level of consciousness, perhaps through exposure to an idea or unexpected research finding – without having the label 'empowerment' pinned to them.

By focussing on gender, this book is not suggesting that gender is more important than any other dimension of individual or group identity: race, age or disability; ethnic, class or religious background. A classroom event in one context that is a function of a learner's gender – say, the type of questions she is asked by the teacher – could in another context be a function of her being, say, the only Turkish Cypriot in the group, or being speech impaired in some way (or both: many learners fit into more than one group recognised as disadvantaged and relatively powerless). There are of course similarities as well as differences between gender and race, age, disability, ethnicity, class and religious background. Gender may thus be capable of acting as a metaphor for some or all of these.

The book is divided into four Quadrants. These four Quadrants are thematically distinct, but pieces of the same pie; they are interrelated, with strands overlapping. Each contains several related contributions, followed by one or two Case Studies. Each Quadrant is preceded by an Introduction, which locates the contributions in the context of existing work and indicates how each advances our understanding, and concludes with a Comment, which identifies and discusses questions the contributions raise.[4]

Quadrant I, 'The English Language', looks at English in relation to both linguistic and human gender: at how linguistic practices can shape human gender, and how human gender can influence linguistic practices. Edward Woods considers what gender means for English grammar in relation to other languages. Deborah Cameron looks at sexist and non-sexist English language and the problems of each. Shân Wareing discusses the sociolinguistic question of where, how and why use of the English language varies with speaker gender. Her contribution is illustrated by two Case Studies on pragmatic variation by gender, the first by Janet Holmes, on compliments, and the second by Julie Kerekes, on expressions of sympathy and advice. All this, of course, is the English language teacher's potential subject matter.

Quadrant II is entitled 'Materials'. It looks at the way textual practices characteristic of textbooks, pedagogic grammars and dictionaries represent and potentially shape human gender. Robert O'Neill, criticised for the sexism of his early textbooks, reflects controversially on the validity of this criticism. David Carroll and Johanna Kowitz illustrate how computer concordancing can expose pernicious and often unrecognised sexist linguistic patterns in textbooks. Christine Mannheim looks at the important question of learners' responses to textbook sexism. Then follows my survey of pedagogic grammars' responses to and representations of non-sexist language change. And Margaret Hennessy shows how new non-sexist and more established linguistic items are dealt with in three new pedagogic dictionaries – and at how they could be. The first Case Study is 'On Balance' – guidelines for ELT publishers on avoiding sexist language and stereotyping in textbooks. These guidelines have been produced by 'Women in EFL Materials', an offshoot of the British organisation 'Women in TEFL'. The second Case Study is Lilie Chouliaraki's interview with Bessie Dendrinos, head author of the recent Greek English language textbook series *Task Way English*, one aim of which was the avoidance of gender stereotyping.

Quadrant III, 'Classroom Processes', looks at how human gender shapes what actually happens in the classroom (and, by implication, how it can itself be shaped by this). It starts with Rebecca Oxford's survey of research into female and male learners' different use of learning styles and strategies – a reminder that difference does not automatically mean disadvantage. This is followed by my own study of differential teacher treatment of female and male students in mixed-sex English classes, and a study of how learner–learner discourse in groupwork can vary with gender, by Janet Holmes. Fran Byrnes then considers the role English language teacher education can play in foregrounding gender, and the relevance of 'masculine' and 'feminine' discourse to teaching and teacher education. The Case Study is William Burns' account of English language teaching with a group of future residents of the USA – Vietnamese women, many of whom were mothers of Amerasian children. This is the only account of single-sex language education in the book, and it is a particularly moving one.

Quadrant IV, 'Beyond the English Language Classroom', starts with Jenny Pugsley's discussion of the management structures which define and contain the English language teaching profession and issues of language and gender which pertain to these structures. Following this, using her own experience of simultaneously teaching, child-rearing and being pregnant, Katie Plumb looks critically and practically at the situation and rights of mothers in the profession. The Case Study is an account of the work of the organisation 'Women in TEFL'.

This brief advance look at the four Quadrants gives, I hope, an idea of the range of writers, the mixture of styles, and the different emphases and positions adopted in this book. The range of writers allows a range of perspectives, appropriate for a book aiming to promote critical reflection. The styles vary from the conventionally academic to the unashamedly subjective. Several contributions include a significant personal component: there is a diary, an interview, interpretations, advice and impressions. This personal dimension lends the book a veracity without which it would be the poorer.

Much of the content of *Exploring Gender* is research based: new, original work or surveys of existing work. Some of the research is quantitative, some is based on qualitative data. Some of the writers are coming from an educational standpoint, others from a linguistic one, still others from a managerial or organisational one. The explicitness of writers' own positions and ideologies varies, as does their commitment to theory. This diversity reflects the complexity and richness of gender studies, as well as the interdisciplinary nature.

An editor always has to select. After selection, she will speculate on further possibilities. Many of the topics that have since occurred to me, however, have only been partially explored. It is therefore in a spirit not of self-flagellation but of constructive suggestion that I offer the following (selective) list of areas for future investigation:

1. The extent to which foreign language classrooms are similar to other subject classrooms in terms of teacher attention, for example in level of difficulty and types of questions asked to female and male students; 'wait time' allowed before an answer is expected from a female or male student; amount and quality of attention paid to male and female students in terms of disciplinary *vis à vis* academic attention, praise, reprimands, encouragement, correction and feedback (all the above in either the first or target language).

2. The extent to which foreign language classrooms are similar to other subject classrooms in terms of learner discourse, for example in the ways female students' questions and comments to the teacher differ from male students' comments to the teacher, and in the ways female students' use of the target language differs from male students' use of the target language, in whole classwork, groupwork and pairwork (both mixed-sex and single-sex).

3. The thorny question of differential proficiency: are girls and women really better language learners than boys and men? Clare Burstall *et al.*'s large-scale survey of learners of French in school suggests they may be (though not necessarily because of an innate superiority) (Burstall *et al.*, 1974), but could these findings have been a factor of the language teaching methodology of the time and/or the tests used? A fruitful area of research might be to assess the current basis for and validity of teachers' claims that girls are better language learners, and to attempt to ascertain whether this superior proficiency (if it exists) is linked particularly to the skill of reading, writing, speaking or listening. Could the apparent difference in proficiency in fact be a difference in learning style or strategy? Also of interest would be to ascertain the extent to which women's and girls' possible superior proficiency holds (a) beyond grades or test results, (b) beyond the mixed-sex classroom (see R.R. Dale,

1974, and Burstall *et al.*, 1974), together with the practical applications of this, and (c) for language learning outside the classroom context.

4. The (related) question of subject choice: why in so many cultures do girls elect to continue with languages longer than boys, often becoming language teachers themselves? It would also be of interest to establish whether schools' and Language Departments' own Equal Opportunities Policies have had an effect on the numbers of boys who actively choose to study languages.

5. The sex of the language teacher: several investigators in the area of gender and classroom processes in non-language classrooms have found that teachers treat male and female students differently, but do so in a similar way to each other. There are, however, counter-claims to this: that male and female teachers *do* behave differently (e.g. Alison Kelly, 1988; Frank Merrett and Kevin Wheldall, 1992). What can be said about the effect of the sex of the teacher in the language classroom?

6. Literacy in developing and developed countries: in much of the developing world fewer girls than boys attend school, and female literacy rates are lower than male rates. Accordingly, many more refugee and migrant women than men must learn to read and write English as a second language without the presumed benefit of L1 literacy. What are the implications for these women's development of literacy in English?

7. Lesbians and gay males in ELT: this issue is relevant to gender roles, relations and identities because there is a conflict between the sexual preference of lesbian and gay people for people of the same sex, and heterosexist expectations of the form sexual behaviour will or should take; it is relevant to English language teaching not only because sexist language may also be *heterosexist* language, but also because a large number of learners as well as teachers must be gay or lesbian, while other learners and teachers may hold and express anti-gay attitudes. Further, lesbian teachers may not be free from sexism on the part of gay males in the profession.

   At the TESOL Convention of 1992 in Vancouver, a Colloquium entitled 'We are your colleagues: lesbians and gays in ESL' (Lisa Carscadden, Cynthia Nelson and Jim Ward, 1992) attracted some three hundred participants, a large proportion of whom, in contrast to other sessions, were men. One question discussed was that of different attitudes to homosexuality within the profession, and whether a lesbian or gay teacher, who may be asked about homosexuality, with the assumption that she or he is not homosexual, can 'come out' to his or her students. Another topic was textbooks, many of which consistently focus on and assume heterosexual interests (but why is AIDS not more frequently a topic? Why are lesbian and gay issues not seen as an aspect of multiculturalism?) A third issue was the value of carefully chosen classroom discussion topics, for example, not 'Should gay people have children?' ('This is not controversial; we do!'), but rather 'What are the best ways to end discrimination against gay people?', 'What problems do gay people face?' and 'What legal rights do gay people have, and not have?' Further work could usefully be done in all these areas.

8. Gender and language testing: this pertains to both 'Materials' and 'Classroom Processes'. Work both inside and outside language testing has shown that gender can be a factor in the areas of 'topic', 'task' and 'tester' (Jane Sunderland, 1993). There may be gender bias (a form of differential item functioning (DIF)) in the topics of reading comprehension texts and multiple-choice items (e.g. Antony John Kunnan, 1990; R. Wood, 1978), bias which actually affects results. If results are not analysed for gender, such bias may pass notice. Task type is important, male students tending to do better than females on objective questions (Roger Murphy, 1980; see also Nancy Jenkins and Jenny Cheshire, 1990; Cheshire and Jenkins, 1991). Effects of the sex of the rater and interlocutor have also been found (M.G. Spear, 1984; Don Porter, 1991; Brendan Carroll, 1991). If language test results vary demonstrably with testee sex, and if proficiency is not thought to be the reason, this should be a major cause for concern. Yet it has been researched less than gender stereotyping in language teaching materials – which has not yet been shown to hinder language acquisition.

9. A full critique of Deborah Tannen's best-seller *You Just Don't Understand* (1991), in terms of its relevance to English language teaching. Though very popular and influential, this book has also been seen as lacking in analysis and social theoretical grounding, and as requiring a more satisfactory explanation of the origin of gender differences in language use and some acknowledgement of the role of masculine power (Deborah Cameron, 1992b; Senta Troemel-Ploetz, 1991).[5]

The relationship between gender and English language education is turning out to be a rich, productive and dynamic one. . . .

Note on the Bibliography

All references from all contributions are given in the Bibliography at the end of the book. This Bibliography is divided into four sections, reflecting the four Quadrants. Each section contains all references given in the corresponding Quadrant, plus others – 'classic' works, or relevant work that is not cited directly. References from this Introduction have been included in the most appropriate section of the Bibliography. (References to gender and language testing are in the 'Classroom Processes' Bibliography.) The Bibliography has thus been in part subjectively compiled. Though it cannot be comprehensive, it is more wide ranging than the book itself.

Notes

1. The phrase 'social construction of gender' is in a sense redundant, since gender, by virtue of the fact that it is not sex, is by definition socially constructed. The phrase is useful, however, as a reminder of the way in which gender is crucially different from sex.
2. Among the processes which shape young children's gender within the family, Eleanor Maccoby and Carol Jacklin include same-sex imitation, internalisation of 'rules of behaviour' (related to but often a distortion of their reality), and socialisation of young children by adults (1974: 364).
3. This practice has been institutionalised by figures such as Danny La Rue, Dame Edna and pantomime dames, who are part of mainstream culture, suggesting transvestism to be part of the male gender role. For transsexuals, unlike transvestites, the issue is more likely to be sex than gender. Transsexuals feel they were 'born into the wrong body', and there may be genetic reasons for this. A man who was originally a woman may however always have had a masculine gender identity, and *vice versa*.
4. All the Introductions and Comments are written by the editor, with the exception of the Comment on Quadrant II: Materials, 'An International Publisher's Perspective'. This is written by David Haines of Prentice Hall.
5. Three contributors to *Exploring Gender* do in fact address the issues Tannen raises: in Quadrant I, Shân Wareing, who contests Tannen's extreme 'difference' approach, and Julie Kerekes, who takes issue specifically with Tannen's claims about sex-preferential use of advice and sympathy; in Quadrant IV, Jenny Pugsley, who rejects Tannen's recommendation that we adjust to the communicative style of members of the opposite sex.

Quadrant I

THE ENGLISH LANGUAGE

Introduction

Language, in its different senses, is the language teacher's subject matter. Three ways it has been dichotomised for teaching purposes are usage and use (Henry Widdowson), competence and performance (from Noam Chomsky) and code and discourse (here, discourse in the sense of one or more utterances or sentences which play a role in communication). Whereas traditional language teaching emphasised usage, competence and code, communicative language teaching has focussed increasingly on use, performance and discourse.

As far as usage, competence and code are concerned, gender is a grammatical term: nouns and pronouns can be referred to as masculine, feminine or neuter. And gender in English is in many ways straightforward: *mother* and *ewe* are feminine; *father* and *ram* are masculine; *moon* and *theatre* are neither masculine nor feminine. English gender is thus often thought of as 'natural'. This is in contrast with languages with grammatical gender, like French and German, in which whether a noun is masculine or feminine (or neuter) has to be learned: *la lune*, *das Theater*. Edward Woods' contribution to this Quadrant develops this point.

English grammar, however, cannot simply be labelled 'natural' as long as English speakers can produce sentences like: 'The applicant should sign his name in the space below.' In this, probably written, sentence, 'the applicant' may be female. 'His', in this sentence, is therefore an example not of natural gender, but of grammatical gender, and is intended to be sex-indefinite or generic, i.e. inclusive of males and females. Other words sometimes similarly intended to be sex-indefinite or generic include *he*, *him*, and '*man*-words': *men*, *a man* and *-man/-men* in compounds (*chairman*, *spokesman*, *milkman*). This usage does not exist as a syntactic property of English, since alternatives such as *he or she* are equally grammatical. It is, however, currently manifested in some people's spoken and written English, and is still prescribed in some English grammars.

The story does not end with some words in English potentially having grammatical as well as natural gender. Given the sentence, 'Man breastfeeds his young', native and non-native speakers of English alike concede that it sounds odd. This oddness illustrates how *he/man*-words have only limited generic potential, genericity depending on context. There are two other problems. Though a speaker or writer may intend a word generically, that word may not be thus understood (see Jeanette Silveira, 1980). Secondly, it is easy for a generic word to slide into being a sex-specific one, the classic example being Erich Fromm's claim that 'man needs food, water and access to females' (e.g. Wendy Martyna, 1978: 132). And the story of gender words in English continues. Deborah Cameron in her contribution to this Quadrant challenges even the gender inclusiveness of neutral words such as *adult* and *neighbour*.

In addition to English gender not being straightforwardly natural, masculine bias of a lexical nature is apparent in some pairs of nouns referring to people. These nouns can have very different denotations: *governor* and *governess*, for example, and *mayor/mayoress*: a *mayoress* is only married to a *mayor* (if a woman holds the position then she is a *mayor*). In many other pairs the feminine item has different or additional connotations to those of the masculine. In *master/mistress* only the feminine form has sexual connotations (true also of *king/queen* and *sir/madam*); in *manager/manageress* the masculine form connotes a company, the feminine form a tea shop; and in both *poet/poetess* and *doctor/woman doctor* the feminine form is marked, suggesting that a female individual thus referred to is a rather unusual version of the male (see Muriel Schulz, 1975). Though the meaning of a given word is not fixed, there are constraints on using or interpreting any of the above lexical items without its masculine or feminine trappings. (For a discussion of vocabulary, linguistic gender and language teaching see Jane Sunderland, 1990.)

This situation did not go unnoticed by the modern Women's Movement. As early as 1970 Emily Toth took issue with 'generic' *he* and one-man tents (see also Germaine Greer, 1971; Robin Lakoff, 1973, 1975). Recognition of linguistic sexism accordingly prompted the use of alternatives: *he or she*, *s/he*, *she or he*, 'singular' *they* instead of 'generic' *he*; *people* and *humankind* instead of 'generic' *man*; *fire fighter*, *poet* and *author* instead of *fireman*, *poetess* and *authoress*; and the revival of *Ms* as an alternative to *Mrs* or *Miss*, to refer to or be used by a woman who chose not to indicate her marital status. Non-sexist language did not and does not have to mean gender-neutral language, however. An alternative strategy is to promote women's *visibility* linguistically through the conscious use of items such as *woman doctor* (with, to avoid 'marking', *man doctor*), and, more unusually, 'generic' *she*.[1] Deborah Cameron discusses both strategies, together with the question of standardisation, and suggests how such linguistic reform may (or may not) contribute to combating sexism.[2]

Is there evidence for real non-sexist language change? This must be of concern to teachers of EFL who have no English-speaking environment to test claims of change against. One American study demonstrates change in the language of newspapers and magazines published between 1971 and 1980: Robert Cooper (1984) and his seminar group found 'a dramatic decline in the rate of androcentric generics', especially *man* (but see also R. Fasold, 1988; Susan Ehrlich and Ruth King, 1992a). Cooper did not find a compensating rise in *-person* words – though in my own examination of a 1989 issue of my local paper, the *Lancaster Guardian*, in the 'Employment' section I found the following *-person* items: *delivery person*, *handyperson*, *groundsperson*, *warehouse person*, *route planning person* and *bar cellar person*. Other studies demonstrate change in written classroom work by native speakers of English and in the speech of politicians and academics (Cathryn

Adamsky, 1981; Anne Pauwels, 1989b; Sandra Purnell, 1978; Barbara Bate, 1978). And *Ms* is now demonstrably a frequently used written honorific for women.

These studies do not indicate language change in gender words to be firmly established and encoded throughout the English-speaking world. What is clear is that linguistic variation in this area is well established. In some contexts 'generic' *he* is still used, apparently unquestioned;[3] in others, for example some television documentaries, non-sexist English is now the norm, sexist language the marked alternative; and some politicians carefully use *he or she* when interviewed. Even Margaret Thatcher in a television interview with David Frost was heard to use the phrase 'one person one vote'.

Importantly, non-sexist language is now documented in grammars and dictionaries (see Jane Sunderland and Margaret Hennessy, Quadrant II), whose representations provide indirect evidence for change. It is also advocated in publishers' and other institutions' non-sexist language policies and guidelines (e.g. 'On Balance', Quadrant II; see also Sally Robertson and Sara Mills' 'Gender-free language: guidelines' written for the University of Strathclyde). Such guidelines presuppose that sexist language can be reformed within a sexist society. They tend also to share a belief that language can influence as well as reflect thought and accordingly that language change and social change can go hand in hand (see Cameron, 1985; Marlis Hellinger, 1991). Grammars, dictionaries, policies and guidelines may all play a role in promoting non-sexist language change.

Non-native speakers of English, not unreasonably, tend to be sceptical of change that seems ungrammatical; they may be willing to accept *he or she* as an alternative to 'generic' *he*, but less willing to accept 'singular' *they*, since this runs counter to what they have been taught about number concord. This raises the question (also addressed by Cameron) of which forms English language teachers – most of whom are non-native speakers of English – should teach. This question has implications for the content of language teacher education programmes.

Recent work on language and masculine bias has mostly been on the performance/use/discourse end of the dichotomies, rather than at the codified end. Within this, there have been studies of what Cate Poynton (1989: 70) refers to as the 'phonological stratum', the 'lexico-grammatical stratum' and the 'discourse stratum', the first two being traditional concerns of sociolinguistics. An interesting development in the lexico-grammatical stratum is the study of word frequency through linguistic corpora: in the COBUILD corpus *he* is the twelfth most frequent word and *she* the thirtieth, with less than half as many occurrences (Jane Willis, 1992). This difference cannot be explained by the additional but minor generic role of *he* (Wendy Martyna, 1983: 32).

Many recent investigations in all three strata have been prompted by 'folklinguistic' beliefs about women's and men's speech. These investigations aim first to identify empirically gender differences in language use and second to show how these reflect and can perpetuate inequality (dominance) and/or how they constitute an authentic female language, or different linguistic subculture (difference) (see Cameron, 1992a: 37). Shân Wareing's contribution summarises these studies (see also Poynton, 1989: 70) in the context of the difference and dominance approaches to the explanation of linguistic gender differences. Questions raised by the two approaches include, respectively, 'To what extent and how do women and men draw on different linguistic subcultures?' and 'What is the nature of the relationship between men's and women's speech styles and the power they have at their disposal?' These questions are central to our understanding in this area. It is difficult, however, and may be unproductive to generalise about actual gender differences in language use, since context is such a large determinant of what is said, how, and to whom, and, most importantly, of what is meant.

In the discourse stratum, language is seen as a vehicle for discourses. A discourse in this sense is a way of representing. Some discourses are characteristic of contexts, for example teacher talk in the primary classroom and courtroom discourse. In the area of gender, discourses include discourses of masculinity, heterosexuality and maternity as well as feminist and sexist discourses. Women and men may both draw on all these discourses, but may do so differently. In the language classroom itself there are both public discourses (debates, questions to the teacher, performances of role plays) and private discourses, for example information-gap pairwork. In many subject classrooms, boys have been shown to have more access to, and make more use of, public discourses than girls (see Janet Holmes, 1992b), though it is unclear to what extent this is true of language classrooms.

Janet Holmes' and Julie Kerekes' Case Studies take the speech acts (language functions in language teaching terminology) of compliments, and advice *vis à vis* sympathy, respectively, and show how women and men differ in their use of these. Whether and how such studies can usefully inform the teaching of receptive and productive language in the EFL/ESL classroom are important questions. These Case Studies may help readers think through their own position and possible applications.

Notes

1. See Cathryn Adamsky (1981) for a study of an increase in use in and changes in attitudes towards 'generic' *she*. A further strategy, adopted by some public speakers and writers of published texts, is to alternate between 'generic' *he* and 'generic' *she*. This strategy assumes they are in fact equivalents, equally capable of genericity. To operate fairly, this strategy requires an equally frequent use of *she* and *he*, and no association of these pronouns with stereotypical gender roles.
2. There is now a derogatory term to describe language which hopes to promote equality – 'politically correct' (PC). On the surface a positive phrase, its use is to denigrate such language and their users, i.e. to make it impossible to be 'politically correct' and correct in any general sense. Its existence is in part a reactionary backlash to established non-sexist linguistic items as well as to the much caricatured newer items such as 'differently abled'.
3. Including, amazingly, by some applied linguists, who *cannot* by now be unaware of how masculine generics can exclude and/or offend.

Grammar and Gender

EDWARD G. WOODS

Introduction

Individuals and society have become more aware of sexism and the discrimination that is involved, and legislation such as that for 'equal opportunities' has tried to effect a shift in attitudes (see Deborah Cameron, this Quadrant). It is often, however, the language itself which creates a sexist interpretation. In many cases, both men and women are not even aware that what they are saying could be considered sexist. Traditionally, generic terms are thought of as neutral and natural and not possibly the outcome of the way the language developed in a patriarchal society.

An Indonesian student at the Institute for English Language Education at Lancaster University made the following comment:

> In Bahasa Indonesia, there is no distinction or discrimination in treatment concerning genderism (*sic*) because of regular clear-cut usage of gender and neutrality. For example, Bapak for Mr and Ibu for Mrs. Sandera, Anda, Kamu – neutral for the second person. . . . However, people tend to exclude female from male by adding the suffix 'i' to the word.
>
> For example:
> Mahasiswa = neutral/male student;
> Mahsasiwi = female student.
> Sandora   = neutral/male – second/third person;
> Sandori   = female – second/third person.

In these examples, the masculine form is the commonly used generic form; but this contradicts the opening remarks that 'there is no distinction or discrimination in treatment concerning genderism (*sic*) because of regular clear-cut usage of gender and neutrality.'

Thus an aspect of the grammar of Bahasa Indonesia, as with the grammar in many other languages, discriminates in favour of the masculine form.

Natural and grammatical gender in language

English has been described as a language of natural gender, i.e. animate things are male or female and inanimate things are neutral. Other languages, such as French or German, are described as languages of grammatical gender, where inanimate things may be masculine or feminine, e.g. *table* in French is feminine, *la table*, and in German masculine, *der Tisch*. The gender is indicated by the determiner, in these cases by the definite article.

In English, on the other hand, there is no indication of gender by the use of determiners. The only way gender is shown grammatically is through a reference word such as a pronoun or possessive adjective:

1. Careful, when you open the door. *It*'s just been painted.
2. *She*'s a very good writer.
3. *He*'s the top student in *his* year.

However, there is no singular pronoun or adjective which covers both feminine and masculine genders. This can give rise to such statements as:

4. A young doctor has to spend *his* first years working almost eighty hours a week.

This is not a statement about male doctors, but a general statement about doctors. There are both male and female doctors, but the use of *her* instead of *his* in the example above would be seen as a marked form. And it is generally the case, that the masculine form is considered to be the unmarked form (see also Greville Corbett, 1991; and Luise Pusch, 1980).

It is the same situation with indefinite pronouns:

5. Everyone has the right to *his* own opinion.

David Graddol and Joan Swann (1989: 120ff.) comment that problems of this nature arise in English because English is a language of natural gender. They also recognise, however, that the same problem can arise with languages of grammatical gender. Pusch (1980) noted that in German, which is a language of grammatical gender, where there is a distinctive form to distinguish the gender of the participant, e.g. *der Student*, *die Studentin*, it is the masculine form which is considered unmarked, so that when a person wishes to refer to a student generally irrespective of sex, *der Student* would be used. This is very similar to the English use of *doctor* and *woman doctor* (see Cameron, this Quadrant; see also Marlis Hellinger, 1989).

Custom and change

How people use or react to the use of language which contains sex bias can depend on the context of their lives. The following actual exchange is between the booking secretary (female) of a coach company and the driver of one of the coaches (male) over a mobile telephone.

Booking Secretary: Is there someone in charge on the coach?
Driver: Yes.
Booking Secretary: Can I speak with him, please?

The person in charge was, in fact, a man; but the use of *him* by the booking secretary at the other end of the telephone without seeing the person in charge upset a woman sitting behind the man in charge. However, in the context of the booking secretary's life, all people in charge were men.

This is an example of how what speakers are accustomed to affects the way they use language. If the booking secretary had worked in an office where both women and men could be in charge, then she might have been more circumspect in her choice of pronoun.

Most readers will be more than aware of the language change that is going on in this area (see Cameron, this Quadrant; Jane Sunderland and Margaret Hennessy, Quadrant II). However, this change may not please the grammar purists, as this recollection of a discussion in the novel *Talking It Over* by Julian Barnes illustrates.

Stuart, the narrator, talking about the people in the book, has commented that 'everyone else around here has changed their name.' He deliberately uses *their* and asks the reader's opinion of its use after the singular indefinite pronoun. He then recalls an argument between himself, his wife Gillian and their friend Oliver.

> Oliver said that words like *everyone* and *someone* and *no-one* are singular pronouns and must therefore be followed by the singular possessive pronoun, namely *his*.
>
> Gillian said you couldn't make a general remark and then exclude half the human race, because fifty per cent of the time that *someone* will turn out to be female. So for reasons of logic and fairness you ought to say *his or her*.
>
> Oliver said we were discussing grammar not sexual politics.
>
> Gillian said how could we separate the two, because where did grammar come from if not from the grammarians, and almost all grammarians – probably every single one of them for all she knew – were men, so what did we expect; but mainly she was talking common sense.
>
> Oliver rolled his eyes back, lit a cigarette and said that very phrase *common sense* was a contradiction in terms, and if Man – at which point he pretended to be extremely embarrassed and corrected himself to Man-or-Woman – had relied on common sense over the previous millenia we'd still be living in mud huts and eating frightful food and listening to Del Shânnon records.
>
> Stuart then came up with a solution. *His* being either inaccurate or insulting or quite possibly both, and *his or her* being diplomatic but awfully cumbersome, the obvious answer was to say *their*. Stuart put forward this compromise suggestion with full confidence and was surprised by its rejection by the rest of the quorum.
>
> Oliver said that, for instance, the phrase *someone put their head round the door* sounded as if there were two bodies and one head, like in some frightful Russian experiment. He referred to the displays of freaks that used to take place at funfairs, mentioning bearded ladies, deformed sheep's foetuses and many similar items until called to order by the Chair (= me).
>
> Gillian said that in her opinion *their* was just as cumbersome and just as obviously diplomatic as *his or her*, but why was the meeting being so squeamish about making a point anyway? Since women had for centuries been instructed to use the masculine possessive pronoun when referring to the whole human race, why shouldn't there be some belated corrective action, even if it did stick in a few (masculine) throats?
>
> Stuart continued to maintain that *their* was best, being representative of the middle course.
>
> The meeting adjourned *sine die*.

(Julian Barnes 1991: 3–4)

In the discussion reported here, Oliver pedantically sticks to a purist grammar view, ignoring Gillian's comments that the use of *his* in these circumstances reflects an attitude to the roles of men and women in society and particularly the dominant role that men have hitherto claimed; and that it suggests that women are a subdivision of men in the human race.

Grammar as a meaning resource

The significance of grammar as a resource for meaning and not simply the formalised structure of the language is something which is lost on a large number of people. It is not uncommon to hear a native speaker telling non-native speakers having difficulties with the language that they need not worry about being grammatically correct, as long as they can communicate their information.

There are, however, two things we have to distinguish in the way we use language. We use language to convey information and this is often done very carelessly with little concern for accurate grammar:

6. *I goed to the park.

A child's or non-native speaker's mistake such as this is very easily understood by the native speaker-hearer. The information about going to the park is conveyed, even though the past simple form of the verb *to go* is incorrect.

However, when we communicate we do not merely convey information. Information is only a part of a message. Let us take this example:

7. Norman Tebbit, a former Secretary of State for Trade and Industry . . .

Here, the use of the indefinite article in describing Tebbit's ministerial post is unusual and, therefore, marked. It is usual when referring to former government ministers, however long since they held the post, to use the definite article. Thus the journalist is not only giving us information, but also displaying an attitude towards either Tebbit or the position he held. We are getting more than just information. The information is wrapped up in the bigger package of a message.

In the case of:

8. Everyone else around here has changed their name.

the use of *their* is not accurate according to traditional grammar since it flouts the rule of grammatical concord (Randolph Quirk *et al.*, 1985: 342–3) but, when spoken, would probably be acceptable to most people. The information is clear, but it is also packed within a more subtle message which in this case shows Stuart's attitude to the role of language within gender relations and to the receivers of his message.

Dwight Bolinger (1977: 4) makes the following point:

> Linguistic meaning covers a great deal more than reports of events in the real world. It expresses, sometimes in very obvious ways, other times in ways that are hard to ferret out, such things as what is the central part of the message as against the peripheral part, what our attitudes are toward the person we are speaking to, how we feel about the reliability of

our message, how we situate ourselves in the events we report, and many other things that make our messages not merely a recital of facts but a complex of facts and comments about facts and situations.

What is at issue when we use *his* rather than *their* or *his or her* (or when any masculine form is used as a generic form) is an important part of Bolinger's thesis that, within the message, we convey more than information, we also convey an attitude. While grammar helps us to form messages, it is through our messages that we show our attitudes, and this makes the form we choose important.

Conclusion

If we look at grammar as purely prescriptive, then it might be true to say that the grammar itself contains the elements of sexual bias. But it is probably truer to say that grammar is a description of the way language is used at any one point in time. If we take this view, then accepted lore that the indefinite pronoun is followed by the singular pronoun or possessive adjective, and that the use of the feminine instead of the masculine form indicates a marked comment, merely reflects a traditional use, which in turn reflects a traditional attitude to the roles of men and women in society. As attitudes change, the uses which now help to avoid sexual bias will become more acceptable as the correct forms to use.

Problems of Sexist and Non-sexist Language

DEBORAH CAMERON

Introduction

Recent debates about sexism in language have led to observable changes in English usage, in western Anglophone countries particularly. Over the last fifteen years, many individual language users have deliberately adopted novel conventions for marking gender in the English language, and some institutions – the university where I work, for instance, many trades unions, certain newspapers, various journal editorial boards and academic publishing houses – have gone so far as to recommend or even prescribe elements of 'non-sexist language' in printed texts (see 'On Balance', Quadrant II).

It should be noted, though, that this upheaval does not (yet) amount to any overall consensus replacing the old norms with an agreed set of new ones. Rather, what we have at the moment is a proliferation of variants, and a sociolinguistic situation in which every alternative is politically loaded, because the meaning of each is now defined by contrast with all the other possibilities. Clearly, the adoption of non-sexist language conveys a message about the speaker's political sympathies; but so does the retention of traditional language. Conservative speakers may protest that they are merely using English as they have always used it, but rightly or wrongly, others will see their conservatism as the result of conscious choice. The real change, then, has been to eliminate any 'neutral' option in respect of English gender marking.

This situation poses problems for ELT professionals. The need to give language learners clear guidelines on what is acceptable or appropriate usage is not something teachers can lightly dismiss. But in the area of gender, matters are not clear, and any prescription is contentious. It hardly seems fair to make students inadvertent sexists by prescribing traditional usage; nor does it seem right to impose a pro-feminist line on them without comment. Furthermore, non-sexist language is a linguistically complicated phenomenon. Avoiding sexism in language use calls not only for political judgements but for a high level of linguistic and stylistic sensitivity.

All in all, then, it is important for teachers of English to have a clear understanding of the issues at stake. Rather than simply describe current practices I will try in what follows to clarify the underlying issues.

Sexism in language

Sexism is a system of beliefs and practices which affirm the dominance of men over women.[1] Apprehended by most people as 'only natural', as common sense, sexism pervades social relations and institutions, affecting everything from people's domestic arrangements to their career expectations, from the contents of their wage packets to their treatment by the law – and, indeed, their everyday language use.

When feminists have protested against sexism in language, they have often been accused of pursuing a red herring, on the grounds that language is not itself the problem, it merely reflects pre-existing realities. This argument seems to me a red herring in its own right. Languages *are* social institutions: language using *is* a social practice. There is no reason why language should not be a focus for feminist activism (and no reason why such activism should impede other campaigns against, say, rape or low pay). Moreover, it is arguable that language is a peculiarly significant social practice, since it mediates so many others. Our beliefs are publicly communicated, our social and sexual relations conducted, our laws made and our wages negotiated, through linguistic interaction. Perhaps, then, a language organised on sexist principles insidiously primes its users to take gender inequality for granted in every sphere – in which case language should be seen as actively reproducing sexism rather than merely reflecting it.

Sexism in English

Gender is a salient distinction in English, its importance underlined in ways so obvious we hardly notice them. For example, men and women in English-speaking cultures are given different personal names; have distinct address forms; are denoted by gender-marked pronouns and sometimes occupational titles (e.g. *manager/manageress*); differing adjectives may be preferred to describe their attributes (e.g. *pretty/handsome*) or the same adjectives may have a different range of meaning applied to men and women (compare *an honest man* with *an honest woman*: the latter can have the additional meaning *chaste*. Many words have specifically sexual implications when applied to women.) Linguistic convention thus encourages English speakers to pay attention to gender whether or not it is immediately relevant. We have guidelines prohibiting gratuitous reference to someone's race in media reporting, but these would not work in quite the same way for gender. If a particular individual is being referred to, it is almost impossible to avoid specifying their sex. Of course, it is not necessarily sexist merely to acknowledge the existence of gendered beings. But the idea of gender difference as always and everywhere significant is a founding principle of sexist ideology.

Not only does English call attention to gender, it does so in a way that makes the masculine gender normative. This can be seen in the language's grammar. Where paired terms exist, it is almost always the feminine term that is morphologically marked (e.g. by the addition of the *-ess* suffix in *manageress*), and thereby identified as the exceptional or deviant case. The masculine term is the generic term: *manager* can subsume *manageress*, denoting the whole class of people who manage, but *manageress* can only denote a woman. (The two exceptions to this rule about occupational titles are, not coincidentally, *nurse* and *prostitute*.)

A similar patterning affects third person singular pronouns, with *he* prescribed for generic and indefinite use, as Edward Woods (this Quadrant) explains. The item *man*, too, denotes both the male of the human species and the species as a whole, as well as being a suffix used to form agent nouns and occupational terms (*foreman*, *fireman*). If the paired terms make women appear deviant, the generic pronoun and *man* make them invisible.

The discussion below will focus on the issue of generic masculine terms in traditional English usage. Although a number of other problems could be raised, pertaining to various other linguistic subsystems (such as titles, address terms, insult and endearment forms, etc.[2]), it is this question of grammaticised gender distinctions which has attracted most attention and inspired most attempts at linguistic reform. Partly, this reflects the commonness of the problematic usages; partly, too, it reflects an assumption that grammatical rules are suitable cases for treatment: their generality and regularity make it possible to legislate on acceptable usage. Most particularly, though, the attention given to the sexist implications carried by grammatical markers reflects a widespread belief among feminists that this form of sexism is especially insidious and damaging.

Many feminists have claimed that the use of generic masculine terms is more than just a symbolic declaration of women's lesser (deviant, invisible) status – though, of course, that in itself would be sufficient grounds for feminists to favour change. It is arguable, however, that the use of the English generic masculine is more directly damaging to women's interests: that it impedes communication and encourages discrimination.

If generic masculines are interpreted by contemporary English speakers as masculine rather than generic, as some research has suggested (e.g. Jeanette Silveira, 1980), then it is clear miscommunication must routinely be occurring. Moreover, this kind of miscommunication could quite easily have discriminatory consequences. If, for example, an advertisement uses a job description like *chairman* or *foreman* with subsequent pronominalisation as *he*, and readers of this text interpret the masculine forms as non-generic, qualified women might be discouraged from applying for a given post. An accretion of similar texts might signal to the public at large that certain positions are and always will be occupied by males, thus perpetuating traditional career expectations on the part of both women and men. For these reasons, the Sex Discrimination Act that came into force in Britain in the mid-1970s specifically prohibited the use of masculine terms in the vast majority of job advertisements.

Gender-neutral language

There are various strategies one might use to address the problem of the English generic masculine. Over time, however, the strategy which has met with most support has been to replace masculine with ungendered terms, producing what is variously labelled 'gender-neutral', 'gender-free' or 'inclusive' language.

De-gendering is achieved by means of various substitutions, which are widely accepted now in even the most formal written texts. For example, *man* as a label for the species becomes *humanity* or *humankind*; suffix *-man* is replaced by *person* (e.g. *spokesperson*) or some more precise designation (e.g. *firefighter* in place of *fireman*); compound words in *man-* are replaced by synonyms (e.g. *staffing* or *personnel* for *manpower*; *artificial* or *synthetic* for *man-made*). The pronoun problem is resolved either by pluralising whole sentences (e.g. *any student wishing to consult his tutor* becomes *any students wishing to consult their tutors*), or – in Britain anyway – by using 'singular' *they* (*anyone wishing to consult their tutor should make an appointment . . .*)[3] with disjuncts like *he or she, her or his*, etc. available if these genderless variants are for some reason unacceptable.

The range of alternatives mentioned here is important, and in choosing among the various options there are clear linguistic and stylistic patterns which teachers might find it useful to be aware of. 'Singular' *they* in British English is preferred for the indefinite antecedents *anyone, someone, everyone, no-one*; indeed in this context it is often preferable to *he* on independent grounds, since indefinite pronouns may have a plural element in their meaning: such hypothetical sentences as *everyone came to the meeting and I was glad of his support* and *no-one brought his car since he knew there was nowhere to park it* are bizarre, and only slavish adherence to the prescriptive norms of correctness could induce native speakers to entertain them. By contrast there are some sentences with clearly singular constituents, where the co-occurrence of a plural pronoun (especially if it comes close to its antecedent and is in a form other than the subject case) may strike many native speakers as of dubious acceptability: e.g. *the yuppie who snorts cocaine in their lunchbreak will soon have trouble supporting their habit*, which is more likely to be made gender neutral by judicious rephrasing or pluralisation.

These strategies undoubtedly solve the purely technical problem of avoiding *he* and *man*, and given the range of alternatives encompassed by gender-neutral language there is no reason for the resulting expressions to be obfuscatory or inelegant. But the technical problem is not the real underlying problem. The technical problem has to do with linguistic form: eliminating some forms and finding suitable substitutes for them. The real underlying problem, however, is meaning. Unfortunately, there is not a perfect mapping between the two. Gender-neutral forms do not always carry gender-neutral meanings; language can be gender free in the technical sense without being truly free of gendered connotations, and without being inclusive in the sense of including women.

Problems of neutrality

Some feminist proponents of gender-neutral language (e.g. Casey Miller and Kate Swift, 1980) have failed to take their analysis of sexism in language to its logical conclusion. They have correctly identified a pattern in English whereby masculine terms are the norm and can be used generically; but they have not considered the possibility that this pattern might apply not only to formally masculine terms like *man*, but also to terms without any formal gender marking.

There is considerable evidence suggesting that the pattern 'unmarked = male' does commonly apply to the interpretation of terms that are in principle neutral or, more technically, of dual/common gender. We can deduce this, for instance, from the following examples taken from news reports (Cameron, 1992a):

> The lack of vitality is aggravated by the fact that there are so few able-bodied young adults about. They have all gone off to work or look for work, leaving behind the old, the disabled, the women and the children.
>
> *(Sunday Times)*

> A coloured man subjected to racial abuse went berserk and murdered his next door neighbour's wife with a machete, Birmingham Crown Court heard today.
>
> *(The Guardian)*

Adult and *neighbour* are not formally marked as masculine or feminine: their sense is, theoretically, inclusive. Yet in the texts quoted above, quite clearly we have to interpret *adult* and *neighbour* as referring to men only. Why? No-one could argue that these particular words denote stereotypically masculine occupations (an argument sometimes used to explain why theoretically neutral words like *surgeon* or *astronaut* are so often interpreted as referring only to men). The sexism here would not be eliminated by replacing the words *adult* and *neighbour* – it is not a problem with these specific lexical items. Examples like these suggest that the inclusiveness of formally neutral language is something of a myth. We need to remember that language is contextualised in discourse, where words that are neutral in theory can become sexist in practice.

On the other hand, discourses can also offer opportunities for linguistic resistance. In 1989, the US Supreme Court upheld a Missouri statute restricting abortion rights. A pro-choice pressure group, NARAL (National Association for the Reform of Abortion Laws), took a full-page advertisement in the *New York Times* to protest:

ON JULY 16, AMERICANS LOST A FUNDAMENTAL LIBERTY.

The text went on to refer to continuing or terminating a pregnancy as 'the most personal decision an American can make'.

This might just seem like an admirably thoroughgoing example of inclusive language. NARAL does not specify the gender of 'Americans' – who in this instance are quite obviously women rather than men – because the word *Americans* can simply be taken to mean, in the appropriate context, 'American women'. If we look more closely, however, the omission of the word *women* has a rather different meaning. In a subtle way, the advertisement is precisely pointing out that 'American women are Americans too', so that their constitutional rights and liberties should not be curtailed by a sexist court. The text plays deliberately, for rhetorical effect, on the fact that *Americans* is not conventionally interpreted as meaning 'American women'. If *Americans* were unproblematically a neutral term with an inclusive meaning, our knowledge of this, added to the contextual information that this text concerns abortion rights, would make the use of *Americans* to mean 'American women' unremarkable and without rhetorical value – whereas in fact the rhetorical value is an important component of NARAL's message.

To get rid of sexist forms while leaving sexist meanings intact is a hollow victory. Gender-neutral language represents an advance in some areas of language use, but it does not always challenge the underlying convention which makes the masculine gender the norm. If the problem with many traditional usages is that they render women invisible, feminists can hardly rest content with reforms which likewise fail to ensure women's visibility.

The visibility strategy

Aware of this difficulty, some feminists have advocated not gender-free language but gender-explicit language with a bias towards women – in effect, the deliberate use of feminine terms as generics.[4] This strategy is known as 'the visibility strategy', and although it is perceived as more radical than gender-neutral language (and therefore by some people's standards less acceptable), it has nevertheless gained some ground. (I have yet to see it prescribed in a stylesheet, but most editors will at least tolerate it.)

The point of the visibility strategy is to raise people's consciousness. Arguments that it is unfair (like traditional sexist language in reverse) or inaccurate (it makes men invisible, though they constitute about half of the population) miss crucial points about language and power. To use the feminine pronoun *she* generically is essentially a symbolic gesture: rather than actually excluding or marginalising men, it draws attention to the way women are excluded and marginalised by the traditional convention; by undermining our normal expectations as readers and listeners, it forces us to ask why we take those expectations as natural, and therefore to acknowledge sexism for what it is. (The NARAL text works in much the same way, though it uses apparently neutral terms rather than gender-specific ones to subvert the reader's expectations.) If a time ever comes when feminine generics do not violate anyone's sense of what is natural, normal and right, that will be the time to abandon the visibility strategy as outdated.

Conclusion

The varying usages, problems and strategies discussed above bespeak a complex sociolinguistic situation in which users of English are compelled both to make choices and to be judged by the choices they make. While some are passionate advocates of non-sexist language, and others equally passionate in their defence of traditional forms, I suspect that a majority would prefer simply to be told once and for all, by a suitably authoritative expert, exactly what is 'correct' in each problematic case. Over time, their wishes may come true: as the relevant authorities update and revise their texts, it is possible that points of dispute will be resolved, and no-one will ever again have to ask themself, 'What pronoun should I use?' (As that last sentence suggests, my money would be on gender-neutral variants emerging as the new codified standard.)

This may seem like good news for hard-pressed English teachers, but standardisation has its own drawbacks. Throughout this discussion I have tried to bring out the crucial point that sexism in language exists below the surface, so that superficial reforms (like proscribing some finite set of offensive forms or making all terms formally gender neutral) are insufficient to combat it. Many instances of sexism are manifested not in single words or specific constructions but through an accumulation of discursive or textual choices; this kind of sexism will always elude the mechanical application of a standardising rule. Furthermore, a great deal of sexism exists at the level of our interpretative behaviour, and this, too, needs to be addressed in a different way.

In order to challenge non-surface sexism, speakers and writers must choose a mode of expression that blocks the expected, conventionally sexist reading. In some cases (e.g. NARAL's use of *Americans*) a formally neutral term has this effect; in many cases the sex-explicit language of the visibility strategy is more effective. In all cases, though, making the appropriate choice requires careful thought about the goal you are aiming at and the best way to realise it given the context, subject matter and probable audience.

The feminist-instigated debate on sexist language has had the great virtue of forcing English speakers, whether feminist or not, to think; they have had to grapple with language and its implications at a level of conscious awareness that may be unprecedented, and I believe the experience has been a valuable, educational one. The most effective way to combat sexism – and every other objectionable 'ism' – in language and life is to insist on people thinking more carefully than most are accustomed to do about the implications of their behaviour. The reform strategies discussed above do, of course, contribute to that process of reflection. They cannot, however, be a substitute for it.

Notes

1. Actually, sexism is a disputed term. The definition I have given is close to the one feminists coined the term to express; but in the individualist cultures where feminism has had most impact, not surprisingly an alternative definition – 'treating people unfairly on account of their sex' – has come into being. This second definition suggests that men too can suffer sexism. It is liberal and individualist in the sense that it does not acknowledge the power imbalance between social groups, in this case, men and women. For feminists, it is obviously crucial to recognise that men and women are not equally affected by sexist beliefs and practices. (Which is more serious: not being able to cry, or not being able to vote?) My definition reflects this.
2. For an account of these and other issues in the debate on sexist language, see Deborah Cameron, 1992a, Chapter 6.
3. This usage is far less acceptable in the USA. Ann Bodine (1990, first published 1975) found it strictly

proscribed in grammar texts, and a more recent survey (Sharon Zuber, 1990) found that despite a move away from the traditional *he*, composition handbooks still felt unable to recommend the 'ungrammatical' 'singular' *they*. Conversely, guidelines for authors issued by UK publishers such as Routledge and Simon and Schuster specifically suggest *they* as an alternative to 'generic' *he*.

4. A weaker form of this strategy is sex-explicit language in which disjuncts are used in generic cases (e.g. 'the man or woman in the street has his or her own views on capital punishment'). This has been a preferred strategy in British job advertisements since the Sex Discrimination Act – advertisements use paired terms like *manager/manageress* to indicate openness to either sex (note that because the word *manageress* exists, the neutral choice, *manager*, is too strongly marked as masculine for advertisers to risk it). Legal requirements aside, though, there are problems in using this strategy consistently. Because disjuncts are long winded, many writers of texts other than job advertisements prefer to avoid them. The sex-explicit strategy also raises the question of the ordering of masculine and feminine terms: writers who do use it very often place the feminine term first to show awareness of the sexism of conventional orderings ('The woman or man in the street . . . ').

Gender Differences in Language Use

SHÂN WAREING

Gender differences in language use have been extensively documented, the literature spanning many cultures and many languages. A distinction can be made between 'sex-preferential' and 'sex-exclusive' differences. Anthropological work has investigated speech communities where it is reputed that certain linguistic forms are restricted in use to only female, or only male speakers – sex-exclusive language. Under this sex-exclusive heading come some aspects of Japanese. In Japanese, speakers are expected to indicate their sex by their choice of words: a male speaker refers to himself as *wasi* or *ore*, while a female speaker uses *watasi* or *atasi* for herself. Among the Carib Indians in the Lesser Antilles of the West Indies, men and women have been reported as actually speaking different languages – although in fact these differences appear to be sex-based characteristics within a single language (D.M. Taylor, 1951, discussed in Ronald Wardhaugh, 1986).

Sex-exclusive differences in language use have also been approached from a feminist perspective. Feminists from a variety of disciplines have proposed that a form of women's language exists, which is in some way superior to patriarchal language. Subscribers to this philosophy have included modernist writers Dorothy Richardson and Virginia Woolf, and the psychoanalytic philosophers and writers Luce Irigaray and Julia Kristeva (see Deborah Cameron, 1990; and Toril Moi, 1986).

However, it is sex-preferential differences which I will concentrate on here. These refer to the different ways female and male speakers tend to make use of the same language system. Such differences have long been discussed in relation to English, though early work relied on the writer's intuitions, and perpetuated folklinguistic myths about language. The extract below was published in 1922:

> There is no doubt . . . that women in all countries are shy of mentioning certain parts of the human body and certain natural functions by the direct and often rude denominations which men, and especially young men, prefer when among themselves. Women will therefore invent innocent and euphemistic words and paraphrases.[1]
>
> (Otto Jespersen, 1922: 210)

Robin Lakoff's later, feminist, work, *Language and Woman's Place* (1975), fell into the same trap as Jespersen of making linguistic claims based on empirically untested stereotypes.

It is only relatively recently that substantive empirical research into gender differences in language use has been carried out. Although studies have disproved some of the original claims, untangling the myths and preconceptions surrounding gender and language use is an ongoing concern for feminist linguists.

In what follows, I will review the differences which have been found to exist between the language use of male and female native speakers of English. I will outline arguments in favour of seeing these differences as evidence of women's subordinate social status, and evidence which defends women's communicative competence as successful in its own terms, or even superior to men's.

Gender-linked phonetic variations in English – differences in pronunciation – have been revealed in numerous studies. Peter Trudgill's work (1975) has been particularly influential. His findings indicate that for any given social class, if the variable of context is held constant, women are consistently closer in their pronunciation to the prestige form (RP in British English) than men. This finding has been repeated in the work of Jenny Cheshire (1982), Suzanne Romaine (1978), Lesley Milroy (1980), and others. The explanation first offered for this phenomenon was that women's class loyalties were weaker, and they were more swayed by the positive social connotations of the prestige form. This was supposedly because of the perceived need to 'set a good example' of language use in child-rearing, or because, being dependent on husbands or fathers for social status (within the traditional sociological model used in these studies), their own social aspirations remained unfulfilled. Working-class men, on the other hand, were thought to have stronger class ties, and to be affected by the norm of 'covert prestige', which gave higher status to forms marked as non-standard.

Feminist linguists have, however, argued that the explanations put forward for the phonological differences between women's and men's speech have themselves been influenced by folk beliefs concerning gender roles which undermine their explanatory power. For a critique of these explanations, see Coates and Cameron (1989: 13–26). Milroy's 'social network theory', developed through fieldwork in Belfast communities, provides a more satisfactory explanation. In working-class communities where the men are employed locally, socialise with colleagues, and live near kin who share the same employment and social activities, the vernacular form of the language is used with greater regularity by the men than by the women in the community, the women's social structures being looser. This is in keeping with Trudgill's findings. However, in areas where there is high male unemployment, but where the women in the community share a place of employment and socialise together, the pattern is reversed (Milroy, 1980; see also Beth Thomas, 1989). It appears, therefore, that in the case of Milroy's fieldwork, the gender differences in pronunciation are due to employment patterns, and life within the community – rather than an inherent male class loyalty, or female anxiety about social status (see also Jenny Cheshire, 1982). There has been a tendency in some research to regard women as a homogeneous group and to disregard differences between women, such as age, class, ethnicity and sexual orientation. Work such as Lesley Milroy's illustrates the importance of recognising the complexity of social identity.

With respect to lexis, most work has been on perceived, rather than real, gender differences in lexical use. Lakoff, who suggested that women used less assertive lexis than men – including *Oh dear* instead of *shit*, and *lilac* and *mauve* instead of *purple* (1975) – used her own intuition, not empirical research. While her work is often cited, and was admittedly very influential in foregrounding gender differences in language use, it has no real basis. Carole Edelsky's (1977) work on lexis was concerned with the extent to which people believe words to be male appropriate, or female appropriate. She found that, from childhood onwards, people acquire beliefs about which terms are typically used by women, and which by men, although these beliefs may be contradicted by their own usage. Both these studies (Lakoff's unintentionally) provide evidence of how deeply people believe that gender affects lexical choices. There is, however, little evidence for this.

Gender differences are increasingly being investigated in discourse and the pragmatics of language (see Janet Holmes and Julie Kerekes, this Quadrant). Linguists interested in evaluating and revaluing women's conversational style, and how power is achieved and maintained through discourse, have focussed on:

1. Backchannel support (when the listener makes *mmmm*, *yeah*, *uhhuh* sounds), and other markers of active listening such as nodding and leaning forward.
2. Hedging and epistemic modality (expressions like *perhaps*, and *I suppose*, and modal auxiliaries such as *could*, *might* and so on).
3. Turn taking: the proportion of time for which any speaker holds the floor, average length of turns, latching (when speakers exchange the floor without overlap and without any perceivable gap between turns), pauses between turns, interruption, overlap and repetition.
4. Tag questions.
5. Topic introduction and development.

Gender differences have been found in all the above, but their significance is disputed. Theories for a while fell into two camps, giving rise to the label 'the difference v. dominance debate'. The dominance theory of gender differences focussed on the distribution of power in society, and suggested that women's speech reflects their subordinate position. Pamela Fishman, for example, suggested that in conversations women ask questions, introduce topics and make active listening signals, while men interrupt, delay or omit backchannel support, reject topics offered by women and hold the floor longer (1983). The strength of this approach is that it accounts for how power is wielded in conversations, between a married couple, for example.

The main problem with this approach is that there is no place within it for the value and strengths of any speech style associated with women: all the identified features are seen as markers of submission, or as lack of assertion. There is also the danger of a circular argument, whereby the forms identified as typical women's language are considered 'weak' because they are used by women – the fallacy of which Lakoff's work is guilty, and which William O'Barr and Bowman Atkins' (1980) study of the speech of witnesses in Carolina courtroom cases sought to expose. O'Barr and Atkins showed hesitation, hedging and other indications of self-doubt were in fact typical of insecure or powerless speakers of either sex. These features also occurred in the speech of the inexperienced witnesses (male and female) in court cases, while the more experienced witnesses (male and female) used them less.[2]

In contrast to the dominance line of thinking, the difference model rests on the idea that an important part of our socialisation occurs in single-sex peer groups, and that male and female groups have different norms of communicative competence, boys' being based on competition, girls' on co-operation. These differences have been shown to develop in very early childhood (see Amy Sheldon, 1990, 1992). The strength of this theory over the dominance approach is that women's speech styles are no longer viewed negatively as the product of powerlessness and signals of submission. The potential advantages of co-operative conversational styles over competitive speech styles can be recognised: the choice not to compete for the floor, not to interrupt, not to withhold backchannel support. These can be seen as a strength of women's conversational style, not a weakness, and suggest a different sense of social relations and responsibilities.

Significant work adopting this approach includes Jennifer Coates' studies of conversation in all-female friendship groups (see 1986, 1987, 1989a, 1989b, 1991) and Daniel Maltz and Ruth Borker's 1982 study. The latter suggests that women and men understand backchannel support differently, and that this can lead to misunderstanding, frustration and communication breakdown. Their theory is that backchannel support is a sign amongst women of active listenership – it means 'I'm listening, I understand you, go on', whereas for men, the same markers mean 'I agree with you'. As a result, in mixed-sex conversations, women wonder why men appear not to be listening to them, and men wonder why women indicate they agree when listening, and then disagree when they hold the floor.

A further example of a conversational feature which can have different significance for men and women is overlapping speech. Whereas women listeners are likely to overlap the speaker to indicate support, men tend to interpret the overlap as competition for the floor (see revised 1993 edition of Coates, 1986).

This approach, however, tends to side-step power – the effect of the different speech styles in both public and private domains.

A recent, and well-publicised, illustration of the shortcomings of the difference approach is Deborah Tannen's best-seller *You Just Don't Understand* (1991). Using largely anecdotal data, Tannen makes a case for gender differences in conversational norms which lead to communication breakdown between the sexes. Asymmetrical power relations, or their maintenance, are not mentioned as being influential factors. The book's theoretical basis has also been attacked for neglecting to explain why and how gender differences in language came to exist in the first place. In the following Tannen extract, Earl has asked Zoë to tell a joke. As soon as she begins, he interrupts her, claiming to recognise the joke, and telling it himself. Not only has he interrupted the turn he proffered her, and told the joke he invited her to tell, but it turns out to be not Zoë's joke at all but a sexist one about 'a doctor fucking his secretary' that Zoë finds offensive. Tannen glosses this exchange as follows:

> Most people would agree that Earl's interruption violated Zoë's speaking rights, because it came as Zoë was about to tell a joke and usurped the role of joke teller. But Zoë yielded quickly to Earl's bid to tell her joke. . . . [I]t was obvious that he had a different joke in mind. But instead of answering 'no' to his question ' . . . that one, right?' Zoë answered 'I'm not sure. This might be a different version,' supporting his bid and allowing for agreement where there was really disagreement. Someone who viewed conversation as a contest could have taken back the floor at this point, if not before. But Zoë seemed to view the conversation as a game requiring each speaker to support the other's words.
>
> (Tannen, 1991: 213–14)

It is easy to see why this kind of analysis has provoked feminists to receive Tannen's work so negatively (see, for example, Senta Troemel-Ploetz's well-argued review (1991)). Everything about the above scenario points to asymmetrical power relations – Earl's interruption, the subject matter of his joke, and Zoë's acquiescence. However, Tannen's analysis, which seems to suggest that the remedy is that Zoë alter her behaviour – she should treat the conversation as a competition, tell Earl his joke is not the one she was going to tell, and take the floor back from him – also contributes towards the maintenance of patriarchy.

There is no doubt that research such as Maltz and Borker's, which sees women as a subcultural group whose conversation styles reflect and reproduce their differences from the dominant group, has provided many useful insights into conversation. However, feminist researchers cannot afford to follow Tannen and ignore the relationship between conversational interaction and patriarchal power – how conversation both manifests and helps maintain patriarchy. An alternative framework for research must be found – one that can take account both of patriarchal power and the strengths of women's speech styles.

Notes

1. This quotation is taken from an extract from Otto Jespersen's book *Language: Its Nature, Development and Origin* (1922). The extract can be found in Deborah Cameron's excellent anthology of articles on language and gender (1990).
2. Further studies which have pursued the issue of 'women's language or powerless language?' are H.M. Leet-Pellegrini (1980), Geoffrey Beattie (1981), and Nicola Woods (1989).

Case Study 1:
The Role of Compliments in Female–Male Interaction

JANET HOLMES

Compliments are positive speech acts which are used to express friendship and increase rapport between people, as the following example illustrates.

> Context: two good friends, meeting in the lift at their workplace.
> Complimenter: Hi, how are you. You're looking just terrific.
> Recipient: Thanks. I'm pretty good. How are things with you?

A range of studies, involving American, British, Polish, and New Zealand speakers, have demonstrated that compliments are used more frequently by women than by men, and that women are complimented more often than men (Nessa Wolfson, 1983; Janet Holmes, 1988; Barbara Lewandowska-Tomaszczyk, 1989; Robert Herbert, 1990).

My own analysis of New Zealand patterns was based on a corpus of 484 compliments collected by students using an ethnographic approach (Holmes, 1988). In this corpus of compliments between mainly middle-class Pakeha New Zealanders, women gave and received significantly more compliments than did men, as Figure 1 illustrates.

Women gave two-thirds of all the compliments recorded and received three-quarters of them. Women in fact complimented each other twice as often as men complimented them. Compliments between males were much less frequent, and even taking account of females' compliments to males, men received considerably fewer compliments than women. Research in other places confirms these patterns, though the differences between women and men are not always so dramatic (Herbert, 1990).

In general, then, complimenting appears to be a speech act used much more by women than by men. This is consistent with extensive research which suggests that women's linguistic behaviour can be broadly characterised as affiliative, facilitative and co-operative, rather than competitive or control oriented, concerned with 'connection' rather than status (Philip Smith, 1985; Holmes, 1990; Deborah Tannen, 1990). If compliments are considered expressions of rapport and solidarity, the finding that women give more compliments than men illustrates the same pattern.

Figure 1
Compliments between the sexes

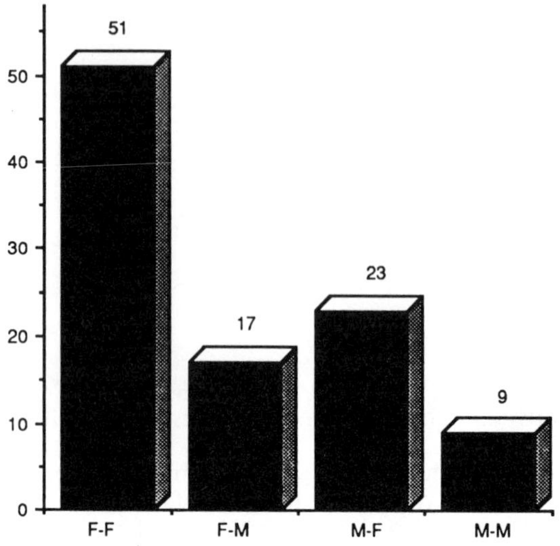

Topics of compliments

Most compliments refer to just a few broad topics: appearance (especially clothes and hair), a good performance which is the result of skill or effort, possessions (especially new ones), and some aspect of personality or friendliness (Joan Manes, 1983; Holmes, 1986; Herbert, 1990). In the New Zealand data the first two topics accounted for 81.2 per cent of the data.

Women tend to receive most compliments on their appearance, and they compliment each other most often on aspects of their appearance. Over half of all the compliments women received in the New Zealand data related to aspects of their appearance, and 61 per cent of all the compliments between women related to appearance, compared to only 36 per cent of the compliments between males.

New Zealand men do receive compliments on their appearance (40 per cent of all compliments they receive). It is interesting to note, however, that the vast majority of these (88 per cent) were given by women. According to Wolfson (1983), the American pattern is different. Though men rarely compliment each other on appearance in either community, the appearance of American men seems not to be an appropriate topic of compliments from men or from women. Wolfson comments that only when the male is much younger than the female does this occur at all, and in general she says 'there seems to be a rather strong if not categorical constraint against the giving of appearance-related compliments to higher-status males, especially in work-related settings (1983: 93). A further interesting feature of the New Zealand data was a distinct male preference for complimenting other men on their possessions rather than women on theirs.

Vocabulary and grammatical patterns

Compliments are remarkably formulaic speech acts. Most use a very small number of lexical items and a very narrow range of syntactic patterns (Wolfson, 1984; Holmes, 1986; Herbert, 1990). A small range of adjectives, for instance, is used to convey the positive semantic message in up to 80 per cent of compliments. In Wolfson's American data 'two-thirds of all adjectival compliments in the corpus made use of only five adjectives: *nice, good, beautiful, pretty* and *great*' (1984: 236). In the New Zealand data, the five most frequently occurring adjectives were *nice, good, beautiful, lovely* and *wonderful*. Most of the non-adjectival compliments also depended upon a very few semantically positive verbs (*like, love, enjoy* and *admire*) with *like* and *love* alone accounting for 86 per cent of the American data and 80 per cent of the New Zealand data.

The syntactic patterns used in compliments are also drawn from a remarkably narrow range. Four syntactic patterns accounted for 86 per cent of the 686 compliments in Wolfson's American corpus, for example, and 78 per cent of the New Zealand corpus. While many of the syntactic patterns used in compliments seem to be pretty equally distributed between women and men, there are some patterns which differ, as Table 1 illustrates for the New Zealand data.

Table 1
Syntactic patterns of compliments according to speaker sex

Syntactic formula	Female		Male	
	No	*%*	*No*	*%*
1a NP BE (INT) ADJ	121	42	51	40
b BE LOOKing	19		13	
e.g. *That coat is really great*				
You're looking terrific				
2 I(INT) LIKE NP				
e.g. *I Simply love that skirt*	59	18	21	13
3a PRO BE a (INT) ADJ NP				
e.g. *That's a very nice coat*				
or	38	11	25	16
b PRO BE (INT) (a) ADJ NP				
e.g. *That's really great juice*				
4 What (a) (ADJ) NP!				
e.g. *What lovely children!*	26	8	2	1
5 (INT) ADJ (NP)				
e.g. *Really cool ear-rings*	17	5	19	12
6 Isn't NP ADJ!				
e.g. *Isn't this food wonderful!*	5	2	1	1
Total	285	86	132	82

Women used the rhetorical pattern *what (a) (ADJ) NP!* (e.g. *what lovely children! what a beautiful coat!*) more often than men, while men used the minimal pattern *(INT) ADJ (NP)* (e.g. *great shoes; nice car*) more often than women. The former is a syntactically marked formula, involving exclamatory word order and intonation; the latter by contrast reduces the syntactic pattern to its minimum elements. Whereas a rhetorical pattern such as pattern 4 can be regarded as emphasising the addressee- or interaction-oriented characteristics of compliments, the minimal pattern represented by formula 5 could be regarded as attenuating or hedging on this function. It is interesting to note that there are no examples of pattern 4 in male–male interactions, providing further support for the association of this pattern with female complimenting behaviour.

In another study of American English, Herbert (1990: 206) found that only women used the stronger form *I love X* (compared to *I like X*) and that they used it most often to other women. And in students' written reviews of each other's work, Donna Johnson and Duane Roen (1992) noted that women used significantly more intensifiers (such as *really, very, particularly*) than men did, and that they intensified their compliments most when writing to other women.

Cross-cultural differences in complimenting behaviour

Should English language learners be taught to use compliments as native speakers do? Or should they compliment others according to their own sociolinguistic norms? This is finally a question learners must decide for themselves, but in order to do so they need information on the areas of cross-cultural contrast.

Paying compliments and responding to them appropriately is an aspect of learning English which can be troublesome for those from different cultural backgrounds. Indonesians in the United States, for instance, comment on the very high frequency of compliments between Americans (Wolfson, 1981). Malaysian students in New Zealand are similarly surprised at how often New Zealanders pay each other compliments, while for their part New Zealanders tend to feel Americans pay far too many compliments and, judging by their own norms, assume that American compliments are often insincere. South Africans apparently respond similarly to American complimenting norms (Herbert, 1986; Herbert and H.S. Straight, 1989).

The patterns of cross-sex complimenting behaviour described above obviously compound the potential for miscommunication and offence. Women from cultures where compliments are rare, experience them as embarrassing. They often respond inappropriately to compliments from native speakers of English by disagreeing or rejecting them. On the other hand, they may not offer enough compliments, by the standard of native speakers, especially to their English-speaking women friends. Conversely, men from different cultures may embarrass their English-speaking male friends by the frequency of their compliments.

Wolfson (1983: 90) suggests that in America the safest compliments to offer to strangers relate to 'possessions (e.g. *That's a beautiful car*)' or to 'some aspect of performance intended to be publicly observed (*I really enjoyed your talk yesterday*)'.

This advice appears to be particularly useful when complimenting male addressees. But it would not be appropriate in some Polynesian cultures as the following example illustrates.

> Context: Pakeha New Zealand woman to Samoan friend whom she was visiting.
> Complimenter: What an unusual necklace. It's beautiful.
> Recipient: Please take it.

The complimenter was very embarrassed at being offered as a gift the object she had admired. This was perfectly predictable, however, to anyone familiar with Samoan cultural norms with respect to complimenting behaviour.

The exchange in this example occurred in New Zealand where there is a relatively large Samoan population. When sociopragmatic norms differ, cross-cultural misunderstandings involving compliments are perfectly possible between ethnic groups within one country. There is abundant anecdotal evidence, for instance, of embarrassment experienced by Maori people in New Zealand by what they perceive as compliments from Pakeha people which go 'over the top'. The relative strength of what Geoffrey Leech (1983: 132) calls the Modesty Maxim may differ quite markedly between groups.

As illustrated in this paper, most compliments are formulaic: they draw on a very restricted range of vocabulary and a small number of grammatical patterns. The linguistic features of compliments are easy to acquire. Learning how to use compliments appropriately is not so easy, however. Each speech community has norms of use involving the relative frequency of compliments, the kinds of topics which may be the focus of a compliment and the contexts in which compliments are appropriate, mandatory or perhaps even proscribed. These norms interact with the gender of speakers and addressees, so that knowing who to compliment, how, and when is a sophisticated aspect of sociolinguistic competence. *You look wonderful tonight!* may be a welcome compliment from your partner, but your boss may just find it embarrassing.

Case Study 2:
Women and Men, Sympathy and Advice – the Same or Different?

JULIE KEREKES

Towards more effective communication

Gender differences in conversational style have been documented for several decades. The significance of such findings is not simply that differences exist, but that they can be the result of imbalances in power (and a perpetuation of such imbalances), and the cause of misperceptions of illocutionary intent and of miscommunication. Acknowledging linguistic gender differences is therefore only the first step in approaching the problem of gender-related miscommunication.

Progress towards more effective and agreeable communication may be possible if the awareness of gender-related linguistic style is increased. However, understanding gender-related linguistic style and associated miscommunication requires, in addition, the ability to overcome stereotypes and folklinguistic beliefs (Elizabeth Aries, 1982; Patricia Bradley, 1981; Glynis Breakwell, 1990; Penelope Brown, 1980; Deborah Cameron, 1985; Jennifer Coates, 1986; Howard Giles, Philip Smith, Caroline Browne, Sarah Whiteman and Jennifer Williams, 1980; John Gumperz, 1982b; Robin Lakoff, 1973; Elite Olshtain and Liora Weinbach, 1987; Marjorie Swacker, 1975). One direction from which to approach gender-related miscommunication, then, is to make speakers aware that their interpretations of the gender-related linguistic styles they notice may be based on false stereotypes. This will require that information on these styles be well grounded and empirically based, as opposed to anecdotal (and possibly biased).

Sympathy and advice

With regard to recognising gender differences and making speakers aware of them, claims have been made that, in conversations between close friends or intimate partners, women and men respond differently to discussions of personal problems, according to their perception of what is most helpful or supportive (e.g. Deborah Tannen, 1990). Women are claimed to discuss their problems more than men do (Coates, 1986; Tannen, 1990) and, while men tend to use advice more than women do, women purportedly express (and expect to receive) sympathy more than men

44

do. That is, women prefer to respond to someone's troubles by giving comfort, describing similar personal situations and offering matching troubles (Tannen, 1990).[1] In *You Just Don't Understand*, Tannen claims that women see this (sympathy) as a way of showing support, while men respond negatively to it, preferring advice. Supported by rich anecdotal evidence, Tannen explains this by maintaining that women tend to focus on the connection element of a conversation, while men focus on status, or saving face; consequently, their interpretations of a given speech act can be quite contradictory. This explanation may reflect culturally biased interpretations and expectations (i.e. that women prefer sympathy when men prefer advice), as opposed to taking heed of the importance of reducing miscommunication by overcoming false stereotypes. It is also questionable whether such generalisations are applicable across cultures, age groups, and socioeconomic classes. To date, due to a lack of empirical evidence to support claims about gender differences in the use and perception of sympathy and advice, it has not been determined to what extent they are projections of stereotypes (perpetuated, for example, by the media), and to what degree they are accurate.

Evidence

This study investigated how female and male subjects differentiate between sympathy and advice as ways of responding to someone with a problem, and whether their perceptions and use of sympathy and advice vary according to their gender (see also Julie Kerekes, 1992a, 1992b, 1992c). In order to support Tannen's claims about gender differences regarding sympathy and advice, it would have to be shown that at least in certain contexts women do indeed use more sympathy than men, and that men use more advice. It would also have to be shown that in such contexts women perceive sympathy as a more supportive way of responding to someone's troubles than giving advice, while the opposite would be shown for men.

For this preliminary examination, 140 university students of diverse cultural, ethnic and native language backgrounds (and from a range of academic fields) completed written discourse completion tasks and listened to tape-recorded dialogues between American women and men discussing problems and situations in their everyday lives (Kerekes, 1992c). The topics discussed pertained to school and other personal experiences with which most students are familiar, such as minor health matters and lack of time for everyday activities.

The subjects were instructed to imagine themselves talking on the telephone to a friend (of the opposite sex) who was describing a problem, and to write what their response would be. Responses were subsequently categorised as sympathy, advice, a combination of both, or neither. Sample responses, taken from the data, can be seen below. Advice responses commonly began with 'Why don't you . . . ' or 'You should . . . ' and contained direct suggestions as to how the person with the problem might go about solving it. Sympathy responses were those in which the subject related a similar experience in her/his own life (as in 'I know how you feel . . . ' and 'Yeah, I know . . . ') and/or used phrases such as 'I'm sorry', and 'That's too bad.'

Sample discourse completion task with sample responses:

A: My housemates are really annoying me. They never wash their dishes!

B: Why don't you have a house meeting and discuss it? (*advice*)

B: I know how that goes. I have the same problem. (*sympathy*)

B: That's too bad. Why don't you tell them to do it and no buts about it. (*both*)

B: Oh, how do you feel about that? (*neither*)

Contrary to Tannen's (1990) claims that females offer more sympathy and males offer more advice, the female and male subjects in this database did not differ significantly in their choice: females and males chose to respond with sympathy and advice with essentially the same frequency. On the other hand, the subjects as a whole did make differential use of sympathy and advice, in that 'advice' responses were offered by the subjects, both female and male, much more frequently than 'sympathy' responses. Advice was chosen approximately 64 per cent of the time over all, sympathy only about 16 per cent of the time. There was no statistically significant difference between female and male subjects' responses (these results do not include the small amount of data from those subjects whose responses were combinations of sympathy and advice ('both'), or whose responses were neither sympathy nor advice ('neither')).

Supportiveness ratings of sympathy and advice

In order to determine whether women and men differ in their perceptions of sympathy and advice, the same 140 subjects listened to tape-recorded dialogues (of a format similar to those in the discourse completion task). Each consisted of a woman and man conversing with one another. In each, one person had a problem and the other responded by offering advice or sympathy, as previously defined. After listening to these dialogues, the subjects rated each response on a scale from 1 to 7 for supportiveness, i.e. how emotionally supportive the second speaker's response was.

Here, again contrary to Tannen's claims, female and male subjects did not differ significantly in their perceptions of the supportiveness value of sympathy and advice responses. In fact, both women and men rated sympathy responses as significantly more supportive than advice responses.[2] This is interesting in light of the fact that even though the subjects perceived sympathy as more supportive than advice, the majority of them chose to offer advice over sympathy – with no significant gender differences.

A need for further investigation

Empirically based inquiry has just begun to probe claims and propose explanations of whether, how and why women and men differ in their use and perceptions of sympathy and advice.[3] Investigations of this sort can help to dispel folklinguistic beliefs which influence people's interpretations, consequent misunderstandings and potentially damaging views, and to encourage a more objective acceptance of cultural, gender-related and individual differences in linguistic style. Findings from this study indicate that claims such as those made by Tannen may not apply to a wide range of people and cultures.

No one kind of investigative approach has a monopoly on validity (David Brinberg and Joseph McGrath, 1985; Craig Chaudron, Graham Crookes and Michael Long, 1988), and controlled investigations as well as more naturalistic ones are necessary. Naturalistic studies of female and male speaking styles in real situations, where women and men do not necessarily communicate in exactly comparable contexts or about exactly comparable topics, would help place the findings presented here in perspective. It may also be that the categories of sympathy and advice are more complex than their representations here, and that a more discriminating system of categorisation is necessary. The use of questions, for example, as they relate to sympathy and advice, has yet to be analysed (but see Alice Freed and Alice Greenwood, 1992, for gender-related differences and similarities in the use of questions). Finally, results of future investigations should be disseminated through the media and education as one contribution to help reduce the impact of stereotypes and false folklinguistic beliefs about women's and men's communicative styles.

Notes

I am grateful to Craig Chaudron, Graham Crookes and Gabi Kasper for insightful comments on an earlier draft of this chapter.

1. For the purposes of this discussion, such responses are included under the category of sympathy, in contrast to advice.
2. Sympathy items were rated 5.373 by all subjects, and advice items were rated 4.867; $F = 17.463$, df $(1,128)$, $p < 0.001$. For further details of the statistical analyses, see Kerekes, 1992c.
3. Some psychological studies have touched on sympathy, advice and/or gender issues in conversational style (Elizabeth Aries and Fern Johnson, 1983; Leslie Baxter, 1984; Francesca Cancian and Steven Gordon, 1988; Nancy Eisenberg, Richard Fabes, Mark Schaller and Paul Miller, 1989; Bernice Lott, 1987; Clifford Notarius and Lisa Herrick, 1988), but no conclusions have yet been drawn specifically about gender-related style regarding the uses and perception of sympathy and advice.

Comment

Conscientious English language teachers have a lot on their plate. The obligation to teach English as it is used, it is suggested, now extends to teaching a balance of traditional and non-sexist language. And non-sexist language is unlikely to be just a fashion. This means that regardless of a teacher's personal opinions about non-sexist language change, these forms should be taught – as should any reasonably established aspect of language. Yet support and guidance are needed, in the form of pre- and in-service education, textbooks and teachers' guides to those textbooks, as well as grammars and dictionaries. Such support is especially necessary for teachers of English working in areas where the only English spoken is in the classroom.

The development of non-sexist language described in this Quadrant points to the interrelatedness of the Sausseurean dichotomy of synchronic and diachronic in respect of linguistic variation. Non-sexist language began as a form of synchronic variation, i.e. linguistic items used by certain groups at a certain time. In this case, these groups and the time were feminists in the early 1970s who were interested in language and its effect on consciousness, and in practising what they believed. This synchronic variation did not die out; rather, it spread, resulting in diachronic variation – linguistic change over time. Non-sexist language change thus has not been homogeneous. On a practical level, this very heterogeneity has made an increasing number of people think about the language they use, what it really means, and the effect it has – a valuable educational experience, as Deborah Cameron suggests.

Because of the common sense understanding of the 'generics' *he* and *man* ('of course I mean *she/woman* too!'), and the increase in use of alternative forms, non-sexist language change is an excellent candidate for language awareness work, particularly critical language awareness (see Norman Fairclough, 1992). It is important for learners to realise that the recent change in gender words is not an isolated phenomenon, but rather that all aspects of language – phonology, lexis and syntax – are capable of change. It is also important for them to be aware that language can change indirectly, through natural processes, or through conscious change leading to deliberate intervention, followed by conscious or unconscious change in still other individuals and groups (see Barbara Bate, 1978). Third person singular pronouns have been a target not only of twentieth-century feminists but also of early grammarians, who were variously concerned about order (male before female), inclusiveness (*he* includes *she*) and 'singular' *they* (to be replaced by 'generic' *he*) (see Ann Bodine, 1990).

A further aspect of critical language awareness in the area of gender is an understanding of resistance to change, in the form of the arguments raised against it. These include 'it's a trivial concern', 'language is not sexist anyway' and 'non-sexist change is stylistically unacceptable' (see Maija Blaubergs, 1980; Nancy Henley, 1987). Several such arguments are illustrated in Julian Barnes' fictional discussion in Edward Woods' contribution. (Many teachers will have had similar discussions in their own classrooms.) Also needing recognition are the 'strategies for containment' of non-sexist language, including marginalisation of its users' trivialisation of the issue (Norman Fairclough and Marilyn Martin-Jones, Lancaster University lecture handout, 1993 unpubl.). One particular strategy for containment, which can perhaps best be described as sensationalisation, represents a confusion between, on the one hand, identification of sexist language and complaints of exclusion, and, on the other, enforced prescription/proscription. Women's claims that they are excluded by titles such as *The Ascent of Man* are a challenge to traditional, sexist language and a form of resistance to it: they are rarely translated into a requirement that people should be forced against their will to change their language use. Contrary to the beliefs of those who see (or maliciously represent) the advocation of non-sexist language as 'thought-policing', people cannot normally be made to write, speak, or think differently.

Most non-sexist guidelines and policies are voluntary, one exception being those of *ELT Journal*, whose 'Guide for Contributors' includes: 'The use of 'he', 'his', etc. (or 'she', 'her', etc.) is acceptable only when a definite individual is referred to. Please use 'he or she', 'his or hers', etc., or plural nouns: 'teachers', 'students', etc.' Certainly, the role of non-sexist guidelines in language change needs research. One question guidelines such as those produced by the National Union of Journalists, and by Sally Robertson and Sara Mills for Strathclyde University, raise is the effectiveness of guidelines alone, and whether they need to be part of a package of measures, including 'staff development' sessions and consultation with staff at all levels (see Susan Ehrlich and Ruth King, 1992b).[1]

Conscientious English language teachers, it is also suggested, need to be aware of sex-preferential language as uncovered by work in pragmatics, and to decide if findings should affect what they teach their male and female students. Most teachers would probably claim that the language use they teach is not sex differentiated, and that it should not be. Yet the studies summarised by Shân Wareing suggest that women and men, boys and girls have different discoursal norms when it comes to communicating, and Janet Holmes' and Julie Kerekes' studies remind us that there *are* sex-preferential pragmatic gender differences in language use. So *should* teachers teach conversational skills and language functions in a way they feel is appropriate to the gender of their learners?

One concept that can be brought into play here is that of communicative competence, developed by Dell Hymes (1971) to include sociocultural factors, and a goal of much modern language teaching. Associated with communicative competence is the notion of 'appropriacy', which is central to the notion of 'sociolinguistic competence', claimed to be one of the components of communicative competence (Michael Canale and Merrill Swain, 1980; Canale, 1983). Canale and Swain refer to 'sociocultural rules of use', the primary focus of which 'is on the extent to which certain propositions and communicative functions are appropriate within a given sociocultural context depending on contextual factors such as topic, role of participants, setting and norms of interaction' (1980: 30). 'Role' may include language users' gender – but it is hard to conceptualise 'norms of interaction' within gender relations since these are fluid and continually being negotiated. Further, norms of interaction that do exist in gender relations rarely assume gender equality. To give a crude example, if men take more and longer turns than women in much mixed-sex conversation, and if most women and men do not experience this as inappropriate (whether they question it, or not), is this what we should teach?[2]

Compliments are an interesting case in point. Do we accept Holmes' data, say 'Well, women compliment more, that's nice, and they compliment each other more than they compliment men – that's female mutual support, isn't it?', and do more work on compliments with girls than with boys? Not necessarily. Frequency is not the whole story: also important is what is intended by a compliment, and how it is received. What may appear on the surface as a male–female 'compliment' may be verbal sexual harassment, intended as such and unwanted. A compliment is like any speech act: what may look like a compliment in terms of its lexical or grammatical exponents may be intended and perceived as one in one context (depending on who is speaking to whom, where and when), and neither intended nor perceived as one in another.

'Appropriacy' is thus a problematic notion for English language teaching. There is certainly no guarantee that it is a justifiable or even useful pedagogic goal. Norman Fairclough questions it on the grounds that it always begs the questions 'appropriate for whom?', and 'appropriate according to whom?' (1992: 52). The only real judge of the appropriacy of a compliment would seem to be the recipient, who will make such a judgement in the light of the context and her relationship with the complimenter. This fact can be taught, with implications for giving and interpreting compliments – though this may be unnecessary, since the same situation is likely to obtain in the first language. Certainly, providing students with a league table of who is most likely to compliment whom would seem to be missing the point as far as learning to express and interpret compliments is concerned.

Whether or not we teach gender-characteristic language also begs the question 'gender-characteristic through difference or through dominance?' To accept even in part the dominance model would suggest that girls' and women's communicative norms are related to their lack of power in many contexts. Whatever combination of processes is responsible, in a male-dominated society (however this is measured), any gender difference identified in language use seems unlikely to have come about without being related to masculine power and the gendered nature of beliefs and social practices. And because of the 'two-way process' relationship between gender (roles, relations and identities) and social practices in language, gender differences in language use may act to reproduce patterns of male dominance. Children's socialisation is a case in point. As Deborah Cameron points out in her review of Deborah Tannen's *You Just Don't Understand*, our society is primarily 'heterosocial', and the 'homosocial' relations enjoyed by young children are precisely a preparation for this (Cameron, 1992b). Leaving aside the fact that gender differences in language use are highly context specific, trying to reflect findings of differences in the language classroom would be to risk recycling and reproducing those heterosocial power relations.[3]

A suspicion of the difference approach does not, of course, mean refusing to sanction the teaching of gender-characteristic language. As Shân Wareing reminds us, the study of women's speech in both mixed-sex and single-sex contexts points to women's strengths – the provision of feedback, the relatively few interruptions – which should be replicated. Janet Holmes (Quadrant III) recommends the teaching of these strengths to both male and female learners – and recent work on testing oral English as a mother tongue (Jenny Cheshire and Nancy Jenkins, 1990, 1991) suggests this can be done.

Notes

1. Feminist theorists of a psychoanalytic persuasion may claim that since language as a whole set of signs and meanings constructs sexual difference, the replacement of a single identifiably sexist word by a non-sexist variant is misguided as far as genuine social and psychological change is concerned (Maria Black and Rosalind Coward, 1990; Julia Kristeva, 1986). Their analysis may be a valid one for an understanding of the social construction of gender. But it is precisely this replacement of a sexist word by a non-sexist one that English teachers have to deal with.
2. In that we tend to pay more attention to male students, this is in effect what we do (see Jane Sunderland, Quadrant III).
3. There may be exceptional areas of language use in which teaching male and female learners different things is justified. One such area may be phonology, since this may be a factor of sex as well as gender: Ruth Brend (1983) comments on her male students having 'feminine' English intonation after learning and only hearing English from her.

Quadrant II

MATERIALS

Introduction

Published English language teaching materials, particularly those intended for TEFL, have for many years now been analysed for their representation of female and male characters. Most studies have been of textbooks, though work has also been done on dictionaries, pedagogic grammars and tests.

One of the main roles of a textbook is to provide samples of use, which illustrates usage. Dictionaries and pedagogic grammars, in contrast, usually provide information about language usage (definitions and rules) before use (examples), giving dictionary and pedagogic grammar writers less scope for creativity than textbook writers. The wording of those dictionary and pedagogic grammar entries which refer to 'gendered' language uses and usages is discussed in my own and Margaret Hennessy's contributions to this Quadrant. Gender can be found in language tests in both content and tasks, either of which, results suggest, may favour female or male testees. (Tests are briefly discussed in the main Introduction to this book. For references, see the 'Classroom Processes' Bibliography at the end of the book.)

In what follows, I will be referring mainly to textbooks, which seem the most prototypical as well as the most researched of language learning materials.

Content analyses of English language textbooks have uncovered different dimensions of sexism, in texts and visuals. These can be categorised as follows:

(a) Invisibility, i.e. fewer female than male characters (e.g. Karen Porecca, 1984).

(b) Occupational stereotyping, in both type and range of jobs, i.e. women characters not only in fewer and more menial occupational roles than men, but also in roles that offer them a worse deal in the job market than they actually have (e.g. Betty Schmitz, 1975). Kata Ittzes observes of Hungarian EFL textbooks, '[they] tell us how women perhaps lived twenty or forty years ago' (1978: 23). When men are shown performing housework tasks, they may do these badly: the 'inadequate male' stereotype (Joy Pascoe, 1989).

(c) Relationship stereotyping, i.e. women seen more often in relation to men than men are to women, usually in a relationship of flaunted heterosexuality or a perpetually happy nuclear family, and associated strongly with the domestic sphere (e.g. Pat Hartman and Elliot Judd, 1978). Jenny Pugsley notes the irony of this in the light of the claim that 65 per cent of the world's work is performed by women (1988: 3).

(d) Personal characteristic stereotyping, e.g. women as over-emotional and timid (e.g. Sandra Talansky, 1986).

(e) Disempowering discourse roles for female characters, i.e. women and girls speaking less than boys and men, initiating less in mixed-sex dialogues, and exemplifying different and less assertive language functions (e.g. ETHEL, 1980).

(f) What Betty Schmitz (1975) has described as 'degradation' – blatant sexism often to the point of misogyny.

Referring to one particular 'major coursebook', Pugsley observes that:

> within the space of some fifteen pages [it] offers us the following examples . . . girl in short skirt creating havoc among traffic, biography of a woman teacher (sewing, cooking, marrying, producing children – but no teacher training), the brassiere of Jane Russell, and – example by omission – the grammatical area of comparison, taking nationalities as a topic, but without a single female national. (1988: 3)

Studies of textbooks thus suggest that the fictional female characters who exist in their pages are neither authentic nor positive role models – two possible (though often non-compatible) models for female characters in a progressive language textbook (see also Question 2, below).

Textbook sexism is not only revealed through content analysis. Linguistic analysis itself may also be revealing. Joy Pascoe (1989) found for example that of the 'sex-specific' uses of *he* in *Streamline Departures* (1978), 75 per cent referred to male characters. In the newer *Headway* (1986), however, only 45 per cent did so. Computer concordancing can also investigate linguistic patternings that would not be otherwise accessible, and which may be particularly pernicious – as David Carroll and Johanna Kowitz convincingly demonstrate in their contribution to this Quadrant.[1]

Although the textbooks surveyed may by now be twenty years old, or older, this does not mean they will have been removed from school storerooms and library shelves. In many countries a set of books must last until it falls apart, not until a more appropriate book comes onto the market.

Producing a non-sexist textbook is not, of course, straightforward. Case Study 2 in this Quadrant, Lilie Chouliaraki's interview with Bessie Dendrinos, head author of *Task Way English*, illustrates this. One reason may (still!) be lack of awareness on the part of a writer of what teachers and students can find offensive, unacceptable or just plain silly. In response to this possibility, and with the intention of obviating it, there now exists in Britain a set of non-sexist guidelines for EFL publishers and authors, 'On Balance', which has the blessing of the British ELT Publishers' Association. 'On Balance' is reproduced in full in Case Study 1. Importantly, 'On Balance' is not recommending a sanitised, perfectly egalitarian textbook world, but rather that 'the books we produce are fair and balanced in their portrayal of all members of society', i.e. that they portray the world as it is.

A second reason is that the production of a sexism-free textbook is not just a matter of carefully avoiding sexist stereotypes. Despite authors' and publishers' good intentions, there are, crucially, 'market forces' constraints. David Haines in his Comment on this Quadrant, 'An International Publisher's Perspective', observes that 'the content of material is determined more and more by the market it is intended for'. And the operations of these markets are themselves social practices – which means it is unlikely that a coursebook will become sexism free while the country or countries ordering it are not.

A third reason (or set of reasons) is that the foreign language textbook lends itself to sexism in rather particular ways. Firstly, the current emphasis on spoken language often means a book includes several practice dialogues – which authors can and often do, however unintentionally, make male dominated (see (e), above; also Question 5, below).

Secondly, in most textbooks, there is a great deal of repetition – not necessarily language drills, but activities involving going over and over a phrase, sentence or paragraph in order to process it or perform an operation on it. Anastasia Zografou, analysing the textbook *Turning Point* (1976), quotes the following punctuation exercises:

> Darling she asked sweetly do you think I could have a little extra housekeeping money this week

> Arthur had hidden the tin-opener . . . [Mary] had given him nothing but tinned meat tinned vegetables and tinned sardines . . . and he suspected she was going to give him tinned spaghetti.

Zografou observes that this 'can become a kind of brainwashing' (1990: 19).

Thirdly, an author's intention to promote practice of a particular aspect of language may distort fair representation of the sexes: for example, by showing a majority of women only in a unit on honorifics, to illustrate the use of *Mrs*, *Miss* (and *Ms*?), or by omitting female characters during dialogue practice in Business English textbooks.

Fourthly, foreign language textbook writers in the past have used gender stereotyping extensively with the intention of either amusing and thus motivating language learners, or of providing something which the learners can relate to, to aid comprehension. These pedagogic aims are important; I will return to them in Questions 1 and 5, and Robert O'Neill also discusses them in his contribution to this Quadrant.

Despite the particular potential for sexism within the language textbook genre, many publishers, editors, teacher educators, teachers and students in the world of ELT now oppose, at least in principle, sexist teaching/learning materials. A 1990 survey of teachers gives some idea of the extent and nature of their opposition. 'Women in EFL Materials' (a subgroup of the British organisation 'Women in TEFL') produced a questionnaire which was printed in a range of publications for teachers of EFL. Responses were returned by 385 teachers – native and non-native speakers of English, working in Britain and abroad. Of these respondents, most

(8:1) said they were aware of sexism in EFL materials and most of these (11:1) were concerned about it. Further, on a 1–4 scale the nearest whole number expressing degree of concern about each of sexist language, stereotyping and invisibility of female characters was '3', i.e. 'definitely concerned'. Most concern was expressed about sex role stereotyping, followed by sexist language, followed by invisibility of female characters. This order might seem surprising. Stereotyping may have ranked first since it is something people are unlikely to say they are *unconcerned* about, partly because stereotyping of one sex can limit the options for the other. The reason for invisibility of female characters ranking lowest may have been because this did not correspond to respondents' perceived experience. Several respondents actually claimed that EFL textbooks did not have fewer female than male characters at all. (Such a perception may be based on the fact that textbooks include *some* female characters.)

Clearly, then, there is concern on the part of teachers. A response to this may be 'Well, it's only teachers who care; students couldn't care less'.[2] Christine Mannheim's study, in this Quadrant, shows, however, that learners do also recognise and can object to textbook sexism.

It is important that the argument should not stop there. Complaining that 'The amount of sexism in this textbook is unacceptable and I'm not the only teacher round here who thinks so!' is not enough. The fact that there is sexism in current EFL textbooks has been established, and concern is widespread. But in order to make progress, it is necessary to identify what is so bad about sexism in EFL textbooks, and to identify possible ways in which sexism in EFL textbooks may actually hinder language learning – after all, an EFL textbook is written with the intention that it promote language learning, and many teachers and writers will not be convinced by a claim of sexism alone. It is also necessary to establish what can (and cannot) be done in the EFL textbook genre, to develop ideas of what a genuinely non-sexist textbook might be like, and to continue to develop and improve the sensitivity and constructiveness of non-sexist guidelines. The value of non-sexist textbooks in a sexist world also needs to be debated, with, conversely, the use of sexist textbooks in a non-sexist way.

In my answers to the seven questions that follow, I have tried to begin to address these concerns.

1 How important are stereotypes?

Stereotyping can be viewed as 'a received "wisdom", which may or may not contain a "grain of truth"; this "grain of truth" is then distorted and exaggerated to fill the whole picture' (Jeanette Redding, Jacquie Thomas and Sue Tomlinson, 1992). Certainly few people would claim that stereotypes had *no* relationship with reality.

Accordingly, to succeed as a received wisdom, a stereotype must be found across a range of media. A recognisable textbook instance of a stereotype does not exist in isolation. If Robert O'Neill's character Julia Frost (the protagonist of his contribution to this Quadrant) is recognisable as a stereotype, then she is a stereotype in the context of all such other similar stereotypes of women, and as such plays her part in the maintenance of what is largely a myth, in that the stereotype is not generalisable. She is also helping maintain what, to many people, is an offensive view of women.

One textbook stereotype of a woman portrayed uncritically as, say, pretty and empty headed, or unable to make a decision on her own, or middle aged, single and unhappy, 'positions' Reader A as someone who accepts this as a valid and even generalisable representation of womankind. Similarly, the presentation of a woman in a non-stereotypical role – for example, a young woman who is pretty and a rugby player, or one who is contented, single and middle aged – 'positions' Reader B as someone who accepts *this* representation. Either reader may resist this positioning, of course. But if they do not resist, Reader B may be just that little bit more interested in ideas of sexual equality than before, Reader A no more interested. Both readers interact with the text at conscious and unconscious levels. Both are involved in social action. As we have seen, it would be rash to deny the possibility of a relationship between language use (including receptive language use), as a form of social practice, and language users' own gender identity.

The question of resistance is an important one, of course, but resisting stereotypes may not be easy. Inge Broverman *et al.*, in the conclusion to the report of their classic large-scale survey of sex-role stereotypes, write

> Women are perceived as relatively less competent, less independent, less objective, and less logical than men; men are perceived as lacking interpersonal sensitivity, warmth and expressiveness in comparison to women. Moreover, stereotypically masculine traits are more often perceived to be desirable than are stereotypically feminine characteristics. Most importantly, both men and women incorporate both the positive and negative traits of the appropriate stereotype into their self-concepts. Since more feminine traits are negatively valued than masculine traits, women tend to have more negative self-concepts than do men. (1972)

At the time of writing, this study is more than twenty years old, and female and male stereotypes are continually shifting. Yet stereotypes are still with us, as shown by more than just EFL textbooks. It would be a pity if EFL textbooks were actively to contribute to women and girls developing more negative self-concepts than do men and boys, not least since this is unlikely to facilitate their self-concepts as language learners.

It can be argued that stereotypical female characters, on occasion, do have a place in coursebooks: that they reflect some women's real lives and concerns, that some learners will accordingly identify with them, and, therefore, that they are needed in the interests of balance. From the point of view of accurate representation, it would at first sight seem hard to argue against this. A useful distinction can however be made between stereotyping and generalisation, i.e. 'a description of activities which can be found more or less commonly in the society being described' (Redding, Thomas and Tomlinson, 1992). More learners will presumably be able to identify with a generalisation than with a stereotype – and generalisable character portrayals are clearly justifiable. Some learners, however, will identify with neither, and if identification is an aim of a textbook, that textbook accordingly requires a range of female and male types.

Men are, of course, stereotyped in textbooks too. Whether male and female stereotyping are comparable, of the same order and status, and have the same effect, is another question. Robert O'Neill in his contribution suggests they *are* comparable. Readers can make up their own minds.

2 Can textbook characters be/feel authentic?

If greater authenticity can be achieved through, *inter alia*, avoidance of or minimal use of stereotypes, this may make a textbook more interesting. Textbooks do, of course, frequently use authentic texts,[3] which can be non-fictional or fictional, and can accordingly be about actual, authentic women and men as well as fictional ones. But can fictional authenticity be achieved in specially written EFL materials? No fictional character in any text type is ever fully authentic: concerns of personal hygiene, for example, are usually not detailed. Some characters, however – those in soap operas? – are less fantasy based than others – those in science fiction? English language textbook materials can and do borrow from both genres. The authenticity question is explored by Robert O'Neill.

Learners may not expect 'real' characters in a textbook. This does not mean that they automatically welcome stereotypes. Christine Mannheim's study of learners' perceptions of textbook sexism reports some relevant findings.

3 What is a desirable goal for women's and men's occupational roles in textbooks?

One theoretical alternative to occupational stereotyping is a statistically accurate reflection of a society or the societies in which the target language is spoken. Thus, whatever proportion of management is female (and in Britain the figure was 27 per cent in 1989 (EOC, 1991)), and whatever proportion is male, similar proportions of female and male managers would appear in a textbook – these characters being distributed through reading comprehension texts, story lines, role plays, dialogues, guided writing tasks, information gaps, sentence-level exercises and other activities. (The same would apply to the depiction of 'social roles' – gay people, black people, disabled people and single parents.)

Such a statistically accurate representation of society would of course be impossible. To make the management distribution pattern work, for example, there would need to be at least four different managers, three of whom would be male and one female. And management is only one occupational group! This principle could thus work only very crudely in individual textbooks, and only slightly less crudely in a textbook series. Understandably, then, no textbook or series aims to include a full statistical representation of society (though some try to include equal numbers of female and male characters).

Another theoretical alternative is to have as many women as men in each occupation in the textbook – though this would, of course, run into similar problems, such as a requirement of an even number of people in each occupation.

There are other, positive alternatives which take into consideration where a book will be used and the constraints of market forces of that country, though considering cultural norms will not in itself result in a guiding principle for occupational roles. Women characters may be powerless, but very visible; or the quantity of women's roles may be sacrificed for quality; or the proportion of women managers, for example, may be actually slightly greater than reality (a solution described as 'reality + 1'); or the textbook may 'point to some "ideal" future' (Ittzes, 1978: 10). Optimistically assuming women's position is improving (as politicians piously assert it should), what might at first be an inaccurate representation, a set of positive occupational role models (a form of affirmative action?), might later amount to accurate reflection, since textbooks are used well after the date of publication of the first edition.

Weighing up numerical alternatives may of course be missing the point. Joy Pascoe writes of EFL textbooks set in Britain: 'it is important to make our students aware of the fact that, in Britain today, women are employed in virtually every sphere, holding positions from shop floor to management' (1989: 12). This does not require proportional representation or even ensuring the textbook shows at least one woman lorry driver. Regardless of their relationship to statistical accuracy, fictional representations of people are always symbolic, allowing readers to generalise from them. Characters' qualities may be thus more important than percentages. This does not mean aiming only for women who are flawless or 'superwomen', or indeed for perfect 'new men'! (see Question 6).

Consciousness of the number and quality of female and male occupational roles on the part of an author does not mean sacrificing the textbook's primary role of facilitating language learning and teaching. Indeed, the reverse could be true: a more encouraging representation of occupational roles may itself facilitate this process (see Question 5).

4 What is a desirable goal for female and male discourse roles in textbooks?

Discourse role stereotyping requires a different type of alternative to occupational stereotyping. Many studies have shown that in mixed-sex contexts men frequently talk more often and for longer periods than women, and give less verbal support (e.g. Daniel Maltz and Ruth Borker, 1982). Accepting uncritically the communicative competence concern of appropriacy might mean reflecting the findings of these studies in textbook dialogues, in order to teach sex-appropriate or gender-characteristic language (see Comment, Quadrant II). Yet these findings should surely not be regularly mirrored in textbook dialogues, symbolically or otherwise. Firstly, regardless of actual practice opportunities, to do so would be uncritically to reproduce the male dominance model of discourse in the classroom. Secondly, most teachers would presumably agree, at least in principle, that every individual in their class should get as many opportunities to practise speaking as any other, regardless of their sex.

Rather than discourse roles in some way reflecting reality (as we may argue occupational roles should), it would make more sense to advocate male and female characters speaking an equal amount, using the same range of language functions, as far as this is compatible with the (culture-dependent) contexts in the textbook, and initiating dialogue equally often[4] – if only to ensure a fair model of discourse and a fair distribution of language practice opportunities. This is particularly important in mixed-sex classes, in which male and female dialogue roles tend to be assigned to male and female students, respectively (see Question 5). Such a principle of 'gender fairness' regarding the distribution of discourse in textbooks would be more straightforward to operationalise than the problematic distribution of occupational roles to female and male characters. To be completely fair, of course, there need to be equal numbers of male and female speaking characters in the textbook.

5 Does coursebook sexism matter in terms of language learning?

Not all textbook writers oppose or even recognise biased or stereotypical treatment of the sexes. Those that do not will need to feel that textbook sexism can hinder language learning, and is widely believed by teachers and administrators to have this potential, before they are prepared to move away from stereotypical representation.

The writers of 'On Balance' claim that if women are 'represented in demeaning ways' they 'may learn less well'. Demeaning or stereotypical representation of women may certainly alienate female learners (again see Mannheim, this Quadrant). Writing on textbooks for adult learners in the USA, Fairlee Winfield Carroll notes

> Adult women attending foreign-language classes are . . . there because the language is necessary to them for career advancement, university studies or to make homes and find employment in a second language environment . . . When many single and married women are part of the labor force, seeking to enter it, or acquiring foreign language skills to improve their potentials, it is unjust to portray only housewives and future housewives in textbooks. (1978: 55, 59)

Neither can stereotypes automatically be justified on the 'learning' grounds that learners can relate to them, since stereotypes are not identical across cultures (Jenny Pugsley, personal communication).

Returning to discourse roles, sceptical textbook writers (and teachers) might be convinced by being shown examples of textbook practices that discriminate against female learners – the disempowering discourse roles in dialogues which have fewer, shorter, more repetitive and/or less interesting parts for females. The following example is taken from a beginners' French class for adults, which uses a textbook published in 1986. Ali Wyllie (personal communication) recalls playing the female role in a dialogue from the book. The setting is a tour of Paris. Ali is a female tourist; there are two male characters, the guide and another tourist. The guide points things out and explains, the male tourist identifies *un bateau mouche* and asks about particular features of interest, and the female tourist has to content herself with asking '*Qu'est-ce que c'est?*' (three times), '*Quoi par exemple?*' and '*Oh, allons-y, allons-y!*' Of course, a textbook cannot be judged on a single dialogue. Nevertheless, it is surprising to find even one dialogue in a modern textbook based on such 'sex-unfair' discourse roles, when with a little thought and a small measure of rewriting this could have been avoided. Whatever the writer's opinions about occupational, relationship and personal characteristic stereotyping, this gendered distribution of amount and content of speech seems indefensible.

Unless the teacher or students make an issue of a dialogue such as this, where male and female students are working together the male students will not only probably speak most, but will also get practice in a wider range of language functions. *Functions of English* (Leo Jones, 1977) was found to have a male initiating all its mixed-sex dialogues (ETHEL, 1980). Unless this is challenged, male students will also speak first, thereby getting more practice than the female students in the language and act of initiating a conversation.

6 Should guidelines for inclusive language and fair treatment of the sexes allow for unpleasant female characters, clearly oppressed women and satirical presentations of female and male stereotypes?

This is an important question, and O'Neill addresses it, as do the writers of 'On Balance'. It is not simply a matter of artistic and professional autonomy. Guidelines need to allow for, even promote, the (occasional) deliberate portrayal of oppressed womankind. This can challenge learners intellectually and linguistically through class or group discussion. Guidelines also need to allow for, even promote, the portrayal of unpleasant as well as pleasant female characters. Otherwise, they could be shooting themselves in the foot through the resultant creation of endless highly competent women who are free from discrimination of any sort, and shooting the textbook in the foot by making its characters bland and uninteresting. It would also be a pity if writers had to avoid satirical presentations of male and female characters in stereotypical roles, since this can also lead to useful discussion.

Guidelines should therefore aim not only to eliminate textbook sexism and unfair representation of women, but also to enhance a writer's creativity. They should also enhance the foreign language learning and teaching processes. (A challenging marketing task is to ensure they are seen to do this.) This may then counteract accusations of 'stifling creativity' and misguided comparisons with *1984*.

There are, as yet, no non-sexist guidelines for publishers and writers of dictionaries and pedagogic grammars. For such guidelines, Question 6 would need addressing differently. There are unlikely to be recommendations for the provision of satirical presentations of female and male stereotypes, for example, since grammars and dictionaries have little space in which to contextualise examples. Guidelines for publishers and writers of dictionaries and pedagogic grammars could however recommend accurate, positive descriptions of contemporary usage (for example in ways suggested and identified by Hennessy and myself, this Quadrant) and equal visibility of female and male characters in the examples with a wide range of occupational roles, relationships and personal characteristics for both.

7 Is changing textbooks the answer?

A non-sexist textbook cannot guarantee non-sexist teaching: a good teacher's guide and, as Bessie Dendrinos observes, teacher education, are needed too (preferably accompanied by changes in social practices!). It is not necessary to invoke a full-blown 'Death of the Author' theory to recognise that the meaning of, say, a reading text in a textbook depends on how it is interpreted and used. The most non-sexist textbook can become sexist in the hands of a teacher with sexist attitudes – and, importantly, the reverse is also true. One form of remedial action is discussion of the manifestations of sexism in the textbook, using the students' own experience and perceptions. Narratives and activities can also be subverted, through sex role reversal in role plays and dialogues, for example (see Audrone Willeke and Ruth Sanders, 1978; John Abraham, 1989; and also General Introduction to *Exploring Gender*, and Fran Byrnes, Quadrant III).

In addition to these seven questions, one critical perspective must be addressed that so far has only been touched on: that excising traditional gender roles from textbooks amounts to cultural insensitivity. There is clearly a need, widely recognised, for publishers, editors and authors to be sensitive to long cultural traditions. In many societies with social practices considered in Western countries to be sexist, women may actually draw strength and identity from those very practices, and do have considerable freedom and power in many spheres. Further, many of the freedoms Western women are accustomed to – relaxed forms of dress, working full-time outside the home – are perceived elsewhere as forms of exploitation.

And yet – are Western gender roles as shocking to other cultures as is sometimes claimed? Will a male student in Saudi Arabia really turn pale and leave the class when confronted with a picture of a man changing a baby's nappy? (Claims of cultural bias invariably seem to focus on the male student.) All cultures are both fluid and heterogeneous. As Pugsley (1988: 5) notes, many of our learners are young and female, and '[may] not be fazed by a redistribution of roles in the familiar storylines so popular with EFL writers'. And one objective of the 'speaking' class, at least, is to stimulate discussion. . . . David Haines in his Comment claims that

'Accurate representation could and often does alienate the publisher from the consumer.' The extent to which this is true may vary according to whether the consumer is the Minister of Education, the Director of a Language Institute, an English teacher, or a learner of English – and, of course, whether the 'consumer' is female or male.

Much surely hinges on why the textbook users are learning English, especially now that English is, as Haines reminds us, an 'International Language', as well as a second language for some and a foreign language for others. If the learners are to come to an English-speaking country, there is an argument for their textbook reflecting that country's cultural norms (see e.g. Willeke and Sanders, 1978). Many learners, of course, will not be coming to an English-speaking country. . . . This debate is part of a wider one on the English language teaching/learning requirements of ESL and EFL countries (itself now a problematic distinction). A further consideration is the perceived needs of teachers and learners. There may be a conflict between learners of EFL preferring a textbook 'set' in an English-speaking country (which, since this seems more authentic, and may have a certain novelty value, many say they do), and the ability and willingness of EFL teachers to deal with a textbook set in an unfamiliar cultural context.

Figure 1

For writers of pedagogic grammars and dictionaries of British/American English, a response to accusations of cultural insensitivity may be simple: that English is changing, and it is the responsibility of the English teacher to teach English as it is.[5] It is correspondingly the responsibility of writers of pedagogic grammars and dictionaries to help them.

At the time of writing, I am unaware of any published studies of sexism in textbooks, pedagogic grammars or dictionaries of the 1990s. This is a pity: the world is changing, as are levels of awareness on the part of publishers, authors, teachers and learners, and such studies might well make for more cheerful reading than their predecessors. Certainly textbooks published in the 1960s and early 1970s were more guilty of stereotyping than their successors (see Reinhold Freudenstein (ed.), 1978).

Finally, it is important for authors and publishers to recognise that an activity or textbook unit which focuses on gender is not necessarily sexist. Charles and Jill Hadfield's 'History/Her story' activity in *Writing Games* (1990) is a good example of how gender can be discussed with warmth and humour. However, it is always worth considering how any textbook *as a whole* deals with gender issues: if women are ignored on pages other than the ones headed 'Women', then such inclusions could be read as tokenism.

Notes

1. Can textbook sexism always be recognised and properly described? Joseph Graci (1989) bemoans the lack of a systematic, replicable methodology; but assuming such could be developed, it might not be sensitive to all forms of sexism. David Carroll and Johanna Kowitz, who suggest in their contribution that collocations, among other linguistic patternings, can be insidiously sexist, used a systematic, replicable methodology to investigate linguistic sexism, but this depended on sophisticated computer concordancing techniques. Further, what is amenable to such a methodology may be less pernicious than what is not: it is possible to find in textbooks situations which depend on unexplored, common sense assumptions, for example the malicious 'woman hitchhikers accusing innocent driver of rape' stereotype in *Mazes* (Mario Rinvolucri and Marge Berer, 1981: 48). This stereotype would in fact seem to depend on a complete distortion of reality.
2. Even if this were true, it would not invalidate the issue: there are many perfectly valid pedagogic issues, large classes, for example, which are of concern to teachers rather than students.
3. Many non-textbook writers continue to use masculine generics and other forms of sexist language. A single instance of 'generic' *he* may not be a reason for non-selection of a text, but textbook writers may wish to comment on such usage.
4. Another challenge for the materials writer creating a dialogue is what to do about the characters' own use of traditional, sexist language, and newer, non-sexist alternatives.
5. This task is facilitated by evidence accumulating from linguistic corpora (though this will always be selective).

'The Case of Julia Frost' or 'The Lure of the Stereotype'

ROBERT O'NEILL

Julia Frost is about twenty-three years old. She works and lives in an unusual world – perhaps even a bizarre one. In this world it is forbidden even to mention a great many things that in the real world appear constantly in newspaper headlines and in ordinary conversation. For example, pork, sex and drugs are strictly taboo. The world of Julia Frost is a world of houses without lavatories, people without religious views and marriages without passion or infidelity.

Twenty years ago Julia Frost engendered a storm of controversy and even today, although most people have either forgotten or never heard her name, the controversy continues. She was a stereotype, one of several characters in a textbook. I was not the only author of that textbook but I created all the characters in it and wrote all except one of the situations they found themselves in. If there was some offence in them, it was I who was the author of it. I also wrote the continuous story that runs throughout the book and in which additional characters appear.

Before I say a little more about the controversy – indeed, 'scandal' – that surrounded Julia, let me say a little more about some of the other characters. They have a direct relevance to the issue.

One of them is called Fred Collins. Fred gets drunk regularly, is seen in bars with floozies (the occasional consumption of alcohol is allowed in this world, or at least in the versions of it not used in Arab countries) and cannot hold down a job. He is briefly employed as a bus driver but is so incompetent that he is fired on the spot. Eventually he joins the army but does very badly in basic training.

Another is Tom Atkins, a rather ineffectual language teacher and husband. His wife is far more capable than he – certainly she seems to have far more common sense. He frequently makes a fool of himself, as for example when he conducts an oral interview in French (he is a teacher of French but not at this school). When a teacher from the school offers him a cup of coffee, Tom mistakes her for a student and insists on asking her the questions he has rehearsed for the interview.

There are two older males. One of them is Frank Martin, the father of Tom's wife. He is a stereotypical factory worker. His main interest in life is football. When he ends up in hospital with breathlessness and shooting pains in his legs, he asks his daughter to smuggle in a packet of fags for him – the very things that have contributed directly to his health problems.

There are only two people in this world who could be seen in any way as symbols of success. One of them is Sir Arthur Tigers, the other older male. He is a rich industrialist who worked his way up from humble beginnings and, after the death of his first wife, married a far younger woman. Unfortunately Sir Arthur is closely associated with the industry that, at the time he appears in our story, was the most obvious symbol of Britain's decline as an industrial power, the manufacture of motor cars. One of Sir Arthur's other defects as a role model is his grim lack of humour. And he – like Tom Atkins and all the other men who appear in the tale – is something of a fool. For example, his secretary tells him that she is emigrating to Canada with her husband, who is an engineer. When she tells him just how low her husband's salary is, Sir Arthur says that he is sure that he would want to emigrate if that was all he was earning. His embarrassed secretary then tells him that her husband works in Sir Arthur's own company.

The other character, a far more likely potential role model, is an actress called Kate. She is instrumental in helping an escaped convict, Edward Coke, who has been wrongfully imprisoned, to prove his innocence. At one point she even throws a man over her shoulder just as he is about to kill Coke.

The book was called *Kernel Lessons Intermediate* and it was published in 1970. Six years later it was attacked in a now famous article[1] because it seemed to typify the offensive way women were treated not just in this textbook alone but in many others available at the time. The writer of the article focussed on things like Julia's habit of coming to work late – this seemed to imply that this was typical behaviour for all women. (In fact, as we learn at the same time, her boss also comes to work late, but this was not mentioned in the article.)

In other words the charge was that the book was full of unflattering, negative stereotypes of women. This charge was true, in at least one sense. I intended to use stereotypes, but I did not intend them to be unflattering, least of all to women. This may have been insensitivity or naivety on my part but it simply did not occur to me that portraying one of the women as a secretary who had problems in getting to work on time would be perceived as sexist. In any case, the stereotypes I used of the men were no more flattering than those of the women. In many ways, I felt at the time and still feel that they were even less so. I deliberately depicted almost all the males as buffoons or fools. I hoped that the very things that made the characters stereotypical – their predictability and familiarity – would also help students to predict and understand the meaning of the language in the textbook.

Of course, stereotypes can be and often are created with a deliberate intent to wound, to insult, to denigrate. But is depicting a secretary who is often late quite the same as depicting blacks as shiftless and lazy, or Jews as avaricious, or Germans as arrogant, or Italians as Mafiosi? I do not ask this question in order to defend or justify Julia Frost. I ask it simply because I think that the stereotypes that occur in textbooks are rarely if ever intentionally negative.

Nevertheless, it is still true that unintentional sexism can be just as offensive as subconscious racism. So we have to leave aside the intentions of authors and explore the effect stereotypes have on people's perceptions of reality. Is it true, as some people argue, that stereotypes such as Julia Frost will have an unfortunate effect on impressionable users of the textbook? Will they conclude that women are incapable of anything more demanding than secretarial work? Or if some users of the textbooks, let us say those from cultures where women stay at home and never work outside it, already have such stereotypes, is it the duty of EFL textbooks to correct them?

My answer is that stereotypes are sexist only if all the stereotypes of women are consistently negative and all those of men are consistently positive. However, if a writer chooses to create a world of foolish women and equally foolish men, you can perhaps accuse him or her of cynicism, but not of sexism.

But what about the other argument? Have EFL textbooks a duty to offer positive role models? First, I believe the question is mistaken. It is like asking if a child whose physical development has been severely retarded as a result of malnutrition could ever become an Olympic athlete. It is impossible even to begin to answer the question until the child achieves something like normal body-weight and muscular development. My second answer is that the purpose of characters in a textbook should not be to purvey some socially hygienic view of gender relations. The author has a duty only to avoid obvious and deliberate insult or offence to the sensibilities of the students – or of the teachers – using the book. The only criteria I believe are valid in judging characters are the following:

1. Do the characters help to make the language presented more memorable and more interesting?
2. Does their predictability, even if stereotypical, help to make language clearer? For example, suppose a character is consistently rude in a book. Does the character help to code or tag language as 'rude', to be avoided in polite conversation?
3. Do the characters reflect the problems people in the real world have? Can they, in other words, be used as windows which we open on the real conflicts of real people so that we can discuss some of these conflicts?

To do any of these things, textbook characters must have some kind of depth. That is, the author has to have at least some of the skills that, say, the author of a soap opera is expected to display. However, as one perceptive critic has remarked,[2] 'even the cheapest escape entertainment has more depth of character than most ESOL materials'. Most characters we encounter in a textbook are no more than names that occur once or twice and then never reappear. How can such characters be taken seriously either as positive or negative role models? We are often told that we should try to reverse typical conceptions of male and female roles in society so that women can be seen to be strong and decisive and men as caring and compassionate. But strong, decisive, compassionate and caring about what? There is no point in trying to portray characters this way if readers do not believe in them in the first place. To create believable characters, you need believable backgrounds, believable stories and a web of believable relationships that those characters enter into.

There are many reasons why it is difficult to do this in the world of English language textbooks. The present climate of opinion does not encourage writers to try to develop strong, believable characters or to be interested in acquiring for themselves the kinds of skills writers in other mediums regard as indispensable criteria of professionalism. A common prejudice among teachers and teacher trainers is that if materials are not authentic – that is, written originally for native speakers who already possess the full code – they are by definition impoverished and worthless. And so, writers increasingly borrow and adapt material from other sources. Few try to write stories or create characters in the same way that writers of children's books do. Writers of children's books are aware that although their readers are restricted in their language development, it is still possible to write material that will appeal to their imaginations and be linguistically enriching at the same time. If it is possible to do this in children's books without cannibalising adult literature, why should it not be possible to do so in the medium of the English language textbook?

To put the question of authenticity another way, suppose an Englishwoman on holiday in Venice meets an Italian to whom she is strongly attracted. She speaks only a few words of Italian. The Venetian gentleman's knowledge of English, although limited, is much better. He implores her to come and live with him in Venice. She tries to explain to him in English, in language that he will understand, why she does not want to (her work, her friends, other commitments, etc.). Is the Englishwoman using authentic English? And if she is, is it also possible to write English that, although specially suited to the needs of non-native speakers, is just as authentic for such readers? If writers of English language textbooks think so, they are surprisingly quiet about it.

Another reason for this scarcity of believable characters is that in contrast to pulp fiction or soap operas, the aim of creating characters in textbooks is not primarily to tell a story. Characters are usually conceived of narrowly, as names in a dialogue that will illustrate a communicative function or grammatical structure. So, again, textbook authors tend to borrow predictable stereotypes from other sources, such as popular magazines, newspapers and popular films (James Bond spies, dumb blondes, etc.). They are immediately recognisable; their power comes from the associations readers already have. Such stereotypes, of course, tend to re-affirm rather than challenge accepted notions of what a woman's role is or what kind of behaviour is or is not acceptable for a male.

Fortunately, however, it is far easier today, more than twenty years after the publication of *Kernel Lessons Intermediate*, to find examples of successful women in business and politics, to mention only two areas in which the real world has changed since the 1970s. Textbooks published today should and do reflect this fact.

These changes in the real world may not, at least in the opinion of feminists, go far enough. But that does not seem to me a convincing argument for suggesting that we should pretend in our textbooks that women have more equality than they already have. There is only one argument that, if it were accepted not only by the producers of ELT materials but also by their users, would be convincing, and that is the argument that the principal task of an English language textbook is not to help teach foreign students English but to change their views of the world in general and of gender relationships in particular. I, for one, cannot and do not accept this argument for reasons I am about to explore.

There is, in fact, only one role of the textbook which I can accept – primarily to present in interesting, practical and relevant ways realistic, natural English. Textbooks have also to interest students, and to do this they have to reflect – even if only symbolically – the way the world really is. On the other hand, they have to follow an internally consistent syllabus that does not go too fast or too far for their intended audience.

Sometimes there are other requirements, too. In Islamic countries, for example, there are definite taboos in regard to dress, alcohol and so on. In many countries the more the textbook reflects the ordinary realities of the English-speaking or western European world, the greater the risk that it will be rejected as culturally imperialistic, or even propaganda for a degenerate culture.

I believe that there are already far too many restrictions on textbooks. Some of them are self-imposed. Others, like those of the external syllabus and taboos, are not. Each additional restriction, each additional demand that textbooks should pay lip service to this or that political, religious or social ideal makes them less interesting, less useful as vehicles for presenting English in ways that accurately reflect its use and usage in the real world.

I have been concerned here with three main questions. The first is whether the use of stereotypes is ever permissible. The second is whether a language textbook can ever break the chains laid upon it by its pedagogical role and use characters – stereotypical or otherwise – who are interesting and intriguing in their own right. The third is whether an English language textbook should attempt to project a vision of an ideal world of perfect gender equality.

I have tried to suggest that stereotypes in themselves need not be harmful, even if they tend to re-affirm some traditional gender roles. I cannot and do not accept that it is abusive to portray women occasionally as secretaries or to reflect a world in which men often have more visible (if not always real) power than women. I believe that the argument that authors must count heads in their textbooks to make sure that there are as many women in powerful or authoritative roles as men is a recipe for sterility, just as the duty to project Socialist Realism that Soviet writers and artists suffered under for years was a recipe for lies and creative impotence.

I have also tried to make the point that it is far more important to have believable characters that reveal some of the conflicts that people in real life face than it is to project a sanitised, goody-goody world in which an ideal parity and equality between men and women already exists. I do not believe that it will benefit anyone, least of all women who are struggling with real inequalities, if we create the illusion in our textbooks that the battle has already been won – that the barriers that prevent more women from sharing power with their male colleagues have been entirely dismantled. What is the point in pretending that things are different? Do we imagine that by doing so, we will create even one more job in which a woman is paid a salary equal to a man in the same position? The evidence is that only one thing really helps to achieve change. That is action in the real world. If editors or textbook writers seriously want to change things, let them give some of their royalties or salaries to organisations dedicated to bringing about change. That will help infinitely more than bickering about how many women have top jobs in a textbook world that nobody takes seriously anyway.

This does not mean I am unwilling to accept any standards at all. It means simply that the only standards I personally am willing to accept are based on certain common sense notions of decency. For example, women should never be seen as sex slaves nor as generally inferior to men in their abilities. Men should not be portrayed exclusively as bullies or predators. Perhaps there is even an argument that they should not be portrayed as all the men were in *Kernel Lessons Intermediate* – as generally incompetent and foolish. Italians should not be depicted as fat spaghetti-eaters or Germans as Nazis, and so on.

In the real world, some women are gold diggers and nags and many men are fools and scoundrels. Some women still come to work late (just as their bosses do). Some wives behave coldly and unfairly towards their husbands and children. And there are many women just as there are many men who behave like tyrants when they have authority or power over other people. Some women have good jobs and incomes but many continue to work in occupations that are much less rewarding than they ought to be. It is a matter of personal belief that many men suffer as much as women do, if not more so, from some of the stereotypical standards that govern their behaviour.

I, personally, have no interest in prescriptions or guidelines that would make it more difficult than it is already to reflect my perceptions of common, everyday reality. I find that reality infinitely preferable to any sanitised or make-believe world. I feel that our textbooks will be better if we try to portray the world as it is, and not as we would like it to be. In doing so we do not perpetuate inequalities and injustices. On the contrary, by making them visible we make it possible to discuss and criticise them and also to propose alternatives. Portraying the world as we would like it to be would make it more difficult, not less, to reflect the real problems of the world in the last years of the twentieth century.

Notes

1. Hilary Rees-Parnell. 1976. 'Women in the world of *Kernel Lessons Intermediate*'. *ARELS Journal* 2/2: 29–31.
2. James Swan, now at Osaka University of Economics and Law, in a thesis submitted in August 1981 to the graduate division of the University of Hawaii entitled 'Characterisation: an ignored aspect of the social dimension of ESOL materials'.

Using Concordancing Techniques to Study Gender Stereotyping in ELT Textbooks

DAVID CARROLL and JOHANNA KOWITZ

Introduction

Much attention has been given in the past decade to assessing the sexism in and increasing the gender fairness of EFL and ESL materials. (For examples of manifestations of sexism, see Quadrant II, Introduction.)[1] The primary tool for evaluation of sexism in EFL and ESL textbooks has been content analysis. Fernando Cerezal (1991), for example, in a survey of a series of Spanish ELT materials, reported that his unit of analysis was the human character in texts and illustrations, the focus being on age, appearance, protagonism and occupation; he found substantial preference for males in key roles. Johanna Kowitz and David Carroll (1990) analysed the presentation of women in the extended texts in *Excel in English* (Louis Alexander, 1985, 1986, 1987), and found (predictably) that there was a general preponderance of male main characters, that shopping and child nurturing were female preserves, and that, even in apparently 'balanced' dialogues, female contributions tended to be marginal or trivial. Yoshio Narisawa and Tsutomi Yokotu (1991) also used content analysis to identify gender bias in Japanese ELT textbooks, reporting that women tended to be portrayed in stereotypical ways which are not a true representation of their real life roles.

Valuable as content analysis may be, it does not give insight into the significant gender differences that exist at the level of the individual linguistic item. Differences at this level are subtle, easy to miss and difficult to identify. Much of their importance comes from repetition. What might be harmless in isolation can become pernicious in, say, contributing to habitual, unthinking responses (such as pervasive use of masculine pronouns) if repeated frequently, or over a sustained period of time – as can happen in a textbook. For this reason it is important to evaluate the gender balance of ELT textbooks at the linguistic level. (See also Goran Kjellmer's study ' "The lesser man": observations on the role of women in modern English writings' (1986), which makes use of the Brown and Lancaster–Oslo–Bergen (LOB) Computer Corpora.)

The basic problem with studying textbooks using a linguistic unit of analysis is to find a suitable analysis technique. Even the simplest language teaching book will contain upwards of 10,000 words; most will contain 20,000–30,000 or more. Manual analysis is therefore effectively ruled out. Computational linguistics has developed a form of lexical analysis that locates and gives information about all occurrences of a particular lexical item within a text.

Analysis techniques

Four main techniques are commonly used in analysis of concordance data:

1. Frequency counts
2. Distributional analysis
3. Collocational analysis
4. Key Word in Context (KWIC) concordances

Frequency counts

The relative frequency of an item in the text is one basic indicator of saliency. Thus, for example, if male-marked pronouns are significantly more common than female-marked pronouns, this could suggest that males have greater prominence in the text as a whole than females. For this reason, the first step in a linguistic analysis of any text is likely to be extraction of a wordlist with frequencies. Example 1 below is a table of a 'raw count' of the frequencies of occurrence of male- and female-marked subject, object and genitive pronouns across six books in two series: *Welcome to English* (Martin Bates and Jonathon Higgens, 1986, 1987, and Martin Bates, 1988), and *Excel in English* (Alexander, 1985, 1986, 1987).

Example 1
Frequencies of gender-marked pronouns

Pronoun type	*Welcome*			*Excel*		
	1	2	3	1	2	3
male subject (he)	134	295	360	306	202	353
female subject (she)	60	141	141	119	79	92
male object (him)	12	32	50	45	35	46
female object (her)	5	13	23	16	9	18
male genitive (his)	23	73	79	59	47	93
female genitive (her)	16	32	25	19	36	13

Male-marked pronouns are approximately twice to three times as frequent as female-marked pronouns throughout both series. (Other corpus data would suggest that the vast majority of the male-marked pronouns are likely to be specific rather than generic.) In no case does any female pronoun occur more frequently than the equivalent male pronoun. This is *prima facie* evidence of imbalance.

As numerical data, such a table can be refined by basic statistical treatment. Appropriate techniques include:

(a) Conversion of raw frequencies to ratios to show relative prominence. For example, male subject pronouns are 2.55 times as common as female subject pronouns in *Welcome to English*, Book 3, and 3.84 times as common in *Excel in English*, Book 3.
(b) Conversion of raw frequencies into standard frequencies (e.g. occurrences per 1,000 words).
(c) Use of statistical tests to assess whether the difference in observed frequencies might be expected by chance, or is significantly different from the frequencies found in natural language.

Frequency is a useful indicator, but should be interpreted in the light of meaning. For example, frequency counts almost always show *husband* to be less common than *wife* (with the exception of the possessive form – *husband's* is more common than *wife's*); but this is not an indicator that more prominence is given to wives than to husbands. The underlying reason for *wife* occurring more frequently than *husband* is mainly because the stereotypical wife is an appendage.

The following examples are drawn from the Lancaster–Oslo–Bergen (LOB) corpus:

The stereotypical *wife* as an appendage:

(a) the Portuguese engineer and his silent wife;
(b) one sturdy Yorkshireman and his wife;
(c) such is the life of a naval officer's wife;
(d) the solicitor's wife, the schoolmaster's wife, the clerk's wife, the plumber's wife, and the wife of a chap who is doing a stretch in gaol.

Wife as a passive participant, rather than an individual in her own right:

(a) His native gardener was getting too interested in his wife.
(b) Thus began a close friendship with him and his wife.

Defined by *wifely* status alone:

(a) A wife led a perfectly blameless life.
(b) Lula, Tom Holland's most charming wife.

A *wife* as subordinate to her husband, even where it might be supposed that the activity was shared:

(a) Mrs Diana Roberts, wife of farmer John Roberts;
(b) guests of Mr Macmillan and his wife;
(c) some poor baby Hawley and his wife adopted.

Husband, on the other hand, is more likely to be the subject of an active verb:

(a) The husband was a prisoner.
(b) My husband rides him every week with the Cottesmore Hunt.
(c) My husband is inclined to be very jealous.
(d) Her husband took her in their car.

Husbands are also more likely to be defined primarily by some other (often professional) characteristic – 'her architect husband, Graham'.

Distributional analysis

Evidence from frequency should also be tempered by a consideration of distribution – whether the item is evenly distributed throughout the text, or bunched or grouped in some way. If a character appears in every textbook unit, s/he will probably be perceived differently from a character who appears in only one or two. It is a basic pedagogical principle that an item should be recycled to reinforce learning. An item that is evenly distributed throughout the text is likely to get more reinforcement than one which appears very frequently in only part of the text.

Example 2
Welcome to English, Book 2: Distribution of gender-marked subject pronouns by unit

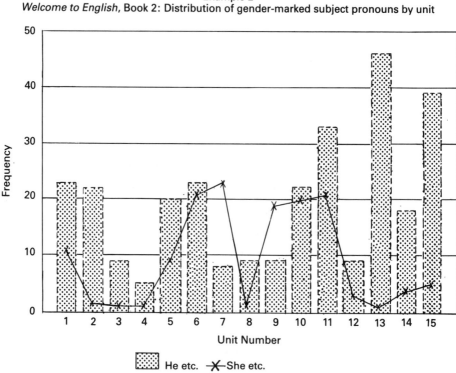

This can be illustrated from the chart in Example 2, showing the number of male and female subject pronouns in each unit of *Welcome to English*, Book 2. The average number of male subject pronouns per unit in the book is 19.67 and the average number of female subject pronouns 9.4. The actual number per unit varies considerably in both cases but, as Example 2 shows, the variation is greater for female subject pronouns than for male. Five units (out of fifteen) have only one female subject pronoun each, while five others have 104 out of the total of 141. Male subject pronouns are reasonably frequent in every unit: only one unit has less than eight. Therefore, gender balance on a unit by unit basis is not achieved, because female pronouns are more irregularly distributed than male.

Collocational analysis

Collocational analysis is a technique for identifying words that occur near to other selected words more or less often than would be predicted from their frequency in the text as a whole. Collocational analysis involves tabulating occurrences of all words within a specified distance (often five words on either side) of all occurrences of the selected word. Inevitably, an analysis of this kind produces a long list of words, only some of which are of interest. Two further steps are needed to turn a raw list of collocates into usable information:

(a) First, a strategy for selection. A rationale has to be developed for retaining words of interest and excluding the others. An initial selection might be done on the basis of form class that is most likely to be meaningfully associated with the target item. For example, subject and object pronouns (*he/she* and *him/her*) would collocate most meaningfully with verbs; possessive pronouns (*his/her*) would collocate most meaningfully with nouns; and nouns (*man/ men* and *woman/women*) would probably collocate best with adjectives.

(b) Second, a method of testing for statistical significance. The method used in the example below is the Z-score, which was devised in its present form by Berry-Roghe and revised by Lancashire and Brainerd (cited in John Bradley and Lidio Presutti, 1990). This treats the total number of collocates (i.e. the total of the ten words on either side of each occurrence of the target item) as a subtext, and assesses the probability, based on the average frequency of the collocate in both subtext and whole text, and the size of subtext and whole text, that the difference in the two average frequencies arose by chance.

One way of using collocational analysis in the study of gender bias would be to investigate the collocates of gender-marked items such as pronouns, names, or words such as *man/men* and *woman/women*. As indicated above, the type of item chosen would to some extent determine the selection strategy for collocates. Example 3 illustrates the kind of information that can be produced in this way. It shows all the personal adjectives which collocated with either *man/men* or *woman/ women*. Adjectives which were not personal, such as *long, hot, hard*, and names of colours and nationalities, were excluded from this analysis. *Long, hard* and *hot* were left out on the grounds that they seemed relatively unlikely to be used in a textbook to describe the essence of a male or female, though outside a textbook they often have a sexual flavour. Colours and nationalities were omitted because it was felt these would not be 'sex bound'. The collocation examples in the table, however, were text generated, not selected.

Example 3
Adjectives collocating with *man* and *woman*
in the *Welcome to English* series.

Type	Type freq.	man/men Coll. freq.	man/men Z-score	woman/women Coll. freq.	woman/women Z-score
poor	17	8	12.641		not found
rich	29	10	11.888		not found
richest	1	1	6.679		not found
young	22	8	10.956	1	2.221
old	126	16	8.093	2	1.259
strong	20	7	10.030	1	2.366
brave	7	2	4.772		not found
tall	23	6	7.838	2	4.703
short	18	2	2.596		not found
bald	9	3	6.386		not found
fat	19	5	7.192	1	2.446
bad	25	3	3.363		not found
lazy	3	1	3.687		not found
important	7	1	2.192		not found
famous	10	1	1.695		not found
busy	5		not found	2	10.744
afraid	28	1	0.515		not found
pleased	18	2	2.596		not found
happy	27	1	0.552		not found
angry	22	1	0.768	1	2.221
beautiful	32		not found	3	6.017
pretty	4		not found	1	5.945

The first, left-hand column contains the adjectives themselves. The second column contains the total frequency of the adjectives in the series as a whole (there are a total of 57,161 words in the three books). The third column contains the number of times that each adjective occurred within five words on either side of either *man* or *men*, and the Z-score, which is an index of how likely this frequency is to have arisen by chance. A positive Z-score indicates that the item is more frequent near the target item than in the text as a whole; a negative Z-score indicates that it is less frequent than in the text as a whole. Statistical significance is indicated by a Z-score exceeding ± 2. If the Z-score is greater than +2 or less than −2, this indicates that there is less than a 5 per cent likelihood that the result arose by chance; a Z-score of ± 3 indicates that the probability of the difference in frequency arising by chance is less than .05 per cent. The final column gives the same information for *woman/women*.

Example 3 shows that all personal adjectives are, predictably, more rather than less likely to occur within five words of *man/men* or *woman/women* than in the text as a whole. Amongst the specific adjectives, the table shows that:

(a) *Rich, richest, poor, brave, short, bald, bad, lazy, important, famous, afraid, pleased* and *happy* collocated exclusively with *man/men*.
(b) *Strong, tall, young, old* and *fat* collocated more strongly with *man/men* than *woman/women*.
(c) *Angry* collocated more strongly with *woman/women* than *man/men*.
(d) *Beautiful, pretty* and *busy* collocated exclusively with *woman/women*.

We may conclude from this that:

(a) Many more adjectives are used to describe men than women. Eighteen of the total of twenty-two are used to describe men, as against nine that are used to describe women.
(b) There is considerable separation between the adjectives used to describe men and women. Of the twenty-two adjectives, only six are used of both men and women.
(c) Statistically, the most important adjectives used to describe women are *busy, beautiful, pretty* and *tall*. Women are never described as *important, famous, rich, poor, afraid, pleased* or *happy*.
(d) Statistically, the most important adjectives used to describe men are *poor, rich, young, old, strong, tall* and *fat*. They are never described as *busy*, and they are relatively unlikely to be described as *angry*.

This collocational analysis shows that even in a series such as *Welcome to English*, where a serious attempt was made to be gender fair, gender stereotyping still persists at the level of language.

KWIC concordances: the cases of *busy/works* and *letter/letters*

Computational linguistics is revealing subtle and complex patterns in language use which were previously virtually unsuspected. For example, the richness of variation in associative meaning amongst different forms of a verb, between singular and plural forms of a noun, or between semantically closely related words, and the underlying logic of these patterns, is now becoming evident.

The Key Word in Context (KWIC) concordance is a useful tool for studying such variations in meaning. A set of KWIC concordance output consists of the key word in a column (usually in the centre of each line) with context to either side of it – the depth of context being determined by the researcher. For some purposes, the context may be a longer unit such as the sentence or paragraph. To the left-hand side of each line information usually concerns the location of the example in the text: a line number, say, or unit and lesson numbers. It is possible to use this locational information for selective analysis, for example of the words of a single character in a dialogue, or the rubric of a particular activity type.

Because this kind of columnar presentation of information facilitates detailed study of underlying patterns, KWIC concordances should be seen as input to a process of analysis, rather than ends in themselves. Generally, concordance data will probably be the input to a process of counting and classification, leading to conclusions about the item itself, or comparisons between items and texts. In the case of Examples 4 and 5 below, partly because they are brief and simple, the likely patterns are easy to see, and show how variations in usage can be relevant to gender. Importantly, they have been selected as representative. (Concordance data is lengthy and limitations of space prevent us from giving complete concordances, but the excerpts given are faithful to the overall pattern.)

To say that someone is 'busy' in English means that they are occupied to the extent that they are not available to do anything else. 'Busy' has no denotation of reward or payment, and can therefore refer to paid or unpaid activity – including the use of excessive energy or (possibly wasted) effort. 'Work', on the other hand, almost always suggests productive, paid labour. This distinction is not itself evidence of gender bias, but there are several ways in which gender bias could become evident. First, the same item may have different connotations for men and women – if, for example, a 'busy man' is in some way different from a 'busy woman', or a 'working man' is different from a 'working woman'. Second, there may be instances where a form is not used for both sexes – a 'working girl', for example, but not a 'working boy'. Third, where there are two items with different connotations, they may be gender segregated – if, for example, a man 'works', but a woman 'is busy'.

In Example 4, the simple present form of work is taught essentially as a masculine verb – 'he works' – with a variety of object complements (on the land, in an office, a theatre or a shop). There is only one example of a woman who works – and she 'sometimes' works as a secretary. However, she is a very busy woman. 'He works' *as* something; 'she is busy', but at what is unclear. A difference in usage which need not have any relationship to gender has implications for gender relations in this specific text.

Example 4
A sample of *busy* and *works* from *Welcome to English*, Book 1.

			busy	3
14	8	Lesson 8 She is a very	busy	woman. Scotland England Wales Lond
14	8	e as a secretary. She is a very	busy	woman. a Where does Jenny's family
			works	9
12	6	e? m He gets up before dawn. He	works	on the land. He sleeps in the aft
12	6	ter dawn. He lives upstairs and	works	downstairs. He finishes work afte
12	6	comes from another country. He	works	in an office. He goes to work in
13	5	an actor. He acts in plays. He	works	in a theater. he also acts with p
13	5	re you can see a shopkeeper. He	works	in a shop. He buys and sells thin
13	5	ctor. Where do they work? Sabry	works	in a theater. What do they do the
14	8	ter them at home. Sometimes she	works	in an office as a secretary. She

'Letter', meaning a message written on paper and sent to someone, shows interesting differences in meaning between singular and plural. 'Letter' in the singular tends to refer to an act of communication – the act of writing, receiving, reading, etc., an individual letter. 'Letters' in the plural tends to be associated more with the production process than with the act of communication – 'writing letters' in general, rather than a letter to an individual, 'typing letters', 'posting letters', and so on. If someone is 'writing a letter', this is more likely to be to a specified individual, with known purpose or content. If someone is 'writing letters', the addressees are unlikely to be specified. In a work-related situation, an individual who writes, reads, types or posts an individual letter is likely to be concerned with the specific message, and therefore an active participant in communication, whereas an individual who writes, reads, types or posts letters in general is more likely to be filling a menial role. An individual who writes and reads work-related letters is also likely to be of higher occupational standing than one who merely types or posts them. Example 5 shows how these ostensibly neutral differences can become gender related.

Example 5
A sample of *letter* and *letters* from *Excel in English*, Book 1.

			letter	39
4	12	them in your answer to George's	letter.	read read read go went gone sho
5	14	ephone rang. She was typing the	letter.	The lights went out. He was run
5	14	hurt his leg. 8. Henry wrote a	letter.	The lights go out. 9. We do our
10	28	to meet you. He's sent you this	letter.	Dr. Field: Thank you. Dr. Fiel
10	30	eld a letter, or not? 4. In the	letter,	does Alan Scott explain that he
12	36	y tomorrow, . . . 2. If I get a	letter	from Mark tomorrow, ... 3. If i
13	38	ation Mr. Pearce has received a	letter	from Mr. James. Mr. Pearce is sp
			letters	25
2	5	g letters NOW! Miss Smith types	letters	every day. Monday Tuesday Wedne
2	5	king coffee. Miss Smith posting	letters.	Talk like this: 1. Look! Miss
2	5	rs every day. now. 2. John post	letters	every afternoon. now. 3. Helen
3	8	day. Write Miss Smith post the	letters	yesterday evening. Miss Smith p
5	14	g suddenly. 10. Miss Smith type	letters.	She make several mistakes
15	45	ing 10 a.m. Asked Helen to type	letters	and post them. Cancelled dentis

With one exception, all references to a singular 'letter' are to writing, sending, receiving and reading specific communications. All have male authors, senders, recipients and readers. The only exception is a female typing a letter, of which she is not the author. All references to 'letters' in the plural relate to the typing and posting of letters by relatively menial office staff – all but one of whom are female.

These examples show how apparently 'gender-neutral' language items can be used systematically in different ways – and how this can have gender implications. They do not suggest immutable laws – such as that *letters* is always associated with secretaries. They do illustrate what can be learned by this kind of investigation into a textbook's representation of gender.

Conclusions

The above examples are specific instances, in specific books. They cannot be generalised to all ELT books, except by further research. Their purpose is to demonstrate that gender bias can and does occur in very subtle ways, and to suggest exploratory techniques which can be used with other textbooks.

This analysis shows that even when a conscious attempt is made at gender fairness, there is gender imbalance at a subtle level: words' frequency of occurrence, distribution, collocates and contexts. It also shows the complexity and protean character of such bias. Gender fairness is much more than a matter of getting numbers of characters and relative roles right: it must pervade the warp and weft of the text.

One major theme of this paper has thus been the subtlety of linguistic variation. A second theme has been the apparently tenuous, but often strong associations which can exist between linguistic variations which are not in themselves pernicious and other factors, in this case gender; associations which can place an entirely different complexion on linguistically neutral differences in usage. A third theme has been the importance of empirical evidence and statistical techniques in defining the nature, scope and quantitative significance of the evidence, and of computer techniques in making this evidence available. It is possible for textbook writers and users to remain unconscious of the complexity of variations in language use, until they are confronted with them in an objective form such as this.

Does this kind of non-random language use matter? Clearly, the authors' view is that it does. The *Welcome to English* books do not lack suitable female role models; these were built in. In spite of this, the image of women portrayed by the language use is overwhelmingly of passivity, physical characteristics, menial roles, irrational worries, constant undemanding activities, and not of economic activity (hence textbook women are not rich or poor).

Such bias is unlikely to prevent a student learning English. It may discourage her, if she sees it as an activity in which she is considered less likely than males to succeed, or as an activity associated primarily with males, in which her role is primarily that of spectator or adjunct. In a world where economic advantage is associated with knowledge of English, considerations of equity alone would require that this should not happen. It certainly should not be the role of English language teachers or textbook writers to deliver to some of their students the message that they are less likely to succeed than other members of the class, should expect to play a subordinate role, or are in any other way less important as people.

Note

1. Gender bias has in fact been found in the texts of most school subjects. Geoffrey Walford (1981) demonstrates sex bias in the illustrations, questions and texts of a selection of physics textbooks, and shows that in some texts physics is presented as a male rather than female subject (see also Sandra L. Ogren, 1985; Gwyneth Britton and Margaret Lumpkin, 1983; and Kathleen Garrity, 1987).

'The Boss Was Called Mr Power': Learners' Perspectives on Sexism in EFL Materials

CHRISTINE MANNHEIM

Introduction

The appropriacy of materials in terms of level and subject matter has always been a concern of teachers and publishers, but there is now also a growing recognition of the importance of both cultural appropriacy and avoiding bias. Sexism is increasingly recognised as one aspect of bias. How not to be sexist is included in guidelines to journalists, for example those published by the National Union of Journalists (NUJ). The equivalent in EFL publishing, 'On Balance: Guidelines for the Representation of Women and Men in ELT Materials' comprises Case Study 1 of this Quadrant.

Most reactions to EFL textbook sexism have come from teachers who have felt uncomfortable with or offended by certain materials or publishers anxious to satisfy a world-wide audience. (See, for example, Jane Sunderland and Margaret Hennessy, this Quadrant; also, David Haines' Comment in this Quadrant.)

There remains however an information gap as regards how EFL students perceive materials. This is now particularly apparent and relevant with the shift in emphasis to more learner-centred approaches in teaching methodology and the realisation that exclusive language, stereotyping and visuals – in this case, so-called generic nouns and pronouns (see Edward Woods and Deborah Cameron, Quadrant I[1]), predictable and outdated stereotypes of women and girls (see Jane Sunderland, Quadrant II, Introduction), and images of women who are fewer, smaller and more formally dressed than men, and again stereotyped – may affect learner image. This paper reports on a study which attempts to begin to fill that information gap.

The informants

There were 72 potential informants: about 60 per cent were European, 20 per cent Japanese, and the other 20 per cent included Israeli state school teachers on sabbatical. The age range extended from mid-twenties to mid-thirties. All were attending intensive language courses (general English or executive courses) at a private language school in London. They came from eight different classes and 32 of them were taught by me. Their language proficiency, determined by a multiple-choice grammar and listening test plus oral interview, was intermediate upwards. Many had not previously discussed the subject of textbook sexism in class.

Research approach

Learners' views on sexism in materials were probed by means of a questionnaire (see p. 90). Personal details and language learning background were asked for, but not names. The questionnaire was supplemented by follow-up interviews with selected respondents.

I first gave an initial oral introduction to the questionnaire to each class as a whole, with time for queries, after which students who wished to completed the questionnaire at home.

The aim of the written Introduction to the questionnaire was not only to explain overall aims and give instructions but also to get students to reflect on the subject of textbook discrimination and sexism. Respondents were encouraged to look through their textbooks and files in order to refresh their memories and to help them to give specific examples before completing the questionnaire.

The questions were designed to cover views on: (a) the proportion of men and women in EFL textbooks, (b) gender stereotyping, (c) appropriacy of language and vocabulary, and (d) the appropriacy of themes and topics, role plays and other classroom activities. Rather than using a scale such as the Lickert Scale, learners were asked, where appropriate, to give examples and specific instances to support their views.

Findings

After introducing the questionnaire, a few of the queries were language based but most were about the purpose of the questionnaire. Some students were quite interested, many were a little suspicious and a few were openly dismissive.

The response rate for the questionnaire was a little over 60 per cent: 45 were returned (14 of the 45 respondents were selected for follow up by interviewing).

Questionnaires

The sex of the potential and actual respondents was as follows:

	W	M	Total
Received questionnaire	46	26	72
Returned completed questionnaire	31	14	45
Follow up	7	7	14

(In this and the tables that follow, W = female respondents and M = male respondents.)

Quantitative responses to questionnaire Items 1–6

1 Proportion of males and females in teaching materials

'too many women'		'too many men'		'about right'	
W	M	W	M	W	M
0%	0%	13%	0%	87%	100%

2 Reflection of reality

Good		Not good		Don't know/blank	
W	M	W	M	W	M
68%	58%	16%	21%	16%	21%

3 Roles and characters of men and women in teaching materials

Differences in —	Yes		No		Don't know/blank	
	W	M	W	M	W	M
(a) appearance?	23%	21%	26%	21%	51%	58%
(b) activities/body positioning?	16%	7%	61%	58%	23%	35%
(c) what they say?	26%	14%	26%	58%	48%	28%
(d) their jobs?	32%	36%	32%	50%	36%	14%
(e) their characters?	6%	7%	0%	0%	94%	93%
(f) how they are talked about by others?	0%	0%	0%	0%	100%	100%
(g) their voices? (on cassettes)	13%	0%	10%	21%	77%	79%
(h) who takes the dominant or leading part?	0%	7%	26%	43%	74%	50%
(i) age?	19%	14%	62%	58%	19%	28%
(j) other positive or negative characteristics?	0%	0%	0%	0%	100%	100%

4 Themes or subjects found to be offensive or uncomfortable

Yes		No		Don't know/blank	
W	M	W	M	W	M
23%	28%	64%	58%	13%	14%

5 Inappropriate language practice – spoken or written

Yes		No		Don't know/blank	
W	M	W	M	W	M
0%	0%	68%	86%	32%	14%

6 Inappropriate activities or role plays

Yes		No		Don't know/blank	
W	M	W	M	W	M
0%	0%	58%	93%	42%	7%

Summary of questionnaire findings

In response to Question 1, whereas none of the male respondents thought there was an imbalance of men and women, 13 per cent of the female respondents identified one. A majority of both sexes felt that the 'reflection of reality' (Question 2) was 'Good'.

Gender differences were perceived in all areas asked about in Question 3 except (f) 'how they are talked about by others', although 'Don't know' and 'Blank' were also the most common answers for (a) 'appearance' (both sexes), (c) 'what they say' (women), (d) 'their jobs' (women), (e) 'their characters' (both sexes), (g) 'their voices' (both sexes), and (h) 'who takes the dominant or leading part' (both sexes). Respondents perceived most gender differences in (d) jobs, (a) appearance, (c) what they say (largely with reference to business-oriented materials), and (i) age – the general feeling also being that materials tended to be biased towards the young. Visuals were often cited as examples and seemed to be especially memorable.

A larger proportion of female than male respondents perceived gender differences in six out of the nine areas – though a larger proportion of females also perceived no difference in appearance, activities/body positioning or age. Polarisation in fact seemed to be a characteristic of women's responses rather than men's: both sexes were polarised for 'appearance' and 'jobs' but women were polarised also for 'their voices' and 'what they say'.

The greatest sex difference in perception was in (b) activities/body positioning (which included shopping, cooking), and in (g) voices, these being perceived by 16 per cent of women but only 7 per cent of men, and 13 per cent of women and no men, respectively.

Approximately one quarter of all male and female respondents had found themes or subjects to be offensive or uncomfortable (Question 4), but no-one identified inappropriate language practice (Question 5) or inappropriate activities or role plays (Question 6).

Interviews

What follows is a selection of comments on and observations by the fourteen students during the follow-up interviews. The quotation marks indicate close paraphrasing taken from notes made, rather than absolute verbatim. (Relevant comments made on previous occasions are also included, indicated with an asterisk.)

Question 1 (Proportion of males and females)

The women who felt there were too many men were all executive course students. The materials about which they made this complaint were 'Business English' materials.

Question 3 (Roles and characters)

Comments included:

'You don't see many older women except where they are grandmothers or a bit strange.'

'The women are mostly young but there are older men.'

'The way men and women are shown is OK, normal, but sometimes it would be good to show the fathers more with children – usually it's the women who are with children. Also it's the same for shopping.'

'Are there any older women in Britain except the Queen? . . . and Barbara Cartland?'

(Speaking about a piece of material that looked at famous women and their achievements) 'I liked this – it was interesting not to learn about the same persons all the time – not just famous men. I didn't know this information before.'

'You see women in some sports like keep-fit, gymnastics, skating, but not enough in the exciting or so active ones like parachuting, climbing, windsurfing, skiing.'

'The books now are more modern but I can remember when I studied English before, in jobs the women were secretaries and the boss was called Mr Power.'

'I would like more listening of women.' (referring to recordings used on an executive course)

(Referring to a role play 'The Right Man for the Job') 'It would be nice to include a woman as a candidate – it's a job that women can do also.'

'Most books show traditional roles.'

*'Men have more respectful names.' (examples: Mr Briggs v. Lulu, Gloria)

*'Sometimes in the pictures women aren't wearing serious clothes, but the men are always wearing seriously.' (i.e. men in suits and women in more glamorous attire)

*'Women's voices on cassettes sometimes sound silly – too high and going up and down a lot.'

Question 4 (Offensive/upsetting themes or subjects)

The topics most frequently cited as causing offence or discomfort were war, politics and religion.

Comments included:-

'Most books, especially for lower levels, describe how a normal life should be – very boring!'

'Why do teachers think marriage is always interesting for women? For me it's not so interesting – I'm bored with discussing it' (resented the expectation that as a woman she was the expert on it). Similar comments were made on food and cooking.

These preliminary findings, both quantitative and qualitative, suggest interesting and fruitful areas for future investigations.

Observations on the research approach

Information such as this is not easy to gain access to. This is partly due to the limitations of written questionnaires, the sensitivity of the subject and the potential for student resistance. Among students' reservations were their difficulties in articulating their thoughts in writing and in English. There may have been reading problems too. In addition, some questions may have been too general. A 'Don't know' or blank response thus does not necessarily indicate a lack of interest. Importantly, different reasons and views may well lie behind similar responses (see also Jane Sunderland, Quadrant III).

Nevertheless, certain approaches can be adopted to facilitate access to information and encourage fuller and more interesting responses. The follow-up interviews proved to be very effective here. Once their trust and confidence had been won, students responded well to a more personal approach and found it easier, language-wise, to express themselves orally. The result was that it was possible to talk through students' answers, obtain more detailed answers, and probe participants' views in more depth. It also enabled more effective use of those questions which did not produce responses, and provided guidelines towards amending them in the future.

As far as changing levels of awareness is concerned, the process of data collection itself may have gone some way towards achieving this. Respondents can also have their questionnaires returned and be encouraged to review their answers. More awareness raising could also take place as part of class activities. Questions such as 'Have you ever thought about the representation of men and women in teaching materials?', 'Have you ever discussed it?', 'Do you think it is important?', could be broached as part of a discussion session.

Conclusion

While uncovering some of the difficulties and issues to be aware of in collecting data in this field, this study also leaves no doubt that some learners at least are sensitive to sexism and bias in EFL materials, particularly in areas such as the invisibility of women in some spheres and the stereotyping and narrowness of certain roles – in relation to elderly women, for instance.

Avenues for further research could include more in-depth investigation of certain areas such as learners' views on expectations of 'reality' in materials. Research and pedagogy could also be combined by making the study of the portrayal of men and women in materials part of group discussions or a class project, or seeing what effect reversing textbook character gender roles and altering stereotypical portrayals would have. This is, certainly, a rich and rewarding area for further research into, among other things, the implications for effective language learning.

Note

1. For another way of understanding 'exclusive language', see David Carroll and Johanna Kowitz, this Quadrant.

QUESTIONNAIRE

Introduction

The aim of this questionnaire is to find out more about what you as students think of the materials that are used to teach English.

We are particularly interested in whether you think these materials discriminate against men or women – whether for example men or women are unfairly represented.

Before you go on to answer the following questionnaire, think for a minute about the materials that you have worked with. Remember these can include videos, cassettes, newspapers, pictures, role-plays and discussions as well as textbooks. Feel free to look through your notes, textbooks or files and to refer to these while doing the questionnaire. Try to give specific examples where possible. Your answers are valuable as they will go towards the future design of teaching materials.

1. What do you think of the proportion of males and females represented in teaching materials?

    too many women   too many men   about right

2. How accurately do you think teaching materials reflect reality?

    Are there things you would add to make the reflection of society more realistic?

    Are there things you would remove?

3. What do you feel about the way men and women are shown in teaching materials – their roles and characters?
    Do you notice any differences in the way they are shown?

    Please consider: Your comments

    (a) appearance
        for example clothes/hairstyle

    (b) activities, body positioning

    (c) what they say

    (d) their jobs

    (e) their characters

    (f) how they are talked about
        by others

    (g) their voices (on cassettes)

    (h) who takes the dominant or leading part

(i) age

(j) other positive or negative characteristics

Comment on as many of these as you can.

4. Are there any themes or subjects that have made you feel uncomfortable, or that have made you angry or offended you? If so, could you give details including why.

5. During controlled language practice – for example accuracy work – have you ever been asked to say or write something that you felt was inappropriate to you as a man or woman, or something that was not relevant to you?

If so give details:

6. Have you ever felt that any of the activities or role-plays you have done in class were not appropriate to you as a man or woman? If so, details please.

Finally, something about your background.

Nationality:

Sex:

Age:

Occupation:

Language learning background
(how long, size of class, where?):

That is the end of the questionnaire. Thank you very much!

Pedagogical and Other Filters: The Representation of Non-sexist Language Change in British Pedagogical Grammars

JANE SUNDERLAND

Introduction

Grammars play an important role in many teachers' and learners' experience of ELT, often consulted as to what can and should be said. Examiners, too, are influenced by them. In the absence (or even presence) of a native speaker of English a grammar is likely to be taken as correct; this is probably as true now as it ever was. Roger Gower notes that 'grammar hasn't been thrown overboard to lighten the load: if anything, after a temporary absence during the "Communicative Revolution", it's been made more complex for being recast in a more subtle, less prescriptive and less formalistic mould' (1981: 53). And this was written even before the resurgence of interest in grammar in the later 1980s and the 1990s.

Grammars have to describe rules for the language, but because pedagogical grammars (henceforth PGs) have to select, and are expected by their readers to provide guidance, they must also be to a greater or lesser degree prescriptive.

Describing language rules is difficult considering that language is in a continual state of change. It is exacerbated when change is rapid, even observable – as are the changes under discussion here. Numerous questions are raised. When is a change well enough established to be documented? What if there is no empirical evidence? What counts as evidence? Do linguistic corpora provide adequate data? What if the change in question is current only among certain groups? How is it best represented? Should changes documented in PGs juxtapose newly established forms with (declining) older alternatives? Should reasons for the change be given? If a change stems from a 'problem', should that problem be identified and glossed? In those PGs whose entries are arranged alphabetically, should 'non-sexist language' have its own entry as well as the integration of different forms in the relevant sections?

Prescribing grammar rules also raises questions, especially since PGs by common-sense definition would seem to have the facilitation of grammar learning as an objective. Learners' needs may conflict here: Sylvia Chalker identifies those of 'accuracy versus simplicity' and 'an awareness of new developments . . . versus well-established descriptions' (1984: 85). How best to deal, for example, with 'singular' *their* following an indefinite pronoun when most readers will have been taught or read in other grammars that it should be *his*? And how can PG writers protect their readers from sounding old-fashioned while at the same time not suggest alternatives which may be current at the time of writing but which may soon become dated?

A little work has been done on sexism and the representation of gender-related words in grammars. Ann Bodine (1990) has traced the history of the representation of 'generic' *he*, Julia Stanley (1978) and Elizabeth S. Sklar (1983) have looked at sexism in descriptions of code in English grammars, and stereotypical examples have been criticised (e.g. Stanley, 1978; Kate Stephens, 1990). This study, however, looks more optimistically at contemporary evidence of the movement towards representing alternatives to sexist language in PGs, the main questions being (a) are these changes represented? and (b) if so, how? Representation can be seen as secondary evidence for a change having 'arrived'; further, the documentation of a change in a grammar (or dictionary – see Garland Cannon and Susan Roberson, 1985; also Margaret Hennessy, this Quadrant) may play a role in the maintenance and perpetuation of that change.

There is some direct, empirical evidence for change in use of gender words (Robert Cooper, 1984; Sandra Purnell, 1978; Barbara Bate, 1978; Cathryn Adamsky, 1981; Anne Pauwels, 1989; see also Quadrant I, Introduction). The amount of evidence is not large, however. Even existing corpora may not provide sufficient information. Renee Dirven claims that 'presently available linguistic corpora are not diversified enough nor sufficiently based on spontaneously spoken language to serve as input for learner-oriented descriptions' (1990: 2).

Which grammars? Which items?

In my original study (1986) I examined twenty British PGs published between 1972 and 1986 and one due to be published in 1987 (though actually published in 1989).[1] All were available in the Resources Centre of Lancaster University's Institute for English Language Education, widely used by overseas students and overseas and British teachers of English – though I read the PG due to be published in 1987 in manuscript form. Two editions of *Practical English Grammar* appeared in the sample, and this was to prove revealing. (For comparison purposes, I also looked at the *Comprehensive Grammar of the English Language*.) The selection was thus done on a pragmatic basis, and corresponds well to Renee Dirven's observation that 'In English, the term "pedagogical grammar" usually covers both learning and teaching grammars' (1990: 1), and to his working definition:

> we can understand pedagogical grammar (PG) as a cover-term for any learner- or teacher-oriented description or presentation of foreign language rule complexes with the aim of promoting and guiding learning processes in the acquisition of that language. This . . . leaves room for various types of pedagogical grammar, i.e. a learning grammar, . . . a teaching grammar, a reference grammar, . . . a university grammar and even some linguistic grammars.[2]

The twenty-one PGs were, in order of publication:

A Grammar of Contemporary English, 1972. (Randolph Quirk, Sydney Greenbaum, Geoffrey Leech and Jan Svartvik) Longman. (*GCE*)

A University Grammar of English, 1972. (Randolph Quirk and Sydney Greenbaum) Longman. (*UGE*)

A Communicative Grammar of English, 1975. (Geoffrey Leech and Jan Svartvik) Longman. (*CGE*)

A Reference Grammar for Students of English, 1975. (R.A. Close) Allen and Unwin. (*RGSE*)

Practical English Usage, 1980. (Michael Swan) OUP. (*PEU*)

A Practical English Grammar, 3rd edn, 1980. (A.J. Thompson and A.V. Martinet) OUP. (*PEG3*)

A Learner's Grammar of English, 1980. (Norman Coe) Nelson. (*LGE*)

English as a Foreign Language, Its Constant Grammatical Problems, 1981. (R.A. Close) Allen and Unwin. (*EFL*)

English Grammar for Today, 1982. (Geoffrey Leech, Margaret Deuchar and Robert Hoogenraad) Macmillan. (*EGT*)

A Basic English Grammar, 1982. (John Eastwood and Ronald Mackin) OUP. (*BEG*)

Oxford Guide to English Usage, 1983. OUP. (*OGEU*)

Cassell's Student's English Grammar, 1983. (Jake Allsop) Cassell. (*SEG*)

Basic English Usage, 1984. (Michael Swan) OUP. (*BEU*)

The Student's Grammar of English, 1984. (Jan E. van Ek and Nico Robat) Blackwell. (*SGE*)

Current English Grammar, 1984. (Sylvia Chalker) Macmillan. (*CEG*)

A Very Simple Grammar of English, 1985. (Celia Blisset and Katherine Hallgarten) Language Teaching Publications. (*VSGE*)

Basic Working Grammar, 1986. (David Bolton, Mats Oscarson and Lennart Peterson) Nelson. (*BWG*)

A Practical English Grammar, 4th edn, 1986. (A.J. Thompson and A.V. Martinet) OUP. (*PEG4*)

Active Grammar, 1986. (W-D. Bald, D.J. Cobb and A. Schwarz) Longman. (*AG*)

Grammar for Everyday Use, 1986. (Ona Low) Collins ELT. (*GEU*)

An A-Z of English Grammar and Usage, 1989 – eventual date of publication. (Geoffrey Leech with Benita Cruikshank and Roz Ivanic) (*AZEGU*)

And, for comparison:

A Comprehensive Grammar of the English Language, 1985. (Randolph Quirk, Sydney Greenbaum, Geoffrey Leech and Jan Svartvik) Longman. (*CGEL*)

This would not normally be considered to be a PG. However, it is sometimes consulted by teachers of English. More importantly, for comparison purposes, it illustrates what a grammar not specifically aimed at learners of English can say about non-sexist items, and accordingly what a grammar aimed at advanced learners of English could come near to saying.

I chose to look first at each PG for mention of the following non-sexist items, and secondly at how those mentioned were represented:

1. 'Pair' forms
   (a) 'dual class gender-neutral' forms, e.g. police officer
   (b) *-person* forms
   (c) a decline in *-ess* and/or *-ette* endings
   (d) *Ms*

2. Alternatives to the following masculine generics
   (a) *man/a man/men*
   (b) *he/him/himself/his*
      (i) *they* forms
      (ii) non-*they* forms

Were the changes represented?

Table 1 shows which PGs mentioned which changes. As can be seen, there was considerable variation, only one (*AZEGU*) mentioning all the changes. Several totally ignored many or most of the changes, even when they included sections in which mention could relevantly be made – no *Ms*, for example, in a section on 'titles'. Representation of a change is indicated in Table 1 by '+' (mention), '–' (no mention, though there was an appropriate section), or 'N/A' (no appropriate section).

Broadly, even where there were appropriate sections, only some of the changes appeared more often than not. Dual class gender-neutral forms were mentioned in only six PGs out of a possible sixteen, and *-person* forms were mentioned in seven grammars where there was an appropriate section and not mentioned in ten. The decrease in *-ess/-ette* forms was mentioned in only three out of a possible seventeen. *Ms* was mentioned in six and not mentioned in five. (Both *-person* words and *Ms* were mentioned more in those grammars published in or after 1983 – the more recent half of the sample – than before.)

Alternatives to 'generic' *he* were given far more frequently than alternatives to 'generic' *man*, which occurred only once out of a possible three times (on *man*, see Linden Salter-Duke, 1983; Robert Cooper, 1984; Jane Sunderland, 1991). *They* as an alternative to 'generic' *he* occurred thirteen times out of a possible eighteen times and non-*they* alternatives ten times out of the same possible eighteen. ('Alternatives to "generic" *he*' has in fact been long established as a topic in grammars, 'singular' *they* hardly being a recent phenomenon: see e.g. Gerry Abbott, 1984.)

Why the variation from one PG to another? Level of audience and intended comprehensiveness are partially responsible (there is a limit to what a grammar for beginners can express, and how), but only partially. Dirven (1990: 2) uses the notion of a 'pedagogical filter' (a 'whole complex set of pedagogical factors') which

Table 1
Occurrence of new non-sexist language items in the twenty-one British pedagogical
grammars (1972–1987)

PG and date	'dual class gender-neutral' form increase	*-person* forms	*-ess/-ette* decrease	*Ms*	*man* alternatives	*they* alternatives to 'generic' *he*	non-*they* alternatives to 'generic' *he*
GCE (72)	+	–	+	–	N/A	+	+
UGE (72)	+	–	+	–	N/A	+	+
CGE (75)	–	–	–	–	N/A	–	–
RGSE (75)	–	–	–	N/A	N/A	–	–
PEU (80)	–	+	–	+	N/A	+	+
PEG3 (80)	+	+	–	N/A	N/A	+	–
LGE (80)	–	–	–	–	N/A	+	+
EFL (81)	N/A	N/A	N/A	N/A	–	N/A	N/A
EGT (82)	N/A	N/A	N/A	N/A	N/A	+	+
BEG (82)	–	+	–	N/A	N/A	–	–
OGEU (83)	N/A	–	–	–	N/A	+	+
SEG (83)	–	–	–	+	N/A	+	+
BEU (84)	–	+	–	+	N/A	+	+
SGE (84)	+	–	–	N/A	N/A	+	+
CEG (84)	–	+	–	+	N/A	+	–
VSGE (85)	N/A	N/A	N/A	N/A	N/A	–	–
BWG (86)	–	–	–	+	–	N/A	N/A
PEG4 (86)	+	+	–	N/A	N/A	+	–
AG (86)	–	–	–	N/A	N/A	–	–
GEU (86)	N/A	N/A	N/A	N/A	N/A	N/A	N/A
AZEGU (89)	+	+	+	+	+	+	+

(See p.94 for names of grammars in full.)

descriptive grammar may (and some would say should) pass through before appearing in a PG. Is it possible that descriptive grammar (itself not free from subjectivity) further passes through the PG writer's 'personal ideology' filter (and other personal filters and publishers' filters) resulting in different writers having different priorities? This is suggested even more strongly in the variation in ways these changes are represented, including the use of unverified claims.

What was said about the changes?

The PGs varied considerably in their representation of the non-sexist language items, making it hard to avoid the impression that many of the descriptions/prescriptions do indeed reflect their authors' own feelings and attitudes.

1(a) 'Dual class gender-neutral' forms

Of the six PGs mentioning these, only three suggested this was an area of change: *GCE*, *UGE* and *AZEGU*. *GCE* and *UGE* talk about 'optional feminine forms' and of certain forms 'no longer in normal use' being replaced by the dual gender forms; *AZEGU* talks of certain endings 'becoming rarer nowadays'. The reason for the change given in *GCE* is that 'more and more positions in society are opened up to both sexes' (the idea of linguistic change reflecting social change).

CGEL (published twelve years later) gives as a reason for the increase the avoidance of sexual bias in language – a far more ideological explanation. Though comprehensiveness and having a linguistically sophisticated audience in mind are no guarantee that the products of non-sexist language change will be described positively and accurately, with an indication of their progressive nature, comprehensive grammars certainly have most potential to do this.

Interestingly, though *GCE* and *UGE* make strong claims for 'gender markers' (*GCE*) and 'sex markers' (*UGE*), such as *male nurse* and *female engineer*, the later *CGEL* has dropped this. *CGEL* further comments that 'introduced' dual class gender-neutral forms (such as *flight attendant*) are used most by speakers of American English.

PEG (both editions) and *SGE* did not imply any change, *PEG* referring to 'most nouns' (*PEG3*) and 'the majority of personal' (*PEG4*) nouns having the same (gender) form. (Interestingly, *PEG3*, published in 1980, reads the same as *PEG2*, published in 1969.) *SGE* observes 'many nouns denoting persons are neutral with regard to sex'. Examples include *doctor* and *driver* (*PEG4*) and *friend, guest, librarian, professor* and *student* (*SGE*).

Dual class gender-neutral forms are well established. Accordingly, grammar writers are unlikely to discourage learners from using them, and new non-sexist items, as long as their morphology is familiar, are accommodated on the same basis.

1(b) -person forms

Potentially productive, *-person* forms are a special case of new examples of dual class gender-neutral forms. However, unlike familiar-sounding occupation terms, such as *flight attendant*, *-person* forms are still conspicuous, marked to the point of being a declaration of the user's politics, in relation to more than just the Women's Movement.

PEG is the most interesting PG here. In the 1969 2nd edition there was, as expected, no mention of *-person* forms. In the 1980 edition (*PEG3*) they receive a very guarded explanation: after reference to *chairman* and *chairwoman* we read the curiously worded claim that 'Recently there has been an <u>attempt</u> to <u>desex</u> these words by using *-person* instead of *-man*. This <u>fashion</u> may not last.' (my underlining) In *PEG4* (1986), the line is that exceptions to dual class gender-neutral forms include *salesman*, *saleswoman*, etc., but that 'sometimes *-person* is used instead of *-man*, *-woman*: *salesperson*, *spokesperson*'.

The idea of change in this area is more overtly addressed by *Practical English Usage*, which refers to 'a move to replace words like [*chairman*] by forms like *chairperson*'.

Users of *-person* words are sometimes specified: 'many people' (*BEU*), 'many people (especially women)' (*AZEGU*) and, questionably, 'feminists' (*CEG*). This claim could be discouraging. In full, *CEG* reads: 'Some words which have a distinctly one-sex connotation, such as *bar maid*, *chairman* are avoided by feminists who prefer such neologisms as *bar person*, *chairperson* and so on.'

CGEL notes that both *-man* and *-person* forms are 'very productive type[s]' of verbless compounds, the second constituent always being a human agent, and that *-man* and *-person* could almost be seen as suffixes. Certainly, *-man* is a weak form in that it is pronounced /man/, and so in speech it is no longer homonymous with the word *man*. Perhaps this is one reason why it seems less 'objectionable', why *-person* has not become more popular, and why grammars describe it with some reluctance.

Further evidence of a difficulty with *-person* is suggested by the paucity of examples: in the seven PGs which mention *-person* words, only four different ones are given: *chairperson* (six mentions), *salesperson* (three mentions), *spokesperson* (two mentions) and *bar person* (one mention).[3] Perhaps this is because, as *AZEGU* points out, 'not everybody likes new words'. Whatever the reason, most PGs are not encouraging about these forms.

1(c) -ess/ette endings

A decline in these endings would correspond to an increase in dual class gender-neutral forms and in *-person* words. However, this was mentioned in only three grammars: the related *GCE/UGE* and *AZEGU*, plus *CGEL*.

The terms used to describe most *-ess/-ette* words are 'optional feminine forms' (*GCE*, *UGE*), 'no longer in normal use' (*GCE*), 'now rare' (*UGE*), and are 'becoming rarer nowadays' (*AZEGU*). *CGEL*, which says these endings have 'no justification', gives as the reason 'changing attitudes to women and to sex discrimination'.

The examples given in *GCE*, *UGE* and *AZEGU* are *poetess* and *authoress*. *CGEL* contrasts these with *actress*, which 'is tolerated', since 'there are roles that must be filled by women'. (Personal observation does indicate that women who act do sometimes refer to themselves as *actors*, however.) *CGEL* also notes 'for other but related reasons, *Jewess* and *negress* are little used'. The 'related' is important here. *Negress* of course has racist connotations (as *Jewess* can have); its superordinate, and 'generic' *negro*, is likewise rarely used.

On the few occasions when *-ess/-ette*-related changes *are* documented, then, there is no ambivalence about change going on here.

1(d) Ms

Several of the six entries for *Ms* clearly indicate it to be an example of language change, in particular 'becoming common in Britain' (*PEU*), and 'becoming more popular' (*AZEGU*). *SEG* had a rather different emphasis with 'a currently-accepted neutral form which can replace Mrs or Miss'. This was in fact an asterisked explanation which followed, as examples of titles, '*Mr* and *Mrs* (or *Ms**). *PEU* and *BEU* explain *Ms* as a referent for 'women who do not wish to have to say whether they are married or not';[4] *AZEGU* claims: '*Ms* is for both married and unmarried women.' *CGEL*, perhaps most elegantly and accurately, describes it as 'a female title which avoids making the distinction between married and unmarried', adding 'women differ strongly on whether they wish to be addressed, or referred to, by *Ms*'. It also provides a plural form, as in 'the two Ms Smith(s)', lending *Ms* further validity.

None of these grammars mentions women's own use of *Ms*, which is perhaps most often on forms when a 'title' is required. However, the above entries suggest that *Ms* is making it into the mainstream code, and there is little here to prevent it from becoming part of learners' productive and receptive repertoires.

2(a) 'Generic' man

Since *man* is rarely covered in grammars, neither are alternatives. *AZEGU* uses the example ' "Men have lived on earth for more than a million years", where men = "men and women" ', noting 'nowadays, many people (especially women) dislike this', and suggests 'avoid the problem where you can, e.g. by using neutral words like . . . *human being*.' *CGEL* introduces the 'sex-neutral' form *wo/man*, which could indeed replace 'generic' *man* – but does not seem to have done so.

2(b) Alternatives to 'generic' he

'Generic' *he* itself is still holding its head high in several PGs. It is acknowledged by *EGT* and *OGEU* (and *CGEL*) to be a source of contention, lending weight to alternatives, which are in ready supply.

The most familiar alternatives are 'singular' *they*, *them*, *their* and *themselves*, which are not new and which occupy more space in grammars than any of the items under discussion here. Their use is invariably in connection with indefinite pronouns such as *everyone* and *nobody*, as in 'Someone/somebody has left their bag there' (*BEG*). There are no references to uses such as 'A teacher should know their class', though *PEU* does include the less indefinite *a person*. On the appropriacy of 'singular' *they*, most grammars are clear: it is used 'often . . . informally' (*GCE*, *UGE*), 'in ordinary conversation' (*PEG3*), 'in informal style' (*LGE*), 'in colloquial English' (*PEG4*), and 'in exams [it] is considered incorrect' (AZEGU) – though we also have the description 'not uncommon but often avoided by careful speakers or writers' (*SGE*). *CGEL* points to language change: 'At one time restricted to informal usage, it is now increasingly accepted even in formal usage' and 'The formal ["Everyone thinks he has the answer"] . . . [is] increasingly ignored now.'

Several PGs point out how these alternatives flout number concord – which is why some non-native speakers of English recoil in horror when they come across them, especially in writing. All the more reason, perhaps, for PGs to include them: Sydney Greenbaum notes: 'I would expect pedagogical grammars to give disproportionate attention to those aspects of grammar that . . . are known to cause problems for foreign learners' (1987: 196).[5]

Reasons for the use of the 'singular' *they* alternatives include avoidance of (a) the sexist 'generic' *he* (EGT, *OGEU*, *AZEGU*), (b) the 'troublesome' 'generic' *he* (*PEG4*), and (c) *he or she* (*GCE*, *UGE*, *PEG*, *EGT*). The reasons given in *CGEL* are (a) and (c), together with the dilemma of knowing whether to use *he* or *she*. Probably largely because of the long educational tradition forbidding it, 'singular' *they* seems hard put to have an existence in its own right. It does, however, seem to be alive and well and deemed appropriate in some contexts.

The other alternatives to 'generic' *he* are new and therefore both stylistically and ideologically marked in comparison with 'singular' *they*. *He or she* is given in *PEU*, *OGEU*, *BEU* and *AZEGU*. Other alternatives include, logically enough, *his or her* (*GCE*, *UGE*, *LGE*, *BEU*, *SGE*) and *him or her* (*BEU*), but also *s/he* (*AZEGU* – also *CGEL*). *OGEU* and *PEG* (both editions) give *she/her* when the people referred to are all female, *OGEU* noting: 'If it is known that individuals referred to are all of the same sex, there is no difficulty; use *he* or *she* as appropriate.' *EGT* suggests rather 'reformulating the sentence in the plural: "All citizens can vote as they wish."' *SGE* similarly suggests avoiding the problem by 'using plurals'.

Descriptions of these forms are numerous but tend to be unfavourable – though *LGE* claims that non-*they* alternatives to 'generic' *he* are less incorrect than 'singular' *they*. *GCE* and *UGE* describe *his or her* as a 'still more pedantic alternative [to 'singular' *they*]' and 'a cumbersome device of conjoining both male and female pronouns': they are all 'frequently avoided' (*PEU*) and 'heavy' (*BEU*); and *he or she* is 'rather awkward' (*SGE*) and 'sometimes awkward' (*AZEGU*). Further, 'several repetitions [of these alternatives] in the same passage are always avoided' (*LGE*); similarly *he or she* 'grows unwieldy with repetition' (*OGEU*). *CGEL* claims that *his or her* 'is particularly clumsy if the pronouns have to be repeated'. One feels the problem is being exaggerated.

S/he is mentioned only in *CGEL*, as an 'experimental form'. Reservations are that it is 'only a written form with no corresponding spoken form; and, still more seriously, there is no objective or possessive form.'[6]

On the whole, then, these PGs suggest that non-*they* alternatives to 'generic' *he* are not widely accepted and accordingly tend not to represent them in a way which lends authority and validity.

An ideological reason for avoidance of 'generic' *he* by either 'singular' *they* or other alternatives is given by *EGT*: that it is 'disliked by those who feel it perpetuates a masculine bias in the language' and that nowadays 'many people (especially women) dislike [using the male pronoun to refer to both sexes]'.

How, then, is non-sexist English represented to learners in British PGs of the period 1972–87? An increase in dual class gender-neutral forms and the disappearance of *-ess/-ette* are mentioned infrequently but unequivocally. *-person* forms and *Ms* are mentioned more frequently but with reservations – though these are disappearing, more so in the case of *Ms*. Grammars say little about 'generic' *man* and accordingly offer few alternatives. Alternatives to 'generic' *he*, itself still largely represented as acceptable, include *they* in informal use, and, to a lesser extent, *he or she* and its variants, though these tend to be represented as stylistically inferior.

The period 1972–87 may be history – but the grammars themselves are not, since books are expensive and in many countries are used years after being purchased. If an examiner's PG is an old one, it is still likely to be consulted carefully in the writing of the exam.

Newer grammars

What of grammars published after 1987? What follows is not a contrastive study of this more recent period with the one surveyed, simply a brief examination of three newer PGs: *Longman English Grammar* (1988) by Louis Alexander, Prentice Hall's *Using English Grammar: Meaning and Form* (1990) by Edward Woods and Nicole McLeod and *Collins COBUILD English Grammar* (1990).

Longman English Grammar does not move far from its predecessors. *He or she* is mentioned but is described, dubiously, as 'becoming less acceptable'. Alexander further notes that 'The tendency is to avoid this kind of construction by using plurals', and later gives the example 'Everyone knows what they have to do, don't they?' – which he claims 'has the advantage of avoiding clumsy combinations like *he or she* and does not annoy mixed groups of people'. *-person* is, however, mentioned as replacing *-man* 'in a few nouns' and 'by some people', and he does note that gender differences expressed through *-ess* are 'becoming rarer', that 'words like *manager* are now commonly used for both sexes' and that 'some words, such as *poetess*, are falling into disuse because they are considered disparaging by both sexes'.

Using English Grammar: Meaning and Form, for intermediate to advanced learners of English, does not mention *-person* words, *Ms* or a decline in *-ess* words. It does however include the following entry for *he or she* and 'singular' *they*.

> You may have learnt that such words as *each*, *every*, *any*, etc. are singular determinants and that they must be followed by a singular possessive determiner. So the correct form of the possessive in older grammars would be his in the following sentence:
>
> > Everyone who applies will receive . . . own copy of the instruction booklist.
>
> [generic] *his* is considered by many people to be offensive since it has a gender bias. There is a general tendency in English today to avoid sexist language. Two ways of avoiding it are either to use both the feminine and the masculine (*her or his*, or *his/her*) or to use the plural (*their*). In informal speech and writing, the second alternative, the use of *their*, is the most usual way to deal with the problem. In formal writing, the first alternative is more

common. Probably the best way to avoid the problem altogether is to put the subject into the plural. For example:

All applicants will receive their own copy of the instruction booklet.

Using English Grammar: Meaning and Form can be relatively comprehensive, making possible the above entry, an explanation of the problem of 'generic' *he* and accurate and positive guidelines for use of alternatives (see also Woods and McLeod, 1992).

Collins COBUILD English Grammar seems to play very safe. It includes *Ms* in the list of 'the most common titles which are used before names'. Of *-person* words, it notes: 'Some people now use words ending in "-person", such as "chairperson" and "spokesperson", instead of words ending in "-man", in order to avoid appearing to refer specifically to a man.' This follows the rather confusing 'Words ending in "-man" are used either to refer to men or to both men and women. For example, a "postman" is a man, but a "spokesman" can be a man or a woman.' There is also a statement that 'Words that refer to women often end in "-ess", for example "actress", "waitress" and "hostess" ' – with no mention of even possible decline.

As with many of the earlier PGs, 'singular' *they* is deemed largely acceptable, with *he or she* in formal or written English. Also mentioned is the possibility of using a plural rather than singular noun because 'Some people consider it wrong to use "they" and "them" to refer to one person', and the predictable 'It is clumsy to repeat "he or she" and "him or her." ' *COBUILD* however does also identify the problem with 'generic' *he*: 'many people object to this use because it suggests that the person being referred to is male'.

Conclusion

PGs face a difficult task when outlining rules of usage and use for language which is undergoing change to learners who may have no other reference point. Dirven (1990: 9) identifies the most important requirement of rule presentations as 'promot[ing] cognitive insight into a given rule and the internalisation of the rule'. But language in a state of flux tends to be a matter of variants rather than rules – *s/he*, *he or she* or 'generic' *he*; *flight attendant* or *stewardess*, for example. This has inevitably made decision making by writers of PGs so much harder.

Prescriptively, it may not be surprising if many PG writers have erred on the side of traditional forms, preferring to take the risk of making learners sound old-fashioned, even sexist, rather than suggest they use language associated with an ideology the learners may not share, and which the writers feel may be only short-lived. The situation may be different with future grammars, when the changes in question may well be more firmly established and documented. In the meantime, lacking empirical evidence, grammar writers will undoubtedly continue to deploy their personal ideological as well as pedagogical filters and let their own beliefs about the Women's Movement, language change and social change, and the obligations of educators in general, and ELT professionals and pedagogical grammar writers in particular, play a role in both their selection and their representation of new and familiar non-sexist language forms.

Notes

1. Though 1972 was still early in the most recent wave of the Women's Movement, from the start it was concerned with language. In 1970 Emily Toth criticised 'generic' *he* and *one-man tents*. In 1971 Varda One coined the term 'Manglish', and Germaine Greer in *The Female Eunuch* noted the semantic derogation undergone by *tart*, *slattern*, *bawd* and *witch*, the use of food images as descriptors for women, and overlexicalisation in (derogatory) words for sexually active women and in *vagina* synonyms (see also Deborah Cameron, Quadrant I).
2. For further discussion on what a PG is and is not, see Sydney Greenbaum (1987).
3. Perhaps *-person* words have become more current since then: in the Employment section of a 1991 issue of my local newspaper, the *Lancaster Guardian*, I found advertisements for a *delivery person*, *handyperson*, *groundsperson*, *warehouse person*, *route planning person* and *bar cellar person*. However, though *-person* words may be becoming increasingly accepted, their use at least in the media suggests them to be mainly the province of left-wing, alternative and women's groups, and some women chairers of meetings still prefer to be *chairmen*, not *chairwomen*.
4. For different readings of this, see Jane Sunderland (1992a) and Michael Swan (1992).
5. Native speakers of English, on the other hand, seem to be more upset by *he or she* combinations.
6. Quirk *et al.* add: 'Generally, it is not certain how far the advocacy of non-sexist language will succeed in discouraging such uses as the unmarked masculine pronoun. What is clear is that the feminist movement in language has made many language users aware of problems of sexual bias which were overlooked by earlier generations.'

Propagating Half a Species: Gender in Learners' Dictionaries

MARGARET HENNESSY

Introduction

Language, society and language change

Many people would now agree that language creates as well as represents reality. It thus has the potential to reflect and shape changing as well as established social values. But to reflect and shape the former, language itself must change.

In the past, reports Ann Bodine (1990: 181–2), language change was seen as unconscious and largely unmotivated, but now, in the light of more recent findings, it appears that people can consciously bring about language change if they have the motivation and the means to do so. Feminists certainly have the motivation to remove sexism from language. And, in English at least, we have devised means of expressing ourselves in non-sexist ways (see Edward Woods and Deborah Cameron, Quadrant I). However, non-sexist English is at present consistently employed by only a minority of users. Do we have the means to bring about substantive language change, to standardise non-sexist English, which, at present, remains a deviation from the sexist norm?

> . . . it is not true that the process of semantic change operates magically, untouched by anything but the collective mind. Whether new meanings and new words catch on depends to some extent on what means exist to disseminate them. . . . Any new terms feminists come up with, in order to be institutionalised in the official and public domains of language use, have to pass a number of 'gatekeepers' – the media, education, lexicography . . .
>
> (Cameron, 1985: 82)

In 1984, the Australian Parliament amended the Acts Interpretation Act to the effect that in legislation either gender may include the other (Anne Pauwels, 1991: 11). Measures such as this, along with the introduction of anti-discrimination laws and the publication of guidelines for the use of non-discriminatory language, have contributed to the dissemination and institutionalisation of non-sexist language. It is worth noting, however, that Cameron does not mention government in her list of linguistic gatekeepers. She may be right: the power to bring about radical language change may rest to a far lesser extent in the action of governments than in the influence of traditional linguistic authorities, including dictionaries.

Lexicographers and language

Lexicographers are indeed, as Samuel Johnson declared, 'unhappy mortals': they have set themselves the task of describing language use without prescribing it. But to describe the ways in which an item of language is interpreted and employed is to set down the prescriptions of others (cf. Donald MacKay, 1983: 40). So, although lexicographers might refrain from expressing their own views as to how language should be used, they cannot avoid presenting the views of others. Neither can they deny 'the significant role of the dictionary as the cultural authority of meaning and usage' (H. Lee Gershuny, 1974: 161). One would expect, however, that they provide authoritative rather than authoritarian accounts of language, by treating language use, or rather, uses, as comprehensively as possible, that is, by recording in their dictionaries conflicting language practices, or, in other words, by describing a range of prescriptions.

Learners' dictionaries

For learners, just as for native speakers, their dictionary is a 'major repository of language usage' (Gershuny, 1974: 160). And, given the nature of the relationship between language and society, learners' and native speakers' dictionaries alike are also major sources of cultural knowledge.

The main difference between learners' dictionaries and native speakers' dictionaries is that the former contain far more information than the latter about such phenomena as grammatical behaviour, appropriateness and collocation. This information is necessarily cultural as well as linguistic. What sort of information about language and gender in English-speaking culture do learners' dictionaries provide?

Learners' dictionaries and gender: a survey

Introduction

This paper does not attempt to answer the above question in any comprehensive manner, but rather restricts itself to an examination of a selection of information provided by three British learners' dictionaries, namely:

> *Collins COBUILD English Language Dictionary*. 1987. London: Collins. Abbreviated hereunder to *COBUILD*[1]
> *Longman Dictionary of Contemporary English*. 1987. Harlow: Longman. Abbreviated hereunder to LDOCE.
> *Oxford Advanced Learner's Dictionary of Current English*. 1989. Oxford: Oxford University Press. Abbreviated hereunder to OALDCE.

Although each of these three dictionaries exhibits characteristics which distinguish it from the other two, they are comparable for several reasons: they share the same audience, learners with upper intermediate to advanced levels of English; they treat a similar range of lexical items, grammatical features and stylistic variations; and they were published within two years of each other.

The dictionary information examined below has been selected for its relevance to a number of phenomena which have attracted attention in the literature on language and gender. (For a comparable survey of pedagogical grammars, see Jane Sunderland, this Quadrant.)

Two pronouns and a noun

'Generic' he

'Although gender in English is now primarily natural,' writes Dennis Baron (1986: 110), 'the rule of the generic masculine shows that non-referential gender still exists.' The problem with non-referential gender is that 'generic' *he* turns females, but not males, into potential non-referents. For example, in English it is possible to say, 'Usually, by the time a baby reaches the age of twelve months, *he* is able to walk.'

The three dictionaries surveyed all include 'generic' *he*. 'Some people dislike this use', notes *COBUILD* mysteriously. *LDOCE* is more illuminating: 'Some people, especially women, do not like the use of *he* with a general meaning.' *OALDCE* provides the most satisfactory explanation for the proscription: 'Many people think that this discriminates against women. . . . ' However, after presenting a number of ways of avoiding the use in question, *OALDCE* adds: 'Note that, to save space in this dictionary, we use *he/him/his* when referring to "sb" [somebody] in definitions, although the person may be either female or male.' (It is worth noting here that space constraints do not exclude 'singular' *they* from the defining vocabulary of *COBUILD* or *LDOCE*.)

'Singular' they

All three dictionaries treat 'singular' *they* in a somewhat disturbing manner. It is characterised as informal in both *OALDCE* and *LDOCE* (under usage notes at *everyone* and *he*, where, because of a typographical error, the relevant text reads 'not in informal [sic] English'). This demeaning characterisation not only mirrors and reinforces the superior attitudes of those who favour the exclusive generic but also neglects to account for the considerable body of opinion which does not consider the inclusive generic to be inferior. *COBUILD* does not label 'singular' *they* in any way, but makes the same mystifying comment as at 'generic' *he*: 'Some people dislike this use.'

By indicating that some people dislike 'generic' *he* and others dislike 'singular' *they*, *COBUILD* signals the existence at least of conflicting language practices in the area of generic pronoun use. Nevertheless, to have described the nature of the rival prescriptions would have enhanced the authority of a book which prides itself on the authoritativeness of its sources.

Girl

In a paper entitled 'The semantic derogation of woman', Muriel Schulz traces 'the pattern whereby virtually every original neutral word for women has at some point in its existence acquired debased connotations or obscene reference, or both' (Schulz, 1990: 135). The term *girl* exemplifies this phenomenon of semantic derogation: while it can be neutral when used to refer to a child, it can be pejorative when it is used to refer to an adult.

In its entry for *girl*, *LDOCE* includes the following senses: woman (labelled informal), woman worker, female servant (signalled as rather obsolescent) and girlfriend (labelled informal and old-fashioned). A usage note at the end of the entry reads: 'Many people, especially women, feel that it is offensive to call a woman a *girl* after she has become an adult.'

OALDCE includes all these senses except for that of female servant, but devotes no space to information similar to that provided by *LDOCE*'s labels and usage note. Yet it does have space not merely to include the secondary headword, *girls*, 'used for addressing a group of women of any age, by market-salesman (sic), popular entertainers, etc.', but also to misrepresent its effect by labelling it as jocular.

COBUILD signals the use of *girl* to mean girlfriend as 'rather old-fashioned', but then goes on to advise: 'You can refer to a woman of any age as a *girl*, especially when you are talking about a woman who is younger than you or when you are in a position of authority over her; an informal use.' Indeed, you can refer to a woman of any age as a girl, and many people do, but surely a learners' dictionary which fails to alert its users to the offense that this can cause is guilty of gross neglect.

Before it even broaches the controversial senses of *girl*, *COBUILD* manages to indulge in what can only be judged gratuitous sexism, when, at its third sense of *girl*, 'a young woman, usually a teenager', it proffers the illustrative phrase, ' . . . calendars showing naked girls'. No doubt 'naked girls' appears again and again in the Birmingham corpus, but it is hard to believe that some other collocation would not have served equally well to illustrate the fact that the noun *girl* can be preceded by an adjective.

It is the responsibility of lexicographers to provide as comprehensive a description of a word's meanings as is possible within the constraints imposed on them by the type and size of the dictionaries they write. Therefore, although many feminists object to the use of the term *girl* to mean an adult woman, it is unreasonable to expect dictionaries, even learners' dictionaries, to ignore this use. But it is irresponsible for dictionaries, especially learners' dictionaries, to ignore the objection to this use. For to record the use without noting its effect is to provide only a partial description of its meaning. Only *LDOCE* provides an impartial account of *girl*. The partiality of the other two accounts imposes on learners a sexist ideology.

Derivatives

Today, the many users of English who recognise the 'trivialising' effect of feminine suffixes (Cameron, 1985: 73) have no hesitation in supporting the recommendation that 'currently existing words with feminine suffixes be dropped from current usage' (Pauwels, 1991: 51).

One way for a dictionary to leave itself open to the accusation of sexism is to include feminine agent nouns which are derivatives of masculine forms without indicating that many users reject such nouns. The three dictionaries surveyed here do just this in the case of *authoress*. *OALDCE* and *LDOCE* do so with *poetess* as well, while *COBUILD* omits *poetess* altogether.

Now some people may argue that through this omission *COBUILD* has failed to provide an adequate account of the language. Others would argue, however, that the absence of the term amounts to a faithful account of its frequency in present-day English. *COBUILD*'s omission of *poetess* seems preferable to the treatment given to the word by *LDOCE*, which includes it, labels it 'now rare', then fails to explain why. A perversely obscurantist approach for a book which declares itself a dictionary of 'contemporary' English.

While all three dictionaries include *Negress*, not one neglects to alert learners to the potentially negative force of the term. As *Negro* is similarly treated, it is all too clear that it is not the sexism of the feminine derivative which is being proscribed.

Titles

Politeness markers, including forms of address, are a source of anguish for language learners. Unfortunately, the explanations of *Miss*, *Mrs* and *Ms* in the learners' dictionaries under review could not be recommended to alleviate this.

COBUILD is simply misleading, advising readers that *Miss* is used 'in front of the surname of a girl or woman who is not married or *who is not using her husband's surname*' (emphasis added), and that *Ms* is used 'especially in written English'.

LDOCE explains *Ms* as 'a title for a woman who does not wish to be called either "Miss" or "Mrs"'. Although it is a pity that the act of choosing is expressed in terms of negative volition, this is the only dictionary of the three to mention that in English it is the right of the addressee to determine whether she will be called *Miss*, *Mrs* or *Ms*. Simply to point out at the relevant entries, preferably in positive terms, something to this effect, and nothing but, would constitute a vast improvement on all the present offerings.

OALDCE proves in one respect more comprehensive, albeit quaintly so, than the other dictionaries when it includes, in the form of an illustrative phrase, what is now a rare construction whose demise is seldom bemoaned by feminists: *Mrs John Brown* is labelled formal and sexist.

Collocations

Amongst her guidelines for non-sexist language, Pauwels (1991: 57) includes the following: 'When describing a couple (woman and man), treat both partners as equals. If mentioning women and men together, do not always list the man first; try instead to alternate the order in which men and women are described.' It seems that the writers of the three dictionaries surveyed here did not have the benefit of such advice.

Mrs Brown makes one of her appearances in *OALDCE*, with, or more precisely, after, her husband, in *Mr and Mrs Brown* (under *Mr*). In *COBUILD*, we come across *Mr and Mrs Clark*, but this time the couple is under *Mrs*. Is this to highlight the notion that *Mr* should always come first?

Phonologists may tell us that the ordering of collocations like 'man and woman' and 'ladies and gentlemen' is phonologically determined, with the word of fewer syllables preceding 'and'. How would they account for 'Mr and Mrs'? Might 'husband and wife' just possibly be following a higher order? This expression is given the status of an idiom in *OALDCE*; it features as a secondary headword in *LDOCE*; and although it does not receive such prominence in *COBUILD*, it does figure under the headword *husband*, in the illustrative phrase, ' . . . the relationship between husband and wife'.

Lexicographers may tell us that to omit collocations such as these is to omit relevant information about 'the' language. But to admit nothing but long-established patterns is to omit equally pertinent information about change.

Associations

In a paper entitled ' "Women are alcoholics and drug addicts", says dictionary', Patricia Kaye (1989) criticises *COBUILD* for choosing illustrative phrases which portray women in a negative light. Alma Graham (1974: 62) reports that lexicographers working on *The School Dictionary*, published in 1972 by the American Heritage Publishing Company, set out 'to avoid gender assumptions that other dictionaries imposed more through custom than necessity'. Gershuny would certainly judge sex-role stereotyping in dictionaries as more a custom than a necessity:

> One could argue . . . that illustrating the connotation and common usage of words in the *best* context implies an unavoidable 'objective' description of the language, stereotypes and all, as it is used. This argument can be more readily applied to 'moral' questions related to 'good' and 'bad' English – the perennial debate between descriptive and prescriptive grammarians. It does not, however, apply to linguistic perpetuation of stereotypes, where the meaning of a word or its usage is generally not dependent on whether it appears with a masculine or feminine gender word. (Gershuny, 1974: 161)

Now, in English at least, women have been stereotyped as hysterical, as domineering, as gossips, as nags. Do the dictionaries under review here go the way of custom rather than necessity by reinforcing these stereotypes?

In *COBUILD*'s illustrative phrases at the headwords *hysteria*, *hysterical*, *hysterics*, *domineering*, *gossip*, *gossipy* and *nag*, 'her thin shoulders' shake in hysteria, 'someone' is in hysteria, 'a man' screams hysterically, there are hysterics 'from her mother', 'she' goes into sobbing hysterics and has a fit of hysterics; 'husbands' are domineering; 'he' is a bit of a gossip and enjoys a good gossip, there is a gossiping 'old woman', while 'old women' and 'Martin's tone' and 'their observations' and 'his book' are gossipy; 'he' nags, and there is a nagging 'wife'.

In *LDOCE*, 'they' become hysterical, 'he' has hysterics at the sight of blood; a 'personality' is domineering; 'she' gossips, 'my sister' writes a gossipy letter, 'a person' is gossipy; and 'you' and 'the children' and 'they' and 'he' do the nagging.

In *OALDCE*, 'fans' are hysterical, 'your mother' has hysterics; a 'husband' and a 'manner' and a 'personality' are domineering; 'she' is too fond of idle gossip, a 'letter' is gossipy; and 'he' nags.

None of the dictionaries could be accused of stereotyping women as hysterical and domineering, or as gossips and nags. Indeed, *COBUILD* could be criticised for over-representing gossiping men, and husbands might object to being depicted in two dictionaries as domineering. All three dictionaries refrain from perpetuating the stereotypes in question. They are to be applauded here for avoiding some customary but unnecessary evils.

Conclusion

The above survey has isolated some of the information about language and gender which *COBUILD*, *LDOCE* and *OALDCE* provide for their users. What conclusions can now be drawn about how users are likely to interpret and apply this information?

Users of *COBUILD* will learn that there is controversy about the use of 'generic' *he* and 'singular' *they*, but they will not discover the nature of the controversy unless they consult one of the other dictionaries. As there they will be told that 'singular' *they* is informal, it would not be surprising if they decided on the 'neutral' *he* option for their own repertoire, thus internalising and perpetuating the established rule that women should remain invisible.

Only users of *LDOCE* will be alerted to and hence be in a position to take a stance on the demeaning uses of *girl*. Users of none of the three dictionaries will learn of the trivialising effect of the suffix *-ess*, and so will have no reason to avoid it. Neither will they find any clear guidance as to the use of titles for women, nor be prompted to challenge the traditional order by putting *Mrs* before *Mr* or wives before husbands. However, neither will they be exposed to the conventional wisdom that it is women who tend to be hysterical, domineering, gossips and nags.

All three dictionaries fail learners in two major ways. Firstly, they do not point out that many of the language practices they are presenting are considered as sexist by considerable numbers of native users of the language. Secondly, they provide little in the way of guidelines and models which would encourage learners to develop non-sexist idiolects akin to those of many of their native-speaking peers.

Until learners have access to systematically reliable and usable information about sexist and non-sexist language, they are denied the choices necessary to exercise their right to freedom of expression on one of the most important issues in the world today. In that same world there are millions more non-native speakers of English than there are native speakers. It is time, then, that the makers of learners' dictionaries acknowledged the magnitude of their responsibilities, and incorporated in their lexicons a thoroughgoing sexicography.

Note

1. Collins Birmingham University International Language Database. This is a large corpus of spoken and written English. The dictionary was produced by researchers in the English Department of Birmingham University using statistical analysis of lexical items in this database.

   The introduction to *COBUILD* notes that the dictionary team had 'daily access to about 20 million words, with many more in specialised stores' (xv). The examples were taken from the corpus 'wherever possible', although some were 'slightly adapted' and, 'on very rare occasions', an example was composed.

   The explanations are 'written in real sentences' and often provide 'an illustration of the word in its typical grammatical context' (xvi). Beside the main entries there is an extra column, designed to provide additional, systematic structural and semantic information without interrupting the flow of the main entries (xvi–xvii).

Case Study 1: On Balance: Guidelines for the Representation of Women and Men in English Language Teaching Materials

JILL FLORENT, KATHRYN FULLER, JENNY PUGSLEY, CATHERINE WALTER
and ANNEMARIE YOUNG

Introduction

The Women in EFL Materials group grew out of Women in TEFL, established in 1986. It took as its objective a study of British materials currently in use for the teaching of English as a foreign language, and the ways in which women and men were differently represented in them. The group designed a questionnaire to investigate interest in sexist language and stereotyping, together with a set of guidelines on how to write materials that treated both sexes with equal dignity and gave them equal coverage. The aim was to present a potentially controversial and relatively undocumented topic to a mixed readership of female and male, native and non-native speakers. The questionnaire was sent to over 650 schools, colleges and university departments all over the world, as well as to British-based publishers, writers and examination boards. Over 400 responses were received, and a clear majority indicated their concern over the issues raised. The guidelines have been extensively revised and supplemented in the light of comments from a wide range of professionals, including teachers in Britain and overseas.

The actual process of devising first the questionnaire and then the guidelines provided the group with the opportunity to explore their own experiences of sexist language and stereotyping, both as providers of learning materials for students, and as working women in EFL-related professions. It was clearly necessary with this, as with any piece of material that can be perceived of as political, to see the audience multi-dimensionally: to consider, for example, their familiarity with the subject, as well as their possible vulnerability, even hostility, in relation to the subject matter and persuasive function of the material.

The group explored carefully the variations of style in which the guidelines might be expressed. There were varying views as to how forcefully the argument should be made for use of non-sexist language as the group perceived it, or whether the examples of sexist language and non-sexist language in the guidelines should speak for themselves. Eventually it was decided to give simple and clear examples of sexist language and stereotyping, and illustrate how the use of alternatives could enhance, rather than devitalise, a text.

On Balance: Guidelines for the Representation of Women and Men in English Language Teaching Materials

Purpose and rationale

These guidelines have been compiled as a reminder to people involved in all aspects of ELT publishing to be aware of discriminatory language and stereotypical images and, wherever possible, to use inclusive language and images which reflect a more balanced and accurate view of the world and of the present state of English. Two issues are involved here:

1. The images and language which are used in teaching, and the extent to which learners can identify with them, have an important effect on how well people learn. If women are under-represented in teaching materials, or represented in demeaning ways, the women who are taught with these materials may learn less well.
2. Language change away from gender bias has been significant in the past few years, and it is important that the language presented to foreign learners of English should not present an outdated and discriminatory version of the language.

Scope

1. The notes that follow are a starting point and are not meant to be exhaustive. They highlight and illustrate areas of concern, and suggest ways of approaching problems rather than trying to anticipate and solve all problems.
2. The points raised apply to illustrations, cartoons, jokes, recorded material and video material as well as to the printed word.
3. The guidelines assume publication for a worldwide audience; materials that are written for and set in another specific country with different cultural values and realities will have to take those factors into account. For example, in materials written for the Arab world, respect for cultural norms will be important; but the spirit of the guidelines can be kept in mind, and, for instance, it can be brought out that women are held in high esteem and often do respected jobs outside the home.
4. While these guidelines focus principally on sexist bias, the ultimate aim is to avoid discriminatory language and stereotypical images in whatever context

(e.g. age, class, ethnic origin, disability, etc.) so that the books we produce are fair and balanced in their portrayal of all members of society.

Guidelines

Images of women

The comments in this section concern all the situations where girls and women appear in EFL materials, and are meant to ensure that female learners are able to identify in a positive way with the characters, fictional and real, that they encounter while learning English.

Visibility

Over half the population is female. This should be reflected in text, illustrations, and recordings. Impressions cannot be relied on – it is necessary to count the relative numbers of male and female characters over a whole book/video/cassette. This includes counting characters
- in illustrations
- in dialogues
- in lists of sentences
- in the voices specified for audio recordings
- in authentic recordings and texts

Stereotyping

For female learners to learn effectively, it is important not to present female characters in a demeaning way.

Avoiding stereotypes
Much can be done to avoid presenting people in a stereotyped way. Here are some checklists:

Physical appearance in illustrations and texts:
- Are people shown as belonging to a range of physical types, or for example, are women always shorter than men?
- Are both women and men shown dressed in a variety of ways, or for example are men usually in clothing appropriate to action while women are dressed in confining and decorative clothes?
- Are women described by their physical attributes ('the attractive brunette MP from Birmingham') in situations where men are described by professional status or mental attributes?

Are both women and men shown in texts, dialogues, recordings and illustrations:
- being bold and assertive?

- being weak, vulnerable or scared?
- instructing, leading, rescuing?
- being instructed, led, rescued?
- displaying self-control?
- responding emotionally?
- being strong, capable and logical?
- being uncertain and in need of reassurance?
- being powerful and able to deal with problems?
- being inept and defeated by problems?
- belonging to a range of emotional types?
- starting dialogues?
- making arrangements?

Vocational stereotyping can perpetuate the notion that if women work at all it is only for 'pin money' and that it is their job alone to keep house and raise children. In fact 54% of women in Britain work outside the home; 42% of mothers with children under five go out to work; 20% of the women who go out to work are the sole or major breadwinners for the family.

In texts, dialogues, recordings and illustrations, are both women and men shown:
- in managerial positions or as artisans?
- caring for children and competently completing household tasks?
- as principal or sole breadwinners for their families?
- occasionally in 'mould-breaking' occupations – e.g. women as lorry drivers or bankers, men as nurses or secretaries? Is it implied that these people's jobs conflict with their femininity/masculinity?

Many learners of English do not belong to nuclear families or take their sense of identity and self-worth from their marital status. Some things to consider:
- Do the materials show a variety of sorts of families, or do all families consist of dad, mum and 2.4 children?
- Are women and men described using the same parameters, or are women described by marital or familial status ('wife of . . .', 'mother of four children') in situations where men are described by professional status or mental attributes?
- Are there some apparently happily unmarried women and men, or are all people over a certain age married?

Confronting stereotypes
A second way of dealing with stereotypes is to face rather than avoid them.

Authentic materials, for example, may well contain examples of stereotyped attitudes. Some questions to ask here:
- Is it clear that the stereotyped attitudes are not those of the author(s)?
- Are students invited to discuss the attitudes?
- Is there a balance between reading/listening/video passages where stereotyped attitudes are exemplified and those where other, more open attitudes exist?

Another way of facing stereotypes is to introduce characters, fictional or (perhaps preferably) real, who have successfully challenged a common stereotype. Depicting women or men in occupations typically supposed to be the domain of the other sex is the most obvious example. However, note:

- Tokenism is a danger, and this is why it might be preferable, where possible, to choose a real character rather than a fictional one.
- Another danger is overdoing it – it would be an unrealistic picture of British or American society if all the secretaries in the book were men, and students would be baffled rather than enlightened.

Women in language

As with stereotypes, language which excludes women can be dealt with 1) by avoiding its use and 2) by dealing sensitively with exclusive language that comes up in, for example, authentic recordings. In the second case it is often enough to suggest that teachers point out that a particular usage may offend many women, and to ensure that other authentic recordings demonstrate inclusive language.

False generics

Studies of native English-speaking college students and school children have shown that the generic use of words like *man* (ostensibly to include all humans), does not elicit mental images of both sexes. When told that 'man needs food and shelter to survive', the great majority of the people in the studies visualised only men. Even with a conscious effort, few people would be comfortable with the sentence 'Like all mammals, man breastfeeds his young.' But the following genuine example demonstrates how ostensibly generic words 'slide' towards a masculine meaning: 'Man's vital interests include life, food and access to females.' Foreign language learners who perceive the word *man* as a term for males will thus be echoing the feelings of native speakers. Building towards a native-like language competence for foreign learners of English will mean either avoiding the use of false generics in teaching materials (for productive use), or confronting them when they appear (for receptive use).

Avoiding false generic 'man'

Instead of	*Use*
mankind	people, humans, humanity
manpower	work force, staff
man-made	artificial, synthetic, manufactured
man-to-man	person-to-person, personally
prehistoric man	prehistoric people
manned by	staffed by

When occupations are being discussed in general terms, job titles incorporating the word *man* can be avoided where another natural alternative exists. Of course if an individual is being discussed it may be reasonable to refer to that individual as, for instance, a *policewoman* or a *policeman*. Note that *chairwoman* is attested in the *Oxford English Dictionary* as being in use since 1699, and it is becoming increasingly unacceptable to call a woman a *chairman*.

Instead of generic	*Use*
businessman	executive
cameraman	camera operator
chairman	chairperson, chair
fireman	fire fighter
foreman	supervisor
policeman	police officer
statesman	leader, politician

Avoiding false generic 'he' and other masculine pronouns
This is a problem that most often occurs in exercise instructions and teachers' books. Note that it is *not* desirable to present material with the disclaimer that masculine pronouns are to be taken as referring to both females and males. Some suggestions:

- Change the pronoun to a plural, so that 'A person generally learns what he uses and forgets what he doesn't use' becomes 'People generally learn what they use . . .'
- Use *they* as a singular pronoun, as in 'Ask each person in your group to say their sentence.' Although this is considered incorrect by some people, it is common in spoken English and has a long history of use in written English (cf. William Caxton, 1470: 'Each of them should make themself ready'; Shakespeare: 'God send everyone their heart's desire'). It is now becoming increasingly common in Britain in formal English (speeches, forms, etc.), so use in EFL texts would reflect authentic usage. The major British grammar and usage books confirm this. (In the US, while spoken usage is roughly the same, singular *they* is still often felt to be incorrect in formal spoken or written use.)
- Use the second person, so that 'Each student should write his answer at the top of a piece of paper' becomes 'Write your answer at the top of a piece of paper.'
- Use an article instead of a pronominal determiner, so that 'Try to make sure that everyone in the group gives his opinion' becomes ' . . . gives an opinion.'
- Replace the pronoun with a noun, perhaps a synonym for a noun used earlier, so that 'Work with another student. Say five things about your family and ask five questions about his family' becomes ' . . . and ask five questions about your partner's family.'
- Avoid the need for a pronoun by recasting, so that 'Ask a bright student. If he can't answer . . .' becomes ' . . . If the question is too difficult . . .' or ' . . . If the question can't be answered . . .'
- Use expressions like *the other*, so that 'You then stand back to back, and each

student says what his partner is wearing' becomes ' . . . each says what the other is wearing.'

- Use *she and he*, *he and she* or *hers and his*, *his and hers*, but not when you have to do it repetitively.
- When referring to an animal whose sex is unknown use *it*.
- There are mixed views, and sometimes strong feelings, over the use of *s/he*; it is neat and economical in writing, but unpronounceable. There may be some argument for it, for instance, in teacher's books that are not meant to be spoken anyway.

Female diminutives of job titles

Female diminutives of job titles are unnecessary, and becoming increasingly rare in general usage.

Instead of	*Use*
conductress	conductor
authoress	author
manageress	manager
poetess	poet

The terms 'girl' and 'lady'

Referring to a woman beyond her middle or late teens as a 'girl' can be patronising and demeaning. Beware of using this term in situations where men would not be referred to as 'lads', 'chaps' or 'boys'.

Likewise, use *lady/ladies* only when you use (or would use) *gentleman/gentlemen*.

Letters

The use of *Dear Sir/s* as the salutation for an unknown person or group of people is becoming more and more uncommon and unacceptable. Use *Dear Sir or Madam* or *Dear Madam or Sir*.

It is becoming increasingly common to use *Dear Jane/Joe Bloggs* rather than *Dear Ms/Mrs/Miss/Mr Bloggs*.

Both these forms of salutation are considered correct by the major EFL examining bodies.

Conclusion

British EFL materials deserve the excellent reputation they enjoy throughout the world. Writers, illustrators, designers and publishers take justified pride in the talent and effort they put into producing materials for effective and enjoyable learning.

The guidelines were written as an aid to this end, and are not intended to voice a criticism or to impose a handicap. We hope that they will be of use.

Acknowledgements

Women in EFL Materials was a voluntary group consisting of Jill Florent, Kathryn Fuller, Jenny Pugsley, Catherine Walter and Annemarie Young, with help and advice from Ann Arscott, Wendy Coleby, Benita Cruickshank, Louise Elkins, Eleanor Gibson, Sue Griffin, Jean Hindmarch and Brenda Sandilands. We would like to express our thanks for help with this project to the hundreds of teachers and others all over the world who took the time to answer the questionnaires that led to the guidelines, and particularly to those who offered further comments and suggestions. We should also like to thank the following institutions and individuals for their help and support: The Bell Educational Trust; The British Council; Cambridge University Press; Collins ELT; The Equal Opportunities Commission; Heinemann International; International House; Longman Group Limited; Oxford University Press; Prentice Hall; The Publishers Association; School of English and Linguistics, Macquarie University; Brian Abbs; Christopher Candlin; Ingrid Freebairn; Judy Garton-Sprenger; Simon Greenall; Kaye Greenleaf; Chris Jones; Leo Jones; Alan Maley; Ray Murphy; Nick Newton; John Soars; Liz Soars; Jane Sunderland; Michael Swan; Peter Viney.

Bibliography

AAUP Taskforce on Gender-Free Language, *Bias-free communication: a select bibliography*, University of California Press, 1988.

Barnes, D., *From communication to curriculum*, Penguin Books, 1976.

Cameron, D., *Feminism and linguistic theory*, Macmillan, 1985.

Cheshire, J., 'A question of masculine bias', in *English Today*, January 1985, Cambridge University Press.

Educational Publishers Council, The Publishers Association, *Sex stereotyping in school and children's books*, 1981.

Freire, P., *Education. The practice of freedom*, Writers and Readers Publishing Co-operative, 1976.

Goldberg, P., 'Are women prejudiced against men?', in Stacey, J. *et al* (eds.) *And Jill came tumbling after: sexism in American Education*, Dell Publishing, 1976.

Gumperz, J., *Language and social identity*, Cambridge University Press, 1982.

Leech, G., in collaboration with B. Cruickshank and R. Ivanic, *An A-Z of English grammar and usage*, Edward Arnold, 1987.

Maggio, R., *The non-sexist word finder, a dictionary of gender-free usage*, Beacon Press, 1988.

Martyna, W., 'Beyond the he/man approach', in *Signs* 5, 1980.

Martyna, W., 'What does 'he' mean? Use of the generic masculine', in *Journal of Communication*, 1978, Vol. 28, no. 1, pp. 131–138.

Miller, C. and K. Swift, *The handbook of non-sexist writing*, The Women's Press, 1980, 1988.

NUJ Book Branch, *Non-sexist code of practice for book publishing*, 1982.

Porreca, K., 'Sexism in current ESL textbooks', in *TESOL Quarterly* 18:4, 1984.

Poynton, C., *Language and gender: making the difference*, Oxford University Press, 1989.

Pugsley, J., 'Teaching English as a foreign language: the female protagonist in EFL literature', unpublished essay, 1988.

Russ, J., *How to suppress women's writing*, The Women's Press, 1983.

Silveira, J., 'Generic masculine words and thinking', in *Women's Studies International Quarterly*, Vol 3, 1980.

Spender, D., *Invisible women*, Writers and Readers Publishing Co-operative, 1982.

Spender, D., *Man made language*, Routledge & Kegan Paul, 1980.

Sunderland, J., 'The grammar book and the invisible woman', Dissertation submitted for MA in English Language Teaching, University of Lancaster, 1986.

Talansky, S.B., 'Sex role stereotyping in TEFL teaching materials', in *Perspectives*, Vol XI, no. 3, 1986.

Women in EFL Materials
c/o Place Farm House
Chilton nr Didcot
Oxfordshire
OXII 0SF
England

Case Study 2: The Case of Task Way English: *Alternative Gender Constructions in EFL Textbooks Interview with Bessie Dendrinos*

LILIE CHOULIARAKI

Second language acquisition (SLA), like any learning process, is a cultural experience and a social practice. EFL textbooks, as parts of the curriculum, are ways dominant culture and sexist ideology may be reproduced, but are also 'sites of struggle' where institutional values can be reinterpreted, and ideology potentially questioned. *Task Way English* consciously aims at systematically questioning sexist stereotypes as well as the social world it constructs for learners.

Task Way English 1, 2, 3 is a three-volume series which has been used for the teaching of English as a foreign language in Greek state schools since 1987–88. The books address students at lower secondary level, aged eleven to fourteen. They were written by a five-member team, Bessie Dendrinos being head author.

The teaching–learning materials which constitute *Task Way English* came out of a five-year research project carried out by the EFL Committee. This Committee was appointed by the Greek Ministry of Education, and later became the author team.[1] The overall aim of the project was to investigate a variety of issues concerning Greek learners and teachers of English and to relate these to specific social and educational needs. On the basis of this, the EFL Committee revised the national EFL syllabus and the nationally determined text and exam specifications, and worked out criteria for materials.

The *Task Way English* series is based on sex-fair attitudes – a conscious aim of the author team. The Introduction in the *Teacher's Manual* accompanying *Task Way English 2* notes: 'there has been particular concern about avoiding sex-role stereotyping and developing behaviour patterns appropriate to functioning as an individual within a collective, conscious of group responsibility,' and in the manual accompanying *Task Way English 3* we read:

> . . . there is an effort to lead learners away from confining persons and personalities into fixed roles. Children and adults, men and women are not defined except in terms of variable roles that respond to different social and personal needs. In fact, there is a very conscious effort evidenced in the materials to present people in sex equitable roles and young people as individuals with various rights, responsibilities and opportunities.

In the following interview with Bessie Dendrinos, I seek to illuminate aspects of this rationale, of the process of producing the materials, and of the problems experienced in the attempt to achieve fairer gender representation.

L.C.: Can we start by exploring the role of the textbook in language education, indeed in education in general. . . .

B.D.: I think we'd agree that the role of any textbook within an educational system is to facilitate the achievement of the goals of a subject-specific syllabus, one component of a curriculum. Now, both syllabuses and curricula, whether they're locally or nationally designed, in my view, aim to a greater or lesser extent at reproducing the dominant culture and ideology. The textbook is an authorised medium which presents students with an officially sanctioned version of the knowledge and culture into which they've been socialised.

The primary aim of foreign language education is to provide learners with the knowledge and experience they need in order to communicate in ways which are thought to respond to social conventions. These ways are selected from within the social reality which I believe any one language helps to construct and reconstruct, shaping the experience, values and attitudes of the users. The articulation of these ways occurs in the language textbook through its texts, which I see as the material realisation of discourses that express the meanings and values of social institutions.

Of course, I certainly don't think that the school is simply an institution where dominant culture and ideology are reproduced, or that language is just an instrument of ideological subjugation. I do see the school as a site where struggle takes place, just as it does in any social institution, since the social experience of groups constantly contradicts the roles that dominant ideology assigns them. And I see language as an instrument for change in ideology. The language textbook in particular has immense importance in changing, for example, the asymmetrical relationships among groups such as teachers and students, boys and girls.

L.C.: That's why in *Task Way English* you chose to make visible a specifically feminist discourse, which is not visible in most other textbooks used in formal education?

B.D.: I don't think I'd accept that *Task Way English* is characterised by a feminist discourse. . . . It certainly reflects an effort to express sex-equitable values, but I don't believe that sexism is really separable from other power relations. My intention was not to deal with sexism in isolation but with all sorts of power relationships, and, where possible, to make the conflicts visible to the students. For example, in *Task Way English 2*, Unit 1 begins with an interview between a male employer and a prospective employee, who's younger than him, and female. After he's asked her several questions with respect to her qualifications he says: 'And now my last question. It's a bit funny, but very important to me. Can you make coffee?' The young woman's response shows she is more than a match for him: 'Coffee? Of course I can. I make my coffee every morning. Don't you?' I see this humorous exchange as one involving power and conflict on at least three levels: the interviewer's 'natural' right to play around with such a question is granted to him not only because he is a man, but also because he takes advantage of his status as an employer and as an older person.

There are other instances where relationships are asymmetrical, or where people are presented in stereotypical roles. This was either to avoid prescriptivism, or because we, the members of the author team, functioned according to the ideological reality that has been constructed for us. We are ideological subjects – and though we make an effort, we don't always succeed in combating the 'common senseism' that is passed on through language use.

L.C.: So, you think that classroom materials and processes, like classroom language and relationships, all play a role in the social construction of the learner? Especially in terms of gender, but not only gender. . . .

B.D.: Everything constructs us as gendered beings. Not only verbal but also non-verbal actions, the way the classroom is organised, where boys and girls sit, how they work and are asked to work together. I remember observing an EFL class assigned the task of constructing a very simple electronic device. The boys wanted to sit with boys and the girls with girls, but the teacher put them into mixed-sex groups. Though boys and girls had the same amount of subject-specific knowledge, the boys took the initiative and started the construction. As difficulties were encountered, though, the girls joined in and finally there was a more or less equal contribution in accomplishing the task.

This experience carried a message through the content students were asked to deal with, through the task, the class organisation, and the expectations of the teacher. And talking about teacher expectations, I have observed classes where teachers expected girls to have better pronunciation in English than boys, and often corrected them more frequently even when their pronunciation was better!

L.C.: And, presumably, you had these sorts of experiences in mind when you were working on *Task Way English*. . . .

B.D.: Yes. If you view language as social practice – a view I share with others – then you are aware of how classroom communication contributes to the social construction and reconstruction of the students, and of the teachers too. And so much of the classroom communication is stimulated by the textbook. So, a primary goal was to create circumstances in the materials for non-gendered social practice.

L.C.: Is that why you believe that it is important to avoid sexism in language textbooks rather than because sexism may hinder language learning – a possibility for which there is as yet little psycholinguistic evidence?

B.D.: Exactly. As an educator I am concerned not only about how students will acquire particular knowledge most effectively; I am extremely concerned about what type of knowledge and experiences we are offering them in school. In the foreign language class the textbook seems to dominate instructional practices, and students are continuously being re-exposed to social contexts and social relations between people. Through the textbook they're taught what is and what is not appropriate to say on social occasions. This necessitates a selection of 'reality' on the part of the textbook writer or writers, and I am suggesting that this selection plays an important role in the social construction of the language learner.

L.C.: So, not only first language acquisition but also second language acquisition constructs you as a social being?

B.D.: Right. You're exposed to totally new social situations, or situations that you already associate with particular meanings and concepts, but you see them from different perspectives. In acquiring this new knowledge learners can develop critical awareness in relation to their own language.

L.C.: So, potentially, learning a second language can be subversive. . . .

B.D.: I'm sure it can.

L.C.: Given that, but also having to work within the particular framework of formal education in Greece, how much space did you have to propose something more progressive than what existed already?

B.D.: Generally speaking, though equal treatment of the sexes is enshrined in the Greek Constitution, there is still no firm movement to combat sexism – which is in fact still strongly engrained. But I think that this acceptance of what we can call a 'dominant gender ideology' is due largely to lack of awareness: an inability to identify sex bias.

Equal treatment of the sexes is also an aim within Greek education – at least on paper. And it's a goal many educators would say they have. But our assumption that most teachers and students were quite unprepared for a critical approach to social education through foreign language teaching, and for negotiable pedagogy, created a dilemma for us very early on: were we to develop a more or less traditional textbook series, or a progressive one? The decision was not easy, but we hoped that the new materials might create conditions for change, and so we opted for progressive materials.

L.C.: And was a teacher education programme organised?

B.D.: Well, unfortunately the textbook series was introduced without the state setting up a training or education programme for practising teachers. What we hoped for then and still hope now is that the materials themselves are becoming a force for change in ELT instructional practices. Moreover, we hope that the type of knowledge and experience that is required for the constructive use of the materials is being provided in English departments of universities so that young teachers at least are prepared to offer this type of foreign language education.

L.C.: I see. But coming back to sex fairness, could you tell me something more about how you dealt with the gender issue in the textbooks?

B.D.: We were concerned to present people communicating in a wide variety of encounters so that learners would be exposed to both gendered and non-gendered social practices; to present certain social encounters which would raise questions related to sex bias in learners' minds. The tasks in Section 6, Unit 1 of *Task Way English 2* are a case in point. The message of the statement in the 'Information' box is that certain jobs may be stereotyped. Task 1 encourages learners to come up with stereotypes that others may dispute. Task 2 then makes students aware of the social reality in their own class. Regardless of stereotypes that students may have about, for example, boys being able to ride a horse, it's unlikely that any of the boys can. In Task 3, in which learners are asked to say one thing that the women on the cover page of the Unit can do – which shows women, and only women, in a range of professions – they are compelled to think of a non-gendered reality.

---

6. CAN THEY DO IT?

INFORMATION
Some people think that only boys can do certain things and that only girls can do others. What do you think?

TASK 1

Instructions   Tick what you think only girls or only boys can do.

BOYS	GIRLS		BOYS	GIRLS	
		play football			understand Mathematics
		make cakes			dance modern dances
		drive			speak many foreign languages
		swim			fish
		sing well			become nurses
		travel alone			become pilots
		climb mountains			go out alone

I was also concerned about how males and females were presented when talking to each other. Would both sexes initiate discussion and introduce topics? Would both males and females pause and hesitate, and speak decisively?

L.C.: So you were concerned with social roles in conversation, with social stereotyping, with how people view men and women and their discourse in particular contexts. . . .

B.D.: How people view others – and through that, how we see ourselves as gendered individuals, and how we act, or react, to that.

L.C.: But you also tried to address the concern through language use in the rubric of the materials, right? I was thinking specifically of your sex-fair grammar. I believe you avoid using masculine so-called generic pronouns, for example. . . .

B.D.: Yes. That was something we as an author team had agreed upon. We had decided to use *he or she* – or, when we were assigning roles to learners, to sometimes use names that could be either masculine or feminine.

L.C.: There must have been issues to do with visibility too. . . .

B.D.: Equal participation of males and females, verbally and non-verbally – because someone could be present in a situation by being shown visually, or simply by being referred to. And of course there was quite a bit of concern in relation to the selected reality shown in the visuals. I had to work very closely with the artists whose gendered ideology frequently reared its head – young teenage boys always taller than girls and girls always neater than boys; boys being active and girls just standing properly.

L.C.: It's interesting that some of the teachers I interviewed picked up the visual cues in *Task Way English 2*, even when they didn't respond to the linguistic ones. For example, they commented on the cover page of Unit 1, and all those women professionals. And most of them did *not* see it as a positive feature. . . .

B.D.: That's exactly the point. If you choose to foreground women in the professional sphere – which is considered to be a male world – you'll get reactions. If that page had been full of men, I don't think many of the teachers you interviewed would have seen it as presenting a false reality – despite the fact that in Greece now there are many women in the work force, including a high percentage in what were traditionally considered male professions. Actually, this page was designed to get students' and teachers' reactions, as a pedagogical strategy.

L.C.: So one way of resolving the dilemma of what to present, i.e. what is versus what should be the reality, is to open up a topic and let the learners react, either spontaneously or prompted – with sensitivity – by a teacher.

B.D.: Well, teachers may not have the sensitivity. If they do not, they will leave an issue untackled, unless some students prompt discussion or convey their own bias, to which other students may or may not react.

L.C.: That's true. From my own interviews with Greek EFL teachers, I didn't get the impression they would readily pick up on different representations of reality and discuss them.

B.D.: I suspect you're right. Even when teachers are dealing with materials which reflect a conscious effort to be sex fair, instructional, or more general institutional practices can be really sexist. One particular class comes to mind, when the teacher wanted to pre-teach the new grammar in a Unit of *Task Way English 3*, and she provided her own examples, most of which were tremendously sex biased.[2] However, I still believe that providing a fair representation of the sexes in textbooks does work on a conscious and subconscious level. And I also believe that it gives teachers and students with interest and sensitivity a good chance to develop critical awareness in relation to gender.

L.C.: Don't you think teachers with low awareness could be helped through more teacher education?

B.D.: Perhaps – though I'm convinced that sex bias in education is a wider issue connected to the gendered roles we are assigned in society. Besides, in a teacher education programme, certain trainees may feel they're having an ideological position imposed on them – without recognising the ideological cast they already have on.

L.C.: Perhaps it depends on the *kind* of teacher education. There are certainly pedagogical grounds for avoiding a reality which seems so strange that it actually inhibits learning.

B.D.: Of course. . . .

L.C.: But in the same way sex-biassed material can hinder learning. One reason many girls respond less than boys in class may be because females tend to be excluded from texts.

B.D.: And that could be investigated, as could the reverse – what happens when males are excluded?

L.C.: One last question. What was co-operation in the team like in terms of gender issues? Did you have any disagreements?

B.D.: Sometimes I and the other woman on the team got into serious arguments with our male colleagues. There were occasions when only after developing and piloting the material did I realise its sexist connotations, or the sexist pedagogical practice that it would probably result in. When I proposed changing it there would often be strong resistance – either with the excuse that the material had worked out fine in class (meaning that it had not created learning difficulties), or with the accusation that this was my constant preoccupation. Then both fronts had to reach a compromise of some sort. . . .

L.C.: How did you feel about that?

B.D.: At the time I'd feel angry, but on the whole I don't think this was negative for the material. It certainly made it nearer our gendered social reality! But I do believe that we did manage to exclude most stereotypes from the series.

L.C.: Bessie – thank you very much indeed for sharing some of the ideas and processes that resulted in *Task Way English*.

Notes

1. The EFL Committee, later the author team, was made up of five members: Bessie Dendrinos, research team leader and head author of *Task Way English*, currently Professor of Sociology of Language and Foreign Language Education in the University of Athens; Sophia Marmaridou, currently Associate Professor in Linguistics, University of Athens; Triantafillos Triantafillou, ELT

specialist at the National Pedagogical Institute; the late Cleanthis Vicas, ELT School Adviser; and Apostolos Ouzounis, state school EFL teacher.

2. For the transcript of this, see Bessie Dendrinos (1992), *The EFL Textbook and Ideology*. Athens: N.C. Grivas Publications.

Comment: An International EFL Publisher's Perspective

DAVID HAINES

Issues such as the effect on readers of gender representation in textbooks and the role of the publisher or author to edify, reflect or change cultural standards, wherever or whatever they may be, are argued elsewhere in this Quadrant. I will not, therefore, dwell on these here but will make two brief points in this respect.

1. I believe it is questionable whether a publisher has an automatic right to influence material intended for international publication according to a chosen set of moral criteria, no matter how desirable they may be.
2. If we do believe that a publisher's role is to help enlighten different societies through its textbooks, the unacceptable representation of women is only one of several areas of discrimination that we have to take into account.

Such considerations constitute important ethical arguments which publishers must and do address, because we accept that textbooks may be instrumental in changing cultural ideologies.

Two issues that do directly concern me here are (a) that some EFL publishers have not always, in the past, taken the opportunity to ensure that there is a fair and balanced representation of women in their materials, and (b) that they still may not always be able to ensure this in the future. I shall explore these further and aim to show that all discussion on this emotive and controversial topic needs to take into account certain interrelated factors in the publishing process. This is not to offer blanket excuses for publishers, but to reply to accusations that are often levelled against us. As Jane Sunderland points out in the Introduction to this Quadrant, it is not a simple matter to produce sexism-free textbooks and the five factors I have chosen are important illustrations of this.

Factor One: We have moved from an author-led era to a market-led era

Some articles in this Quadrant suggest that the content of EFL texts reflects the views of individual authors and/or editors and that texts consequently can and should be amended to correspond to changing cultural values in the country or society of origin. As far as materials originating in the UK are concerned, this is,

Figure 1
Factors influencing publishing decisions

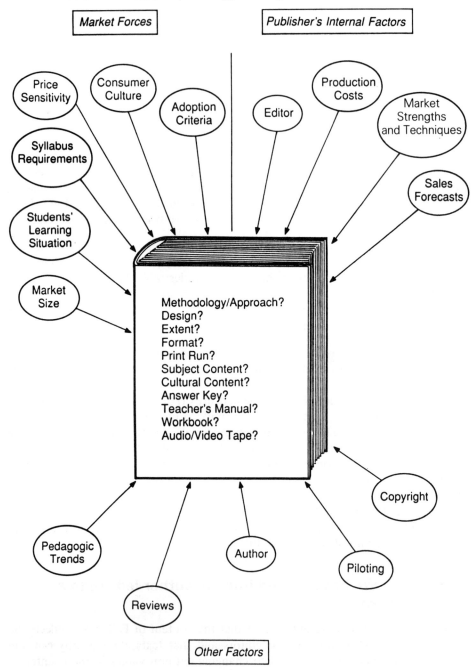

perhaps regrettably, no longer always possible. There are many influential factors during the publishing process (see Figure 1) and the content of material is determined more and more by the market it is intended for. No assessment of material can therefore be made fairly without full recognition of the circumstances and purposes of its publication.

If market requirements do coincide with sex-equitable values, for example as they seemed to do with the *Task Way English* project, fine. But if material is published which does not represent women accurately according to the dominant culture in the country of origin or other similar societies, this may be due to market forces. Accurate representation could and often does alienate the publisher from the consumer and jeopardise sales or even publication itself. Whereas British ELT publishers once had a monopoly in the international ELT market place and could expect to sell what they published, they now have to publish what they can sell. This, in turn, is often influenced by fairly rigid content requirements dictated by schools or ministry syllabuses, themselves reflecting local cultural and sociopolitical values.

This does not mean publishers turn a blind eye to sexism or seek to foster it, as they are often accused of doing. It does mean that there are many occasions when the content of materials just cannot be compatible with what we may see as our own more liberal or enlightened western views, themselves, of course, being culturally relative.

Factor Two: English is an international language, not just one which belongs to Britain

Until relatively recently, the content, scope, design and methodology of EFL textbooks reflected not only the publisher's or author's views, but also the culture of origin. It was assumed that 'foreigners' learned English, for example, in order to speak to the British, to visit Britain or to familiarise themselves with British culture. What was good for a UK language school was good enough for the world. The level and age of users were the only real distinguishing factors taken into account. It was normal, therefore, that these materials reflected certain cultural values at the time which appear inappropriate by today's changing western values. They were certainly unsuitable for many overseas markets for several reasons, gender representation perhaps being the least significant.

The present age of internationalism and greater consumer sensitivity permits language and its cultural origin to be divorced from each other. To publish only texts which reflect our own sociocultural values would be inconsistent with this change. Beginning from the question 'What do we want from our ELT textbooks?' is in itself not only against the interests of sales, but in a sense can be seen as merely another form of that cultural imperialism we oppose. Neither is it sufficient to offer caveats such as 'respect for cultural norms will be important' and 'materials that are written for and set in another specific country with different cultural values and realities will have to take those factors into account.' Herein lie certain major assumptions and considerations which are at the very heart of this discussion. The concept of EIL requires publishers to reflect cross-cultural values; it is not about reflecting societies in which English is spoken as a first language or societies whose culture we happen to find acceptable.

Factor Three: Global EFL textbook publishing is becoming less common or feasible, in favour of indigenous or co-publishing ventures

Hand in hand with the move towards internationalism is the trend towards local publishing, away from a British-based publishing monopoly. We are in an age of greater competition. There are more books for the same markets and European publishers, for example, are now producing EFL materials not only for their domestic markets but also for export. British publishers are having to compete with local editions of textbooks and to look to growth areas. Our textbooks now have to reflect local cultural, linguistic and learning situations, not just for cultural acceptability but in order to sell.

Let me quote two cases I know of: one, a Business English title for the Japanese market and the other for a country in the Middle East. In the former, the book included no women at all; in the latter, all the women were in domestic or servile situations and all the men were in professional positions. Editing these titles to reflect sex-equitable values would almost certainly have made them as inappropriate for these markets as not editing them in this way would have made them for other markets.

Factor Four: It can take longer to write, produce and distribute new EFL material than for cultural values to change

The day an EFL book is published can be at least two years from when the author began writing it. By the time it is first reviewed, it could be up to four years old. By the time an edition is in use, it could be anything up to ten years old. The publishing process is speeding up and EFL books have an increasingly short shelf life, but the time factor of the writing/publishing process has to be taken into account when assessment is made of materials. It is very easy to find relatively old titles to support the argument that EFL materials portray sexist values. It should be increasingly difficult to do so with more recent titles.

Factor Five: EFL textbook materials tend to reflect rather than innovate

Trends in English language teaching come and go and it is difficult to specify a global state of the art at any one time. The network of distributors, consumers, influential teachers, academics and ministry adoption procedures means that many different materials will be in fashion internationally at once. What is 'culture bound' in one market can be considered 'culture rich' in another.

This is not to relegate gender to a fashion, but to show that the best that international publishers can do is to follow directions or at best seek to predict what they will be. It is as unrealistic to expect publishers to reflect all the desiderata concerning the representation of women and men as it is to expect them to reflect accurately any other social, cultural or historical issue. The question is asked in this Quadrant as to whether materials should reflect the world as it is or as some would like it to be. The publisher's dilemma is to decide which world and whose culture to reflect.

UK publishers' books are changing in many of the directions indicated in this book and will continue to do so. The process is slow and publishers are not really in a position to speed it up. The 'On Balance' guidelines are being addressed and used and a new author generation has already emerged in whose materials non-sexist and non-stereotypical content has become the norm rather than the exception. If the resulting materials are absorbed by more and more markets without criticism, this wind of change will have proved successful. But in the meantime, we need to recognise and show respect for other cultural norms in different world markets and maintain our right to publish for these markets.

Quadrant III

CLASSROOM PROCESSES

Introduction

A classroom process, here, is anything that happens in the classroom, from a small event such as a learner looking up the pronunciation of a word in a dictionary, to the whole series of teaching/learning activities which make up a course.

Classroom processes include the approaches and behaviours a learner uses to help him or her learn a new language, i.e. his or her *styles* and *strategies*. Some of these will be automatic and not recognised by the learner. Many will not be observable to a teacher or researcher. Some will be specific to second or foreign language learning, others applicable to learning in general. Rebecca Oxford, whose work has shown that 'styles and strategies are a gender issue', provides a survey of research to date. We now have the possibility of interpreting learners' differences in grades or performance in the language class in terms of differences in their learning styles and/ or strategies.

Classroom processes also include the interpersonal processes of classroom discourse and non-verbal behaviour: the interaction between the teacher and individual learners, the teacher and groups of learners, the teacher and the class as a whole, and between learners. Most important here seems to be the sex of the learners. Findings have suggested that male and female teachers behave similarly in the ways they tend to treat boys, on the one hand, and girls, on the other, and most recent research has accordingly looked at learner gender in mixed-sex classes. (However, see Alison Kelly, 1988.)

Work on gender and classroom discourse can be divided into studies of (a) amount and type of attention teachers give to female and male students, (b) learner discourse in whole-class work, and (c) learner discourse in pair- and groupwork, both 'off-task' and 'on-task'. Findings in one classroom context cannot be generalised to another, but show the different ways in which human gender can affect classroom proceedings, and how in one way or another it usually does.

Studies of teacher attention in different subject classes have frequently found teachers giving boys more attention than girls. Dale Spender (1982) even found this to be true of herself and other teachers who were aware of the tendency and did not wish to be part of it. It is important to recognise, however, that rather than actively favouring male students, teachers may be responding to them.

Attention itself is unlikely to facilitate learning – especially if it is attention to discipline. The more interesting findings concern type of teacher attention in mixed-sex classes. In an early study of classroom behaviour, teachers blamed boys more than girls (William Meyer and George Thompson, 1956). Later studies found teachers making more academic contact with girls in reading and boys in maths (Gaea Leinhardt, Andrea Mar Seewald and Mary Engel, 1979), teachers reprimanding girls more than boys for calling out (Myra Sadker and David Sadker, 1985), girls in maths classes being given more teacher time in terms of 'product questions', boys in terms of 'process questions' (Gilah Leder, 1987), and 60 per cent of the teacher's pupil-directed gaze being towards the boys (Joan Swann and David Graddol, 1988). (See also Thomas Good, Neville Sykes and Jere Brophy, 1973).

Though the above studies are relevant to language education, none were undertaken in a foreign or second language classroom. In my own contribution to this Quadrant, I outline what little has been done, and look at the meaning of differential teacher 'treatment-by-gender' in EFL classes, using teachers' and students' perceptions.

There have been several studies of learner discourse (whole-class work, groupwork and pairwork) in different subject classrooms. Most of these suggest that boys talk more than girls at secondary level (e.g. Sadker and Sadker, 1985; Swann and Graddol, 1988; P. Dee Boersma *et al.*, 1981; Sarah Sternglanz and Shirley Lyberger-Ficek, 1977; Jenny Gubb, 1980; N.M. Webb and C.M. Kenderski, 1985; Elizabeth Aries, 1982; Jane Gilbert, 1992). Again, there are relatively few studies of learner discourse in the language classroom.

Of interest is whether the learning of a second or foreign language affects in a particular way the gendered nature of classroom discourse – in either the first or the target language. Language classroom discourse patterns might be predicted to be special if these classes typically display different forms of interaction from other classes – which, with the emphasis on language functions and the importance of oral skills, and the advent of communicative methodology, they may. But where does this leave women and girls? Girls may tend to get the better grades (on written homework, or in tests), but if findings from other subject classes of boys talking more carry over to the language class, girls are unlikely to fulfil their potential in mixed-sex information gap activities, open dialogues, role plays and simulations, problem-solving tasks, and other 'communicative' activities. In dialogues intended to promote practice of different language functions in the target language, male and female students may get more practice in different functions, depending on the textbook and how the teacher uses it (see Introduction to Quadrant II).

Research on the role of learner gender in the language classroom has looked at differential use of the target language in talk control in pair- and groupwork: turn taking, topic choice and interruptions. Findings on talk control are comparable with those for other subject classrooms. Susan Gass and Evangeline Varonis (1986), working with Japanese learners of English, found that in mixed-sex pairs 'the men initiated the conversation, nominated the topic and took most of the turns at talking.' Janet Holmes found that adult male ESL students in Australia and New Zealand took more and longer turns in mixed-sex groupwork and that the female students provided more conversational encouragement (1986, 1989a, 1989b). Fran

Munro (1987), using some of Holmes' New Zealand data, found in addition that male adult students interrupted more.

Work has also been done on preferred activity types. Julia Batters, looking at modern language classes in Britain, found that the female learners spent more time than the males in 'attentive' activities (listening, observing and reading), and that the male students were dominant in 'oral and participatory activities' (1987). Early in their second year of secondary school, boys have also been found to react as positively as girls to oral work, and more positively to oral work (in French and German) than any other aspect of foreign language learning (Robert Powell and Julia Batters, 1985). These attitudes may not extend beyond the second year – but where they do, may affect boys' talk in the target language in both whole-class work, and group and pairwork. Janet Holmes' contribution to this Quadrant continues the exploration of gendered learner–learner discourse in the English language classroom and looks at whether male students' and female students' questions in mixed-sex groupwork facilitate or inhibit communication.

The topic of 'teacher talk' in classroom discourse is often dealt with in teacher education under 'methodology' and/or 'classroom management'. Bearing in mind gender differences in language use, however, teacher talk is itself likely to be gendered, constituting either 'culturally more masculine' or 'culturally more feminine' discourse. Fran Byrnes, in this Quadrant, looks at how these discourses relate to 'authoritative' and 'negotiative' classrooms. She also illustrates how the different gendered events that occur along the 'materials/processes interface' can be dealt with in language teacher education.

Many language classes throughout the world are composed entirely of women, or men, or boys, or girls, who are taught by a teacher of the same sex. Here, gender does not pertain to gender differences in classroom behaviour, but does pertain to gender identities, and gender roles and relations beyond the classroom. The Case Study in this Quadrant is William Burns' 'Refugee Women Tell Their Stories': an account of teaching and learning in all-female English language classes. The students are Vietnamese mothers of Amerasian children. This contribution concerns the process of awareness raising among teachers, the importance and pedagogic value of the learners' personal experience, and the process of text creation as central to the classroom methodology. The texts are learner produced: the women's own autobiographies which become reading materials for other learners.

La Différence Continue . . . : Gender Differences in Second/ Foreign Language Learning Styles and Strategies

REBECCA OXFORD

Introduction

Learning styles in general have been widely researched recently. They have been defined as 'overall patterns that give general direction to learning behaviour' (Claudia Cornett, 1983: 9). These patterns can be applied in the learning of a new language – or any other subject. Examples of learning style include analytic v. global, visual v. auditory v. hands-on (tactile/kinaesthetic), and reflective v. impulsive. Strategies are the specific behaviours that learners employ, usually intentionally, to enhance their understanding, storage and retrieval of, in this case, second/foreign language information. They include note taking, seeking conversation partners and using gestures to convey meaning when words are not known. Learning strategies and style seem to be related.

Gender differences in learning styles

Research outside second language acquisition has identified many gender differences in learning styles. Several researchers, for example Rebecca Oxford (1990c) and Ronald Schmeck (1983), are beginning to believe that all style differences might represent a dichotomy of human variation: people who are 'globals' and those who are 'analytics':

Globals	Analytics
subjective	objective
feeling	thinking
field dependent	field independent
right-brain dominant	left-brain dominant
extroverted	introverted
co-operative	competitive
impulsive	reflective

(Individuals can of course also be global thinkers, analytic feelers and so on.) Oxford and Schmeck both assert that the global style may be characteristic of females, the analytic style characteristic of males.

These differences may, at least in part, be innate – and thus in fact sex differences – but most are likely to be socioculturally developed (Eleanor Maccoby and Carol Jacklin, 1974).

Learning style as subjectivity–feeling and objectivity–thinking

Mary F. Belenky *et al*. (1986) found that most women they interviewed about 'ways of knowing' preferred a subjective, feeling-oriented, global style rather than an objective, thinking-oriented, analytic style. Likewise, the MBTI ('Myers-Briggs Type Indicator') indicates that females have relatively more of a feeling (values-and-emotions-based) orientation, and males more of a thinking (analysis-based) orientation. Sensing–thinking–judging types (analytic, tied to concrete reality, needing rapid decisions or closure) are frequent among males, while sensing-feeling-judging types (emotions-based, tied to concrete reality, needing rapid decision and closure) appear often among females (see Isabel Myers and Mary McCaulley, 1990).

Relevance to second language acquisition (SLA): males and females might take different routes when learning a new language, with males tending to favour objectivity (rules, facts, logic) and females subjectivity (feelings, cultural sensitivity, empathy).

Learning style as field dependence and independence

Related to the global/analytic dichotomy may be the learning style dimension of field dependence and field independence (sometimes called 'psychological differentiation'). Field independence is related to left-brain dominance and refers to the ability to separate key details from a confusing background. Field-independent people maintain their perceptions even when changes in context are introduced. These individuals tend to analyse situations into component parts rather than acquire a global impression.

Field dependence (or sensitivity) is related to right-brain dominance and is the relative inability to separate details from background. The perceptions of field-dependent/sensitive people are easily affected by changes in context: such individuals tend towards global impressions rather than analysis of different components. Field-dependent people tend to be particularly sensitive to social context (Madeline Ehrman and Oxford, 1988).

Females, especially adolescents and adults, tend to be more field dependent (global) and males more field independent (analytic) (e.g. Thomas Good and Jere Brophy, 1986; Stephanie Shipman and Virginia Shipman, 1985; Oxford, 1990c). This difference may well be associated with child-rearing practices or more general socialisation (e.g. Herman Witkin and J.W. Berry, 1975).

Relevance to SLA: the relationship between field independence/dependence and

L2 verbal learning is not clear cut. Field-independent L2 learners, often males, may have an advantage in analytical reasoning tasks (Oxford, 1990a, 1990c; Jacqueline Hansen and Charles W. Stansfield, 1981). Field-dependent individuals, often females, may have an edge in non-analytic aspects of communicative competence, such as sociolinguistic competence, discourse competence and strategic competence (Oxford, 1990c; Vicki Galloway and Angela Labarca, 1991).

Learning style as relationship with others

Women students tend to favour a two-way or networked exchange of ideas rather than a one-way, hierarchical, lecture-type flow of information from professor to student (Belenky *et al.*, 1986; Maccoby and Jacklin, 1974). Women in many contexts have a non-competitive, non-confrontational social style, while men are more competitive and confrontational (Deborah Tannen, 1990; Oxford, Martha Nyikos and Ehrman, 1988).

Relevance to SLA: women may be more co-operative, less competitive and more sociolinguistically sensitive than men in the classroom. They may also be more interested in social and interpersonal aspects of the target culture.

Learning style as reflection and impulsivity

Reflection is the tendency to stop and consider options before responding, while impulsivity is the tendency to respond immediately (and often inaccurately). Shipman and Shipman (1985) suggest that whenever gender differences are evident and significant, females are usually more reflective (see also Belenky *et al.*, 1986; T. Roberts, 1979).

Relevance to SLA: in research by Ehrman and Oxford (1988, 1989, 1990), the 'perceivers' on the MBTI (learners who could refrain from leaping to conclusions too rapidly and who might therefore also be called 'reflectives') were better language learners than the 'judgers' (those who needed quick closure, rapid decisions and clarity). Perceivers/reflectives remain open to new clues which help them to understand meaning, whereas impulsives can have problems because of their premature, inaccurate responses (Thomas Parry, 1984). However, too much reflective concern for accuracy can become destructive anxiety which can diminish L2 performance (Ehrman and Oxford, 1990). A balance between reflection and impulsivity seems most likely to be desirable for SLA (Oxford, 1990a, 1990c; Galloway and Labarca, 1991; Diane Birckbichler, 1984).

If being reflective is characteristic of female learners, does this contradict the possibility, already raised, that being reflective is also an aspect of the analytic style – a style which may be characteristic of males? Perhaps there are two types of reflection: analytic reflection that deals with structural accuracy and is related to field independence, and global reflection that concerns social and sociolinguistic themes and is related to field dependence. If so, in SLA males may show the first type and females the second.

Learning style as sensory preference

Sensory preference refers to perceptual mode or learning channel: visual, auditory and 'hands-on'. Visual students prefer to learn via the visual channel: they like to read and often prefer working alone. Auditory students enjoy oral–aural learning: they prefer to engage in discussions, conversations and groupwork. 'Hands-on' students need to touch objects, move around the classroom and take breaks frequently.

Relevance to SLA: in the classroom, possibilities include 'hands-on' students being male rather than female (there may be a relationship between a 'hands-on' preference and the spatial ability associated with masculinity; see M.J. Hansen, 1982), with the less traditionally feminine women and girls showing 'hands-on' preferences more frequently than their more traditional sisters. Visual strengths, though prevalent in both males and females, may be slightly more so in males, and auditory preferences might appear more often in females than males.

Style wars: gender differences in teaching/learning style

A student's learning style may be in conflict with the way he or she is taught. The three verbatim narratives that follow illustrate such conflicts in language classes. The students had been exposed to the terminology of styles and had taken at least one style inventory, such as Oxford's 'Style Analysis Survey' (1993), Lynn O'Brien's 'Learning Channel Preference Checklist' (1990), Rita Dunn *et al.*'s 'Learning Style Inventory' (LSI) (1989) or the 'Myers-Briggs Type Indicator' (Myers and McCaulley, 1990). All these instruments help individuals identify their learning style or personality type.

These three students all had teachers of the opposite sex. Though gender was rarely identified as a major issue, when these conflicts occurred between a teacher and student of the opposite sex, the frustration level of both appeared to be higher than when the conflict was 'same sex'. And whether or not the 'different sex' style conflicts themselves were related to gender, they may have been exacerbated by problems communicating about the conflict across gender boundaries (see Oxford and Roberta Lavine, 1991).

Example 1: Female global/impulsive/visual student and male analytic/reflective/non-visual teacher

> My style wars began in a graduate course. The teacher and I are not compatible at all. My style of language learning is causing great friction with his teaching mode. I'm unhappy, I dread the class, and I'm under a great deal of stress in and out of the class.
>
> I'm a visual learner. . . . The teacher never writes anything on the board, in fact, he

never moves from his domain, the chair. . . . I'm a global learner; he likes to have everything detailed at length with no explanation given. I'm having to use rote memorisation in order to study, and that is no joy; nothing has meaning, everything is just a blur.

He is slow, and I'm impulsive, but not to the point that I do not take my studies seriously. He uses over-correction methods which really dampen the atmosphere of learning in the class . . .

I do hope that I will make it to the end of the course without an ulcer or have a nervous breakdown before the exam. This has really been a nightmare and a very forceful style war in my learning career.

Example 2: Female analytical/closure-oriented student and male global/ open teacher

I took a Portuguese class in graduate school in which I experienced 'style wars'. My professor was an intuitive-perceiver [open] (global) teacher. There were many open-ended activities and the class was somewhat chaotic; but fun, I must admit.

I am an intuitive and closure-oriented student. I like organised presentations and detailed grammar explanations. This professor was very animated in the classroom, and he used drama and role plays to teach grammar inductively. We watched a videotape that accompanied the textbook and we learned songs and cultural points of interest.

We did a lot of oral/aural work in the language laboratory. When I finished the course, I wondered what I really learned. I could not reproduce any verb conjugations or many vocabulary words from memory. I enjoyed the class a great deal, but was uncomfortable with his teaching style. I did not learn in an environment with which I was comfortable.

Example 3: Male global student and female analytic teacher

The only style conflict I have ever had in an English class was in the tenth grade. My teacher was very analytical, whereas I am very global. She took every aspect of the class step by step. She never deviated from her plan. She refused to see more than one interpretation for a situation. We had an extremely difficult time communicating, thus I had a hard time in learning because she could not adapt to another style.

Implications of style results for the second/foreign language classroom

What can teachers do about gender differences in learning style?

1. It is useful to assess and acquaint students with their learning styles (see the list of style inventories on p. 143). Teachers and students should not be surprised if gender-related differences appear, but should feel free to discuss possible sociocultural (and biological) factors influencing these. *If* the differences are largely gender (not sex) related, they are presumably not fixed, and it is useful to emphasise that people with different styles may be able to learn from each other, both across and within gender boundaries (see also Fran Byrnes, this Quadrant).

   Students may be able to use information about their learning style to help them seek language learning activities and environments to suit that style (Oxford and Lavine, 1991).

2. By using the style data, teachers may be able to spot and obviate potential style conflicts.

3. Teachers can also vary their instructional techniques to meet the needs of students with contrasting learning styles, using a range of activities to cater for diverse learning styles. In addition, they can help students move beyond their basic style tendencies. Ways include:

   (a) imposing a 'wait time' of 30 seconds to encourage impulsive students (often males) to reflect before responding;

   (b) encouraging reflective students (often females) to be more spontaneous, for example through small-group activities and question games which require rapid answers;

   (c) offering multi-sensory activities allowing all students to move around, handle objects and have both visual and auditory stimulation.

Gender differences in language learning strategies

Learning strategies are the specific behaviours students use, often by choice, to improve their learning. Effective learners, for example, often actively associate new information with familiar information.

SLA researchers have drawn up lists of strategies thought to characterise the 'Good Language Learner'. For example, the GLL (1) willingly guesses, often accurately, (2) wants to communicate, (3) is uninhibited about mistakes, (4) focusses on both structure and meaning, (5) takes advantage of all practice opportunities, and (6) monitors his or her own speech and that of others (Joan Rubin, 1975; see also Neil Naiman, Maria Frölich and Angie Todesco, 1975).

Appropriate strategy use is related to better learning performance (Ehrman and Oxford, 1988; Anita Wenden and Joan Rubin, 1987; J. Michael O'Malley and Anna U. Chamot, 1990; Andrew Cohen, 1990) – though it is not clear which influences the other, or even if the relationship is always causal. Unsuccessful learners may use as many strategies as effective learners, but may do so in a random, almost desperate way (Roberta Vann and Roberta Abraham, 1989). Language performance can hopefully be improved through teaching strategy use in the form of learner training (O'Malley and Chamot, 1990; Oxford and David Crookall, 1989; Gail Ellis and Barbara Sinclair, 1989).

The choice of language learning strategies is related to both gender and style (Ehrman and Oxford, 1988, 1989; Nyikos, 1990; Kenneth Willing, 1988). If learners are not pressed to use certain strategies, they tend to use those congruent with their style.

Analytic, field-independent learners, for example, ordinarily select logical reasoning strategies such as deduction, whereas global, field-dependent learners tend to choose non-analytic strategies such as guessing and searching for the main idea. Visual learners may prefer extensive visual input through reading; auditory learners may engage in conversations and drills; 'hands-on' learners may like using flashcards and labels. Reflective learners may cautiously consider all the angles and the social context before venturing a response, while more impulsive learners may jump right in.

Starting with eighty investigations of second/foreign language learning strategies, Oxford, Nyikos and Ehrman (1988) summarised gender differences in this area using the only four studies to mention them. (Some had not been published but subsequently were.) Robert Politzer (1983) reported that college females used social strategies more often than males. Ehrman and Oxford (1989) found that adult females reported significantly greater use than males of general study strategies, functional practice (authentic language use) strategies, strategies for searching for and communicating meaning, and self-management strategies. Oxford and Nyikos (1989) found that college females used strategies significantly more often than males in three of five possible categories: formal rule-based practice strategies, general study strategies and conversational input-elicitation strategies. Nyikos (1987, 1990) discovered significant collegiate gender differences in mnemonic strategies for German vocabulary learning.

In a later study, Willing, investigating the learning strategies of over 500 adult migrant learners of ESL in Australia, found that although twenty-six of the thirty learning activities he listed were not rated differently by men and women, four were. Learning many new words, learning words by seeing, learning words by doing something and learning by talking to friends in English, all rated highly by both sexes, were rated significantly more highly by women (Willing, 1988).

More recently, Oxford *et al.* (1993) discovered that female high-school students learning Japanese by satellite transmission had higher motivation than males in three out of six possible strategy groups: cognitive, affective and social.

Females seem consciously to use strategies more often than males. However, it may be the qualitative differences in their strategy use that favour women and girls, who often show better classroom performance in a second or foreign language than males. (Studies of informal, non-classroom-based language development within the target language community might reveal different patterns of both strategies and performance.)

Implications of strategy results for the second/foreign language classroom

Teachers can measure the learning strategy use of students and help them become aware of which strategies they habitually use, and why. A useful survey is the 'Strategy Inventory for Language Learning' (Oxford, 1990b). Students are typically eager to learn about their own language learning behaviours, and to know which strategies may be typical of one sex, which of neither. Moreover, they are also usually keen to develop new strategies to improve their learning.

Strategy training can enable students to use more, and more appropriate, strategies, tailored to their needs and the requirements of different language learning tasks. In this way students may discover what is most useful to them. This training can be provided by the teacher and woven explicitly into regular class activities. For instance, the teacher might provide a range of memory strategies (imagery, rhyming, repetition, context creation) for learning naturally occurring vocabulary and point out the value of such strategies (see Ellis and Sinclair, 1989).

This training can stretch students beyond the strategies that fit their style preferences, and perhaps beyond strategies associated with their sex – for teachers will presumably wish to avoid falling into the trap of stereotyping. For example, teachers can help global, feeling-type students, frequently females, to make the most of their empathetic tendencies in conversational settings but also provide them with new analytic strategies, such as deductive reasoning, to infer meaning. They can also provide avenues for analytic students, frequently males, to move in the direction of a greater, global, sociocultural sensitivity (see also Oxford 1989, 1990a, 1990b).

Anatomy is not destiny, as Freud suggested, but a learner's sex – or, more likely, gender – can have profound effects on the ways that learner approaches language learning, ways which may in turn affect proficiency. More research is clearly needed to untie the Gordian knot of style and strategy differences between the sexes and to understand better the relationships involved.

Differential Teacher Treatment-by-Gender in the EFL Classroom: Using Ex-participants' Perspectives

JANE SUNDERLAND

Though EFL teachers may not like to think this of themselves, it appears that we do treat our male and female students differently. Such behaviour may be unconscious or conscious; if conscious, it may be intentional or unintentional (the teacher may become aware of it after the event). If intentional, it may be benevolent – drawing out quiet girls, for example – or malevolent – say, dismissing all students of one sex as bad language learners.

Teachers cannot treat all students identically. Students are individuals, requiring, not only for pedagogic reasons, different treatment. But there is now a considerable body of research which suggests our differential treatment in mixed-sex classrooms is not only by students' individual characteristics, but also by the social characteristic of gender. Since, however, few studies have been done in EFL classrooms, it is unclear whether there are any patterns of differential teacher treatment-by-gender (henceforth 'differential treatment') specific to EFL.

An important finding for classrooms in general is that the sex of the teacher makes less difference to the way she or he behaves than the sex of her or his students, i.e. male and female teachers tend to treat male and female students differently and do so in similar ways (see Lars Ekstrand, 1980; Jere Brophy, 1985; also Alison Kelly, 1988; and Frank Merrett and Kevin Wheldall, 1992).[1]

Studies of mixed-sex non-EFL classes have found differences in both the amount and quality of attention teachers give. As shown in the Introduction to this Quadrant, very often boy students receive more teacher attention than do girls. This does not mean that all boys get more attention than all girls – though if boys on the whole get more attention than girls on the whole, this cuts down on the average amount of teacher attention girls get. Studies have also found that, variously, boys get more blame, approval, disapproval and instructions than girls, and that girls who call out are reprimanded more than boys who call out. In maths, teachers have been found to give more 'wait time' to boys, and to ask girls more 'product questions' ('What's the answer to number 6?'), and boys more 'process questions' ('Why is the answer to number 6 thirty-three metres?').

In her 'meta-analytic review' of 81 studies of gender differences in teacher–pupil interactions, Kelly writes:

> It is now beyond dispute that girls receive less of the teacher's attention in class. . . . It applies in all age groups . . . in several countries, in various socio-economic groupings, across all subjects in the curriculum, and with both male and female teachers. . . . Boys get more of all kinds of classroom interaction. The discrepancy is most marked for behavioural criticism, but . . . [b]oys also get more instructional contacts, more high level questions, more academic criticism and slightly more praise than girls. . . . The discrepancies are just as large in teacher-initiated interactions as in pupil-initiated interactions. . . . (1988)

This question of teacher attention must be kept in proportion. Male students getting more attention is not a classroom rule: some studies have not found this to happen (e.g. Sarah Sternglanz and Shirley Lyberger-Ficek, 1977; Barry Dart and John Clarke, 1988; Merrett and Wheldall, 1992). Where it does happen, learner gender has been found to interact with subject and academic ability (Thomas Good *et al.*, 1973), as well as, presumably, age, ethnicity and class. And where it does happen, as indicated, it is a tendency, not equally true for all boys or men in the class (Paul Croll, 1985), i.e. it is a matter of gender, rather than sex. Most importantly, perhaps, attention in itself does not facilitate learning – blame or disapproval may in fact have the opposite effect. The quality of teacher attention may be far more important than the quantity.

How do these differences in quantity and quality of teacher attention come about? It is certainly easier to understand the former. When a teacher pays more attention to boys, she or he is not simply being sexist. Though readers of Dale Spender's (1982) work may find themselves depressed by teachers' apparent inability to distribute their attention equally among boys and girls, and may even feel guilty about their own complicity in this, recent work on classroom discourse suggests that the process is a collaborative one. Jane French and Peter French, working in a British primary classroom, found the imbalance to be due to 'a particular, small subset of boys taking a disproportionately high number of turns', and 'teacher and pupil acting collaboratively, each simultaneously producing and inviting further talk in response to constraints provided by the other' (1984: 129).

Using video, Joan Swann and David Graddol (1988) identified the importance of gaze: the teacher's eye contact was often with groups of boys or girls; gaze in the direction of boys tended to stay there and when in the direction of girls tended to return quickly to the boys; and the teacher looked more at the boys at critical points, for example when a question was to be answered. One way boys can collaborate in this is by creating discipline problems (or making teachers believe they will), ensuring the teacher is continually scanning their areas to prevent indiscipline, thus increasing the likelihood of selection through eye contact. It is possible to hypothesise from this about quality of attention. Boys seen to have the potential to create discipline problems might, for example, be disciplined more than the girls, or be asked more challenging questions than the girls.

Let us now return to the foreign language classroom. The finding that boys were asked more cognitive (process) questions in mathematics than were girls (Gilah

Leder, 1987) is clear cause for concern. However, the earlier finding that teachers related to boys and girls differently in different subjects (less academically to girls in maths but not reading) (Gaea Leinhardt et al., 1979) is a reminder that what is characteristic of some subject classrooms may not be characteristic of others, and indeed that the language classroom might produce specific patterns of gender-related teacher behaviour. Interestingly, in Kelly's meta-analytic review, less sex differentiation occurred in reading lessons (perhaps the closest to EFL) than in mathematics, science, social studies, general/mixed or other classes. In many countries languages are seen by teachers and students as girls' subjects – and are chosen by girls (Roger Murphy, 1980). If girls are believed to be better language learners, or actually are (see Clare Burstall et al., 1974; Ekstrand, 1980), might this not lead to different interaction patterns in language classrooms? Girls might, for example, be asked more challenging questions than the boys, or might be spoken to by the teacher – or might get his or her attention – as much as, if not more than, the boys.[2]

If there is differential treatment, does it matter? As with textbook sexism, evidence of its existence will not impress all teachers unless they are shown that it may reduce learning opportunities. As indeed it may: if girls get less teacher attention, they may develop feelings of low self-esteem, as pupils can see teacher attention as evidence of interest in them. Teachers get to know those students who (they encourage to) speak – presumably an educational advantage – better than those who do not. If not called on, girls will have fewer opportunities to display their needs or talents to the teacher; and, in the EFL classroom, if their written work is poor, they will have no opportunity to compensate orally. Also in the EFL classroom, not answering or being allowed to ask a question may be a missed opportunity for a learner to test a hypothesis by getting feedback: is the utterance correct or not? (See Michelle Stanworth, 1983; Swann and Graddol, 1988.) The effect of differential treatment on language learning opportunities and language acquisition is hard to research but, again, hypothesising effects is a start.

As yet, there is little evidence for patterns of differential teacher treatment in EFL classrooms (there is more on gendered learner discourse, e.g. Isobel Crouch and Betty Lou Dubois 1977; Jenny Gubb, 1980; Susan Gass and Evangeline Varonis, 1986; Janet Holmes, this Quadrant).[3] Fran Munro (1986) found that teachers in adult ESL classes in Australia asked the male students more questions than the female students (again see Holmes, this Quadrant). Mary Yepez (1990) observed three male and four female teachers of adult learners of ESL and found that six of the seven showed equitable behaviour to male and female students. In addition to Rebecca Oxford's work on 'style wars' (this Quadrant), this was the only work on teacher–male student/teacher–female student interaction in language classrooms I was able to find.

In contrast to the studies of non-EFL classrooms described, which were investigating preconceived forms of differential treatment, I decided to borrow a technique from ethnographic research methodology, and to explore the parameters of differential treatment in the EFL classroom by using EFL students' and teachers' own perspectives, and look for reasons for differential treatment. Ethnographic classroom studies rely crucially on the perspectives of participants in the context being studied; I chose to use the retrospective perspectives of ex-classroom participants. I did this in three ways.

Using ex-participants' perspectives 1: creation of questionnaire items

I asked the 'Language and Gender in the Classroom' (LAGIC) discussion group of Lancaster University, themselves mostly previous learners of EFL, to brainstorm ways differential treatment could occur, based on their own experience, and to 'fantasise' further ways in which it might.[4] The result was a list of twenty-six items – for example 'Expecting a higher standard of written work', 'Expecting higher standards of politeness' and 'Asking [male/female] students to do classroom jobs'. Using this list I designed a questionnaire.[5]

Using ex-participants' perspectives 2: questionnaire completion

The questionnaire was completed by four groups of respondents studying on short courses at the Institute for English Language Education, Lancaster University, in 1991. These were (a) seven students of different nationalities improving their English (three female, four male), (b) thirty-nine Greek trainee EFL teachers (all female), (c) eighteen Austrian trainee EFL teachers (mostly female), and (d) eighteen practising Japanese EFL teachers (mostly male). The mixed-nationality group and the Austrian and Greek respondents were asked to complete the questionnaire as ex-learners of EFL or another foreign language; the Japanese respondents were asked to respond as EFL teachers.

Questionnaire completion with the mixed-nationality group provided a pilot study, and the questionnaire was then improved. However, these respondents had a further important role to play, to which I will return.

Differential teacher treatment which the Greek and/or Austrian respondents most frequently claimed to have experienced included: expectations of higher standards of written work and politeness from the female students, the teacher being more polite to the female students, the teacher usually selecting one of the female students if no student puts a hand up when the teacher asked a question, the female students getting more praise and encouragement about studying the foreign language, the male students being asked easier questions, and the female students often being ignored.

Items to which the Japanese teachers most frequently responded that they differentiated between male and female students were: being more polite to female students, asking a female student when someone was needed to do a classroom job and, if a male and female student spoke at the same time, usually asking or allowing the female student to continue. (Several Austrian respondents reported the reverse for this last item.)

I have not reported the findings of these questionnaire studies in detail since they lack systematicity (but see Sunderland, 1992a). Rather, I wanted to use these preliminary findings to show that, as in other classrooms, teachers in EFL classrooms seem to treat their male and female students differently, and to do so in a range of ways which vary from culture to culture.[6]

These preliminary findings, however, do not seem to resonate with those for non-language classrooms. (Neither, it may be recalled, did Yepez's findings for adult ESL classes.) Much of the differential behaviour indicated here would actually seem to favour female learners. Further studies of differential treatment that might be specific to foreign language classrooms need to be done.

Using ex-participants' perspectives 3: why does differential treatment happen?

Questionnaires are in many ways unsatisfactory for getting at perceptions. Meaning cannot fully be negotiated, the respondents may not be sufficiently interested to complete the questionnaire seriously and sincerely, and their responses may not reflect what they actually perceived, but may have been elicited by the questionnaire itself. If the respondents are non-native speakers of English, and the questionnaire is in English, the respondents may not understand the questions, and in a scheduled class there is little opportunity to fully explain them. Further, although this questionnaire included a box to indicate either details of or reasons for differential treatment, there was no way respondents could do this satisfactorily since completion was subject to the constraints of the respondents' course timetables.

Perceived reasons for differential treatment were therefore obtained in another way from group (a), the seven English language students. Three of these had identified no differential treatment at all. The other four were invited to explain their responses in a recorded interview. The interviews were transcribed. A sample of their interview responses will illustrate the value of this procedure.

All four respondents indicated that a teacher had asked the boys harder questions and the girls easier ones. If this indeed happened, it could suggest that these teachers took the education of the male students more seriously and accordingly challenged them more than the female students. But this was not what the respondents indicated.

Juan (Spain) said that the teacher would ask a boy a harder question to threaten him: 'it's an indirect way to say to him . . . you won't get the results you want.' Marie-Claire (Mozambique) said it was to preserve the male students' egos: 'because of our culture we would like to show all people that the males are good and can answer very well. . . . ' Hassan (Libya) said it was to punish the boys: 'the teacher tried to show that the male students are always noisy and they don't pay attention to the lecture or listen to the teacher so he tried to . . . punish them this way . . . by asking them I mean hard questions.' Mazen (Oman) suggested that the teachers were unused to female students.

Now these respondents may not have inferred what motivated their teachers' behaviour with perfect insight – but students from a particular culture can fairly safely be assumed to understand their teacher's behaviour better than an outside researcher. Juan, Marie-Claire, Hassan and Mazen remind us that what may be the same differential treatment can be differently motivated in different teachers – within the same culture or in different cultures. They also remind us that differential treatment may not be the same as crude discrimination against women or girls. Certainly Juan and Hassan give no indication that their teachers were favouring the male students at the expense of the females – if anything, quite the opposite.

It is likely that different teachers will treat their male and female students in different ways in different cultures for different reasons. The social construction of gender being what it is, it is unlikely that differential teacher treatment will ever not be a feature of mixed-sex classrooms. What is at present unclear, however, is its effect.

Counting and categorising examples of gendered discourse can give a partial account of what is going on in the classroom, but are unlikely to be able to explain it, or its effects, and may mislead. Quantitative approaches can however be complemented by more qualitative ones. Ex-participants are able to retrospect about classroom experiences and their perspectives can be a valuable resource for understanding how learner gender shapes the foreign language classroom (and other classrooms), and can provide insights into how differential teacher treatment might affect learning opportunities and hence language acquisition.

I would suggest that learner gender and classroom discourse operate in an on-going, two-way process: not only does gender influence discourse patterns, but discourse patterns also help shape gender, in terms of gender identities, gender roles and gender relations. The latter is far less demonstrable, requiring, *inter alia*, longitudinal studies. But if foreign language classroom discourse patterns do play a role in the construction of gender, and correspondingly in the reproduction – or transformation – of gender relations, and if the patterns of differential treatment in the foreign language classroom are such that the 'boys get more of all kinds of classroom interaction' tendency is less marked than in other subject classrooms, this would indeed be a progressive characteristic of the EFL classroom.

Notes

1. Merrett and Wheldall's study of mixed-sex classes in British schools found that secondary (but not primary) female teachers 'used significantly more negative responses [than male teachers] to boys' social behaviour' whereas secondary (but again not primary) male teachers 'used significantly more positive responses [than female teachers] to boys' academic behaviour' (1992: 77).
2. My own research in a first-year German class in a British secondary school suggests this can happen.
3. There has also been work on gender differences in language learning achievement and ability (e.g. Ekstrand, 1980; Gunnel Knubb-Manninen, 1988); learners' attitudes to and perceptions of a foreign language (e.g. Julia Batters, 1986, 1987); and the implications of learner gender for EFL/ESL teacher education (e.g. Eleanor Ramsay, 1983; Fran Byrnes, this Quadrant).

4. I am grateful to Dick Allwright for suggesting this exercise.
5. There is not sufficient space here to give details of the questionnaire, the instructions, the full results and the attempt to integrate research with pedagogy. I will be pleased to supply these on request. (Also see Sunderland, 1992a.)
6. Though cross-cultural differences are to be expected, the findings from the Greek, Austrian and Japanese questionnaire studies cannot meaningfully be compared, even for the samples in question: the questionnaire was continually being modified and each time it was used some instructions and items were different; the respondents were answering it from different perspectives and within different pedagogic frameworks. Neither am I claiming that generalisations can be made from these samples to EFL learners in the three countries.

Doonesbury

BY GARRY TRUDEAU

HOW'S NURSERY SCHOOL GOING, HONEY?

OKAY, I GUESS. EXCEPT I NEVER GET TO SAY ANYTHING...

WHAT DO YOU MEAN, ALEX?

THE DORKY BOYS GET ALL THE ATTENTION. MRS. JASPER ISN'T FAIR ABOUT LETTING THE GIRLS ANSWER QUESTIONS.

HMM...

MAYBE I SHOULD HAVE A LITTLE TALK WITH HER.

MOM, SHE'LL NEVER CALL ON YOU! SEND DADDY.

MRS. DOONESBURY! HOW NICE TO SEE YOU HERE!

I'M SORRY TO DISTURB YOU, MS. JASPER, BUT ALEX HAS COME TO ME WITH A PROBLEM.

MS. JASPER!

WHAT SORT OF PROBLEM, MRS. DOONESBURY?

SHE FEELS THE BOYS GET MOST OF YOUR ATTENTION. SHE'S FEELING SHORTCHANGED.

MS. JASPER!

JUST A MINUTE, ERNIE. MRS. DOONESBURY, THAT'S JUST CRAZY. AFTER ALL, I'M A FEMALE MYSELF. IF ANYTHING, I FAVOR THE GIRLS!

MS. JASPER!

WHAT IS IT, ERNIE?

YES, BY ALL MEANS, LET'S FIND OUT.

MRS. DOONESBURY, I'M ACUTELY AWARE OF THE PROBLEMS OF GENDER BIAS IN THE CLASSROOM TODAY. ALMOST ALL TEACHERS ARE...

BUT YOU WOULDN'T BELIEVE HOW FORCEFULLY BOYS CAN PROJECT THEIR PRESENCE. THEY MAKE THEMSELVES VERY HARD FOR US TO IGNORE.

I UNDERSTAND, BUT IT CAN'T BE AT THE EXPENSE OF THE GIRLS' SELF-ESTEEM.

THOSE EARLY, EMPOWERING INFLUENCES ARE SO IMPORTANT. IN MY CASE, I LEARNED FROM MY MOTHER TO BE TOUGH AND INDEPENDENT AND STAND ON MY OWN.

HOW'D SHE TEACH YOU?

WELL, BY...UM... ABANDONING ME. OKAY, BAD EXAMPLE.

I SPOKE TO ALEX'S TEACHER ABOUT GENDER BIAS TODAY...

A CHAT SHE WELCOMED, NO DOUBT.

ACTUALLY, SHE WAS PRETTY COOL ABOUT IT, CONSIDERING.

I MEAN, BIAS IS A PRETTY HARD THING TO TALK ABOUT, MUCH LESS ADMIT TO.

DOES ANYONE THINK I IGNORE THE GIRLS? TEDDY?

SIGH...

Improving the Lot of Female Language Learners

JANET HOLMES

Here are three adult learners of English performing a discussion task in class:

Va.: if they have to go to the jail they very depressed
Is.: yeah it can be the end of their life
Ha.: well I agree with you that going to jail I mean
Is.: yeah
Ha.: it could be very very bad and stressful
Is.: it could be the end of your life
Ha.: because it's not a pretty sight going to jail it's very hard[1]

This interchange occurred in a small group discussion in an English lesson for immigrants. The speakers designated Is. and Ha. were both women. They agree, confirm and build on previous contributions. Contrast this with the following exchange between two male second language learners, doing the same task:

Ch.: yes of course I'm thinking about my son
Da.: but your son is your family
Ch.: no mother and father
Da.: I disagree – son is family too

As these examples illustrate, women and men talk differently. Research in Britain, America and New Zealand reveals similar gender-based patterns of discourse. Women appear co-operative, facilitative participants, demonstrating in a variety of ways their concern for their conversational partners, while men tend to dominate the talking time, interrupt more often than women, and focus on the content of the interaction and the task in hand, at the expense of attention to their addressees (e.g. Jennifer Coates, 1986; Janet Holmes, 1990; Dale Spender, 1980a; Deborah Tannen, 1990; Shân Wareing, Quadrant I).

The strategies which typically characterise female interaction can be described as 'talk-support' strategies, while at least some of those which characterise male talk function as 'talk-inhibition' strategies. In the classroom these strategies have obvious implications for learning opportunities. In the second language classroom they can either promote or restrict language learning opportunities.

Talk-inhibition strategies

Dominating the available talking time

There is extensive evidence that in a range of contexts, and discussing a variety of topics, men retain conversational control simply by talking for longer and taking more frequent turns than women (e.g. Carole Edelsky, 1981; Spender, 1982; Barrie Thorne, Cheris Kramarae and Nancy Henley, 1983; Holmes, 1988, 1992). This is especially true in the kinds of semi-formal settings and interactions similar to interaction in the ELT classroom.

The evidence from classrooms demonstrates the same pattern. Throughout their schooling, boys in mixed-sex classrooms dominate interactions with teachers. They make more contributions to discussions than girls, and they receive more feedback (both positive and negative) from teachers (e.g. Virginia Brooks, 1982; Spender, 1980b; Joan Swann, 1988; see also Jane Sunderland, this Quadrant).

The few studies of sex differences in classroom interaction between non-native speakers of English confirm the pattern for ELT classrooms, and for learner–learner discourse. In the United States, Susan Gass and Evangeline Varonis (1986) found that Japanese men dominated conversations in English between mixed-sex student pairs. In so-called free conversation, the males initiated the interaction or nominated the topic, took marginally more speaking turns and used by far the largest proportion of the speaking time. Observing interaction in Australian ELT classes, Fran Munro found that male language learners not only responded more frequently to the teachers' non-directed questions, made more unsolicited comments, and asked the teacher more questions than the female students, but also talked longer than women in small discussion groups. They also took more turns in most, though not all, groups, and took nearly twice as many long turns as women (Munro 1986, 1987; Holmes, 1989b).

Opportunities to talk and practise using the language are considered very important for most language learners. These patterns of male domination of the talking time in ELT classrooms give reason for concern that women are getting less than their fair share of opportunities to practise using English.[2]

Interrupting

Disruptive interruption also tends to characterise male talk more often than female talk in a variety of settings (e.g. Candace West and Don Zimmerman, 1983; Anthony Mulac *et al.*, 1988; Susan Schick Case, 1988; Nicola Woods, 1989). In the classroom context, Jane Gilbert (1990) analysed the speech of fifteen New Zealand teenagers in a series of discussions which formed part of the work for some science modules. In mixed-sex groups of four or five pupils, the boys talked most, and they were also the most frequent interrupters.

Analysing Munro's (1987) tapes of small group interactions between English language learners in Sydney, I found overwhelming evidence that the male students interrupted more often than the females. The groups were discussing a list of fifteen 'stresses' (such as divorce, a death in the family, money problems) which they were required to rank in order of seriousness. In most of the groups the male students repeatedly interrupted the females and took the floor, as shown in the two examples below. [/ indicates a pause. The words after the square brackets were uttered simultaneously.]

Male (Mo.) interrupts female (Ly.):
Ly.: you still thinking/ [I don't like my mother die . . .   yeah
Mo.:   yes [you feel depressed but no in such great you feel depressed but not as
                you /you have cancer or something like that/

Male (Lu.) interrupts female (Ad.):
Ad.: the friends they gonna bad to you/ that's why (laugh) it's
      more important that [you   m m
Lu.:   [alright we just leave it like this   and we find number eight

In the first of these two examples the man not only interrupts the woman's description of an experience which had caused her considerable stress, the death of her mother, but he contradicts her, asserting his own example is stronger. The second example illustrates an organising and structuring interruption. Men frequently self-selected as group leaders, and then interrupted others to keep the group 'on task', regardless of the feelings being expressed by the speaker or their relevance to the direction and overall goals of the discussion.

These patterns pervaded the discussions. The male students took the floor from the women considerably more often than the reverse. Teachers need to be aware that typically it is women students who are the victims and men the perpetrators of these unsupportive and disruptive talk strategies.

Bald challenges and disagreements

Being polite can mean maximising areas of agreement and minimising disagreement (see Geoffrey Leech, 1983: 138). Yet clearly people do not always agree, and when this happens, women and men tend to approach the problem posed for politeness differently.

Daniel Maltz and Ruth Borker (1982) suggest that men disagree more often and more baldly than women do. In some contexts men seem to maximise disagreements, argue and challenge each other, and even generate confrontation where it could have been avoided (Edelsky, 1981; Koenraad Kuiper, 1991). Women, on the other hand, tend to stress agreement; their talk is essentially friendly (Maltz and Borker, 1982: 209). Maltz and Borker trace these adult patterns back to interactional habits developed in childhood peer group interaction, and Coates (1986), reviewing classroom interaction research, notes that 'girls' sense of their own identity as female makes them feel that the speech acts of arguing, challenging and shouting are inappropriate behaviour for them' (1986: 156; see also Maria Stubbe, 1991).

In the speech of the language learners taped by Munro, challenges and overt disagreements also occurred more frequently in the men's speech than in the women's. Male challenges and disagreements had the effect of discouraging the women from participating as enthusiastically as they otherwise might. In the example below, for instance, we see a woman being asked somewhat belligerently where she stands:

Male (Sh.) to female (Mi.):
Mi.: no it's number nine /(laughter) oh no we're not thinking. . . .
Se.: OK
Sh.: you don't agree with this one number two
Mi.: er
Sh.: you agree or not? you agree with this one number two

The men denied assertions and contradicted opinions expressed by others with little attempt to qualify or hedge their disagreement. 'No, no', and 'I disagree' recur throughout the tapes predominantly in the men's speech. The following is an example of a direct contradiction of a woman's opinion by a male who interrupts her:

Female (Ma.) interrupted by male (Sh.):
Ma.: oh no it's no problem because [when you have a when you
Sh.:   [yeah very problem

Bald contradictions and challenges from both women and men certainly occur in lively arguments between native speakers who know each other well, and this style of interaction also characterises some cultural groups more than others (Tannen, 1990). But such direct disagreement strategies in the classroom appear to inhibit some female learners and discourage them from contributing freely to the discussion.

'Response-restricting' questions

Pamela Fishman points out that 'questions are interactionally powerful devices' (1983: 94): they demand a next utterance, and so they are ways of ensuring at least a minimal interaction. Classroom research has also demonstrated that asking questions gives considerable control over both the structure and the content of an interaction (John Sinclair and Malcolm Coulthard, 1975; Douglas Barnes, 1976; Shirley Brice Heath, 1982).

The length of responses to questions can be influenced by the type of question asked. The traditional distinction is between 'closed' and 'open' questions (Barnes, James Britton and Harold Rosen, 1969). A closed question restricts the addressee's response options: e.g. a *yes/no* question or an *either/or* question. An open question often takes the form of a *wh-* question, apparently giving the respondent much more discretion over the length and content of the response.

Despite the fact that these labels are widely used they are not always easy to apply. A technically closed (*yes/no*) question such as 'Do you have family here?' may in fact serve as an invitation to the speaker to talk about her or his family, while a technically open question such as 'What have you done with "getting fired"?' may be intended to elicit a very specific and short response such as 'number five' (i.e. 'I have labelled it number five.'). In my analysis I found it more helpful to distinguish between what I called 'response-restricting' and 'facilitative' questions, where the main criterion for categorisation was the function of the question in context.

Using Munro's tapes I undertook a more detailed analysis of questions in three groups balanced for sex and drawn from similar ethnic backgrounds. Over all, the men asked 15 per cent more questions than the women, i.e. they were more often taking responsibility for the progress of the discussion. Were they also encouraging others to contribute?

Though both sexes used more response-restricting questions than facilitative questions, there were more response-restricting questions from the men (88 per cent) than from the women (66 per cent). Many of these were 'organising' questions (reflecting the fact that the men tended to take the leadership role more often than the women), asking what order others had put items in, for instance, or whether they agreed with the speaker's ordering. The following are examples of this type of question:

Do you agree with this one?
What you put number four?
What is the most important point family or spouse?

The effect of these questions was to close off and stifle discussion. They give the impression that the questioner is concerned only to elicit a short and very specific answer and proceed to the next stage of the task. Clearly a predominance of this type of question will not lead to extensive discussion, nor therefore to practice in using English, the obvious purpose of such exercises in an ELT classroom.

These strategies, which tend to restrict or inhibit the participation of the addressee in some way and which have generally been found to predominate in the speech of male native speakers of English, may thus equally characterise the discourse of male speakers of English as a second language. In the ELT context, where opportunities to practise speaking English are vital, it is worth considering ways in which one could counteract the negative effect such strategies may have on female learners.

Talk-support strategies

Among native speakers of English, women tend to supply more encouraging feedback, ask more facilitative questions, agree more often and disagree more politely than men (e.g. Fishman, 1983; Holmes, 1989b,). As the first example at the beginning of this article suggests, these patterns also occur in discussions between second language learners. The women provided approximately twice as much supportive verbal feedback as the men, and they used three times as many facilitative questions. They agreed more than the men, and when they disagreed they tended to qualify and modify their statements.

The learning environment these women language learners provided for the men was clearly rather more favourable than the environment they experienced. Fewer facilitative questions were directed to the women by the men than *vice versa*, and while the men had the benefit of attentive, responsive and encouraging listeners, the women received relatively little support for their contributions, and were given less encouragement to continue when they did speak.

Changing things

The research reviewed in this paper suggests that female language learners provide an ideal context for their conversational partners. In mixed-sex interaction, however, they are clearly receiving less than their fair share of conversational encouragement. So what can the ESL teacher do to improve the quality of the classroom environment for female learners?

The patterns of interaction which characterise female and male behaviour reflect and perpetuate the structured inequalities which characterise the relationships between women and men in most societies.[3] We cannot change society quickly enough to benefit our students, but we can manipulate the classroom environment. The analysis here suggests that it is the *male* students whose interactional skills need attention. All too often we are told that women should become more assertive: they should acquire conversational strategies which will enable them to get their fair share of the talking time. But it makes much more sense to focus on the inadequacies in male students' discourse skills. We need to teach men how to be good conversationalists.[4]

Since men appear to lack talk-support skills, they need exercises to help them develop these. Male students need to learn:

1. to be active listeners, giving support and encouragement to their conversational partners;
2. to provide utterances which confirm points made by their partners, elaborating and developing their partner's points from their own experience;
3. to express disagreement in a non-confrontational manner;
4. to ask facilitative questions which encourage others to contribute to the discussion.

These skills can be practised initially in all-male groups so that females do not act as guinea pigs to help male students acquire skills the females already possess. Such skills will enhance their conversational competence, as well as making discussion a pleasanter experience for their conversational partners.

These measures can be seen as steps towards achieving justice and fairness for females in the language classroom. Male domination of various types of classroom interaction is an influential component of the hidden curriculum. In addition to the obvious pedagogical issue of equal access to learning opportunities, there are other sound reasons for attempting to alter these patterns. The subtle message conveyed by male domination in the classroom concerning the paramount importance of male talk and male experience is no longer acceptable to those concerned with the rights and self-esteem of female students. Social justice in the language learning classroom involves providing a receptive environment for female talk.

Notes

1. I am grateful to Fran Munro for supplying the data from which the examples are taken.
2. It is worth noting that both teachers and researchers may be blind to the findings described here. It is easy to believe that such patterns do not obtain in one's own classroom, and that talking time is evenly distributed between the sexes. It is well worth checking the reality (see Spender, 1980a; Edelsky, 1981; Graddol and Swann, 1989).
3. I have not discussed in this paper the ways in which ethnic background may mediate some of the patterns of interaction described. Such evidence as there is suggests that the broad patterns hold over a range of societies.
4. Recent research by Jenny Cheshire and Nancy Jenkins (1991) examining small group discussion in secondary schools reaches the same conclusions.

Issues of Gender in Teacher Education

FRAN BYRNES

The aim of this paper is to examine, with reference to a specific course, issues of gender in teacher education programmes, in particular as they relate to curriculum goals and objectives, content, teaching and learning styles, classroom methodology and materials.

Within this I want to focus on two claims:

1. Fundamental inconsistencies exist in teacher training programmes between the expressed goals and curriculum principles, and the methods and materials used to realise these goals and translate the principles into practice.
2. Traditional teacher education programmes fail to recognise or fully to address the issue of gender, especially the different ways that men and women use language, and how these differences are reflected in, and significantly influence, the nature of teaching and learning.

The course which I will refer to in this paper is the four week pre-service Certificate in Adult TESOL run at the Australian Centre for Languages, in Sydney.[1] I have chosen to use the ACL course for three reasons:

1. My personal involvement with it over a number of years enables me to draw on first-hand experience.
2. A teacher training course in the Australian context provides a particularly interesting and relevant case study. Multi-culturalism as a political and social reality in Australia has contributed to the development of a highly pragmatic approach to language teaching and learning. Language is seen primarily in its social and cultural dimension with linguistic analysis often guided or directed by the social aspects of discourse. This approach provides a particularly appropriate perspective for discussing gender and gender differences in language teaching and learning, since issues of gender are often closely linked to cultural attitudes and to personal world views.
3. Focussing on a real course offers the opportunity to see where gender issues in teacher education have been addressed in practice, and to identify areas where more work needs to be done.

Goals and objectives

Like most teacher education programmes the ACL course has stated aims or goals which attempt to set out practical skills development and teaching competence in a professional or objective way.[2]

The teacher training programs at ACL are designed to:
- inform teachers on an on-going basis of current research developments in theoretical and applied linguistics
- support teachers in making links between theory and their own classroom practice
- encourage teachers to ask questions about their own practice and reflect on what happens in their own classrooms

In the ACL teacher training programs teachers are encouraged:
- to explore the relationship between teaching, learning and language learners
- to develop a greater awareness of their own theoretical standpoint
- to develop specific teaching solutions to the challenges they encounter in their own classrooms

---

Aims
By the end of the course trainee teachers will be able to:
- state clear teacher aims and learning objectives
- use a range of resources and classroom equipment

However, alongside aims like these which are management, organisational or authority oriented, teacher education programmes also set goals where negotiation with learners is an imperative. This perspective is reflected in objectives like these:

By the end of the course trainee teachers will be able to:
- plan and deliver a range of lesson types, modifying the plan during lessons where necessary
- select appropriate materials for learners taking into account learner needs and interests and maximise possibilities for objectives to be achieved
- constructively evaluate lessons
- identify learner errors and use strategies to deal with them
- grade their own language, use questions effectively to elicit language, to focus attention and to focus on concepts

Objectives like these presume highly developed teacher skills of co-operation and collaboration in communication. But in practice most teacher education programmes do not reflect this ideology. Most often we find a competitive curriculum which directs trainers and trainees to focus on the development of teachers as managers and authoritative decision makers. This anomaly reinforces the conflict between the now familiar concepts of communication behaviour that is culturally more feminine and communication behaviour that is culturally more masculine.

Men and women tend to use language in different ways (see Shân Wareing, Quadrant I), and much research shows a more collaborative use of language by women compared to the more assertive and power-oriented nature of male speech, even from very early childhood (e.g. Deborah Tannen, 1990). But the 'male model curriculum' with an emphasis on competitiveness rather than co-operation remains an important part of the practical reality of teacher education courses. The masculine bias in curriculum design, i.e. to develop authoritative, teacher managers, presents serious difficulties for those who believe that a learner-centred approach to language learning, and needs-based syllabuses, are the most effective. Here we have a conflict not only for women but for all teachers or curriculum planners who see teacher–learner negotiation as more important than authoritative teacher guidance.

In relation to the important issue of language and gender I see this as the major challenge for teacher educators. The design and implementation of teacher education programmes must address the issue of integrating the management and authoritative role of the teacher with the negotiating and co-operating role. The expectations of both teachers and learners, men and women, need to be reshaped to allow this to happen; and herein lies perhaps the most pressing reform for teacher education.

Language and language learning

One of the ways teacher education programmes can raise the profile of gender issues is by providing opportunities for teachers to develop a better understanding of their own theories and beliefs about teaching, and to place these personal perspectives in a broader theoretical framework, into theories of language and language learning, of applied linguistics and of cross-cultural communication. The ACL course formally expresses such objectives; but is not detailed enough. In addition to the general objectives about teacher language, like 'By the end of the course trainee teachers will be able to: grade their own language/use questions effectively to elicit language/focus learners' attention on concepts or information', the course curriculum needs to include objectives that focus specifically on the issue of gender difference in teacher talk.

It is important for teacher education programmes formally to address the issue of how men teachers and women teachers differ in the ways they use language to manage classroom activities and procedures. Most teacher education programmes still look at teacher talk in a generic way. Yet there are differences in the ways men and women give instructions, explain, correct, tell stories. How can a teacher training programme approach the task of identifying these differences and develop in male and female trainees appropriate and individually relevant awareness and skills?

The most appropriate focus is the broader one of communicative competence, which incorporates the whole range of communication skills and knowledge. This is especially true in short course programmes where there is not time to analyse in depth all the elements of communication, but rather time only to make trainees aware that communication success depends on a range of communication skills and strategies, e.g. grammatical competence, discourse competence, strategic competence, sociolinguistic competence. Communicative competence, a familiar concept in teacher education, needs to include the concept of the particular communicative competences of women and men and accept that as an essential part of language teaching practice.

Teaching and learning

Teaching involves a large number and a wide range of very demanding roles. The teacher is at different times expected to show competence as course designer and planner, decision maker, negotiator and facilitator, evaluator and assessor, manager, instructor or knower, mediator and counsellor, interpreter (of intentions and meanings) and learner.

Developing and managing this range of roles is one of the most difficult aspects of learning to be a teacher, and it is made even more challenging because the roles themselves are often difficult to reconcile, for example the teacher as decision maker and as negotiator. Accordingly, at ACL an important principle of the teacher education programme has been a formal recognition that:

1. The skills teachers need to develop are often conflicting or at least difficult to reconcile.
2. Men and women trainees bring to the course inherently different ways of operating.
3. Teachers are decision makers and must set the framework for much of the formal learning.
4. Negotiation and co-operation in the teaching and learning process is the only way to reflect the true nature of communication.
5. The skills of negotiation and collaboration, like other teaching skills, are not inherent in trainees.
6. Negotiation and collaboration skills in communication are more likely to be found among women trainees than among men trainees.

Learners need to recognise and develop those strategies of learning which they personally prefer, which are often subconscious and which are linked to cultural views, gender and psychological make-up (see Rebecca Oxford, this Quadrant). A challenging responsibility facing language teachers is this task of developing in their learners an awareness of these preferences, and helping them become familiar with other approaches and strategies for learning, other ways of seeing and doing that other learners in their group, perhaps of the opposite sex, use. In their role as learners, teacher trainees need to be given opportunities to draw parallels between the experiences of their language learners and their own learning experiences in the teacher education programme. They too need to develop an awareness of their own abilities and learning preferences. But teachers also need to develop an awareness of their own teaching abilities and teaching preferences.

The task below, in its original form, was designed to be used with language learners, to assess learning preferences; but it can just as easily be used in teacher education to look at teaching preferences, and to reinforce in a practical way theories of learning principles, differences in teaching styles and strategies, and what teachers can do to facilitate successful teaching and learning.

Task

Teachers can and do teach language in more than one way, but most teachers have ways which they prefer, teaching activities which they like; which they find familiar, comfortable, useful, relevant, non-threatening; which they can do well. These differences result from the person's psychological make-up, and often from the way they have been conditioned or trained to look at things, e.g. men and women often look at things in different ways.

These differences are not determined by ethnic or cultural background. In all language or cultural groups you would find representatives of a range of teaching styles.

Think about some of the choices you have made during the course, and draw some conclusions about your preferred teaching style. Think also about how you have approached the teaching in this course so far – what strategies have you used? how have you organised your teaching? what things have you found easy or difficult? how have you tried to maximise teaching success for yourself? how have you tried to avoid or minimise difficult aspects of the teaching?

Are the reasons for your choices and your preferences clear to you? Are they linked to your cultural views, to your gender, to some other influences?

Content and materials

The choices teachers make about materials, texts and content are influenced by practical, professional, personal and cultural factors that need exploring. The choices are inextricably linked to learner needs, perceived and expressed, and to teacher needs, and these choices may include gender-related considerations.

Trends in publishing are increasingly moving towards the development of generic material for international markets. This means that teachers are often faced with problems in finding material that they feel is appropriate.

Language teaching materials continue to present a relative invisibility of women, stereotyping of gender roles, or male-dominated discourse in mixed-gender conversations (Jane Sunderland, 1992b). The topic of gender has begun to appear but often as a special focus unit or chapter rather than as a naturally occurring part of more general life issues.

An important task for teacher education is to raise awareness of the nature of materials and to develop in trainees the skills to identify and evaluate how gender and gender issues are dealt with in the materials they choose or are directed to use. And, arising out of this, is the need for teachers to develop the same awareness in their learners.

Teacher education programmes must also provide teachers with strategies for dealing with the shortcomings and biases that they find in existing material. One way of doing this would be to include this issue more fully in teacher observation feedback sessions, and to focus on why trainees choose certain material, and how they exploit it in terms of content and of learning tasks.

Teachers need to ask themselves: 'How are people represented in the materials: their attitudes, their behaviour, their language?' They also need to analyse teachers' guides to determine the philosophical bases on which guidance is given and to make judgements about the position presented. And in terms of interaction with text learners need to be encouraged to:

1. analyse what attitudes about gender and gender roles are reflected in the material;
2. examine whether what people do and say and how they do and say things is linked to their position as men or women in society, in the family, in the culture of the workplace, etc;
3. consider role reversals for male and female characters in the situations presented;
4. explore reactions to characters that are not 'gender correct', ways of using language that are not 'gender appropriate';
5. contest existing assumptions about gender and gender roles in communication.

These could be achieved through supplementary, teacher-designed activities where these objectives, rather than specific language acquisition, are the primary purpose of the learning tasks.

Methodology and classroom practice

Teaching is an interaction between teachers, learners and texts, involving collaboration between teacher and learners. But research suggests that teachers often give more attention to male students, and that the rights of female students in language classrooms require careful attention (see Sunderland and Janet Holmes, both in this Quadrant). More research is necessary on these and other gender differences in L2 teaching and learning, but both learners and teachers have experiences and beliefs of their own. These hypotheses can and should be researched in classrooms. Self and peer observation by teachers can provide important insights into what we really do in class.

In the ACL course the issue of gender in classroom interaction is addressed only informally. Its inclusion is left to the discretion of individual trainers. But it needs to be included formally in the lesson observation guides and in trainer observation notes on practice lessons. How do we use language in class? What gender roles are played out in our lessons, by us and by the learners? Do we give learners the opportunities to explore new communication roles, to move safely and confidently outside their gender stereotypes? How can we facilitate this?

Cross-cultural issues in the classroom

Gender is an important part of culture and cultural identity. In the ACL course the underlying curriculum principles clearly reflect a social and cultural view of language and language use.

- the course is designed to explore the relationship of language and culture in the context of adult ESOL teaching in Australia.
- language is social and has meaning only in context . . . the context of culture and the context of situation.

The cultural perspectives of teachers and learners often differ significantly, and learners themselves often bring very diverse cultural views to the learning. These differences provide a good starting point for exploring the link between culture and language, to examine how cultural or world views affect language learning and language use. The following is an example of an awareness-raising task designed to focus attention on cross-cultural differences in language and learning:

Task
Gender issues in language learning are often overlooked but they can also be exaggerated or presented in negative or stereotypical ways.

Discuss in your group what cultural influences, including attitudes to gender, might affect learners in group or individual learning activities, how classroom communication and learner participation in the learning might be influenced, how learner attitude to tasks or content might be determined. Keep in mind that learners react culturally to YOU, to OTHER LEARNERS, to THE MATERIAL, to THE TOPIC OR SUBJECT MATTER and to THE ACTIVITIES OR TASKS.

Class Profile	**Low Level Beginners**
6 Japanese	5 men (from 27 to 56), all from the same electronics company. All want Business English. 1 woman (26) married to an Australian executive in the same company.
2 Hong Kong Chinese	Men, mid thirties. Experience in retailing.
1 Korean	Man, 28. On work exchange to the State Railway Authority as an engineer. Concerned about his practical need for English in the workplace.
1 French	Man, 25. Former social organiser at Club Med. Wants to work in the hospitality industry. Outgoing.
1 Swiss	Man, 23. Travelling. Highly motivated. Speaks a number of European languages. On holiday from his medical studies.
1 Lebanese	Woman, 40. Teacher of French in Lebanon for 17 years. Married to a Lebanese diplomat.

Conclusion

Much work still needs to be done in incorporating issues of gender more clearly into both the theory and the practice of teacher education. One of the most effective ways in which training programmes can do this is to ensure that in their own practice they reflect the methods advocated for classroom language learning in relation to the issues of gender – roles, communicative behaviour and specific language. Theoretical explanations from input sessions should be translated into teaching skills, analytical skills or evaluation skills that are also demonstrated in the methods used by trainers. More attention must thus be given to the importance of gender both in language and in the learning process.

Notes

1. The trainees on the ACL Certificate Course are an extremely diverse group in terms of experience and educational background. There is a significant predominance of women. A significant percentage of trainees are teachers from other areas of the profession, mostly from the secondary school system. Although there are academic prerequisites for the course, there are no teaching prerequisites and many trainees have no teaching experience of any kind. The trainees range from the minimum admission age of 21 to those who are well into middle age. Many trainees have chosen to do the course as a means of changing their lives in some fundamental way. The course seems to offer the chance of a

new direction, a new career, and in this sense takes on an importance beyond itself. This can lead to unrealistic expectations of what the course can achieve and can prove a source of stress if expectations are not realised. It can also cause individual trainees to place extra pressure on themselves in a course which is already very demanding.

2. All texts in boxes are extracts from ACL curriculum documentation.

Case Study: Refugee Women Tell Their Stories

WILLIAM BURNS

> I'm from Bac Lieu City. It's a small city in Vietnam. I quit school when I was 16, because my family was poor. I went to live with my sister in Saigon. I got a good job making clothes. My friend, Lan, had an American husband. He introduced me to his friend, Jay. Jay was in the American military. He was very nice. We began dating. We fell in love and lived together for a year. He left in 1973. After he left, I found out I was pregnant. Now, I have a daughter. She looks like her father. When I look at my daughter, I miss her father. Soon, my daughter and I will be in America. I hope I can find my American boyfriend.
>
> (Thoa Tri Tran, *My Love Story*[1])

This autobiography, used as a text in literacy classes for refugees in the Philippines, illustrates the unique experiences and aspirations that a recently identified group of refugee women bring with them to the classroom. They are the mothers of Amerasian children born as a result of the American presence in Vietnam before 1975. The Amerasian Homecoming Act passed by the US Congress in 1987 granted refugee benefits to tens of thousands of Amerasian children and their families and brought a new profile to ESL classes, both in the United States and at the Philippine Refugee Processing Center (PRPC) where most of these Amerasian migrants receive a six-month pre-arrival orientation in language and culture. Unlike refugee 'camps' which have virtually become permanent residences for disillusioned and hopeless migrants, the PRPC, located in the northwest reaches of the Bataan peninsula overlooking the South China Sea, is energised by constant refugee movement and focussed on readjustment to a new life in the United States. In seeking to respond to the needs of the various waves of refugee migration since 1975, the PRPC had for some time provided special classes for refugee women, but the arrival of Amerasian cases required a reassessment of the whole curriculum.[2]

Women accompanying their now-adult Amerasian children on the way to the United States do not fall neatly into standard placement categories. They are a diverse lot with a wide range of educational and social backgrounds. Some have prodigious fluency and can immediately be tapped to serve as translators. Others seem to have forgotten whatever English they may have known. One group is a particular challenge: those women who have at least latent familiarity with oral English, yet are functionally illiterate even in their native language. In some ways they resemble students in adult native language literacy classes in America. Yet their familiarity with American culture is often minimal and distorted by the years of discrimination they suffered in post-war Vietnam as collaborators of the enemy. Still, they are survivors to the hilt and, unlike many refugee women, hardly need to be encouraged to take a pro-active stance. At first the Filipino teachers at the PRPC were confused about how to meet the needs of these women. Several years of experimentation with special classes and classroom materials like the above autobiography, however, have produced some interesting results.

Well before the arrival of the Amerasian migrants, the language programme at the PRPC had been greatly influenced by the Whole Language emphases on respect for the student and authentic communication based on the students' experiences and backgrounds. Nevertheless, the teachers needed additional help to deal successfully with these women. The greatest stumbling block was one which had plagued the women throughout their migration – an underlying prejudice against them precisely because they were mothers of Amerasian children. Wherever they turned they faced bias: from government bureaucrats, from social service agencies, and from the society at large. The refugees who preceded them had been predominantly male, and often well-educated technicians or professionals. Although the overwhelming majority of these women had been formally or informally married to American servicemen for extended periods (as in the story which introduces this section), they were seen as camp followers or prostitutes. At the PRPC, in-service lectures to eradicate the unconscious prejudice by bringing out the facts achieved minimal results, even among the professional staff. More successful was involving the teachers of the women's classes in case studies and then depending on them to enlighten their colleagues. Several years of such informal research have resulted in a number of case studies which serve as a basis for pre-service and in-service sessions. More important, the process contributes to an awareness and respect for these women as individuals, many of whom have battled an oppressive regime and an unaccepting society to provide sustenance and emotional support for their children. However, teachers still need to address the bias problem consciously and regularly lest they be influenced by the prevailing prejudice of the surrounding community.

Of course, stereotyping mothers of Amerasians as self-sacrificing heroines can be as harmful as stereotyping them as prostitutes. What is needed is for the teacher to be open to these women as people. Including case studies in the ESL approach generates just such a recognition of the student as a person. It also incorporates many aspects of current thinking in literacy education since case studies are most successfully based on student autobiographies. More traditional approaches to reading and writing with these students often led to stigmatisation of the students as 'slow learners' or 'illiterates'. The available workbooks and readers were so divorced from their lives and interests that the students were simply devoid of motivation. When the women found the teachers encouraging them to write about their own experiences and then preserving their stories in classroom libraries as texts for future students, they felt a new pride in themselves as authors and a new desire to produce even more material for the collection. Even first-time writers were amazed to find themselves reading back the stories they had just dictated to their teachers.

The above autobiography of Thoa Tri Tran is an example of student writing that is much more than the display pieces often demanded of ESL learners. It educates the teacher and a wider audience while it affirms the importance and uniqueness of the individual.

Texts generated through classroom composition prompt a variety of further interaction. They provide high-interest culturally relevant materials for individual reading. Teachers often use the illustrations to help students develop prediction strategies. As students see themselves as authors, they increasingly seek the teacher's (and one another's) advice on vocabulary, syntax and style. The stories are frequently dramatised and sequels are created. Formally published stories, like Thoa Tri Tran's, are often purposely left unfinished so that students can discuss significant problems, in this case the wisdom of a reunion with the former boyfriend. One short text stimulates many hours of authentic communication and leads to further composition on related topics.

As oral and written composition in class focussed more and more on the women's experiences, teachers began reporting an unexpected emotional intensity in the classes. There were outbursts of weeping and gestures of sympathy among classmates which the teachers had never experienced before. Students often introduced topics which frightened the teachers. One woman might describe dealing with her child's refusal to attend school because his classmates continually taunted him as the son of a 'Yankee whore'. Another would respond that her daughter had used the same epithet directly to her. Teachers were at first fearful of their own emotions in such discussions and tended to steer the class onto safer ground. But once aware of the supportive environment in which they now lived and studied, the women would insist on discussing such issues. It seemed that their ESL literacy class had become a support group, releasing emotions pent up for fifteen or more years.

Teachers without particular expertise in counselling began asking for further help in understanding and meeting the emotional needs of their students. Psychologists, both from the Center's counselling team and from the United States, encouraged the teachers to allow the women to express the emotions they wanted to vent. Center counselling staff were pleased to have co-opted the teachers (though they were careful to provide teachers with guidance in identifying and referring cases in need of professional care) while US resettlement workers stressed the importance of alerting students to the benefits of such informal support groups during their upcoming transition to American life.

The typical composition of the classroom support group has been surprising to some. While special classes are provided for women at the PRPC, Amerasian cases are not segregated from ordinary refugee cases. (It had been decided early on that segregation would poorly represent the resettlement realities.) Thus literacy classes composed predominantly of mothers of Amerasians would also ordinarily include several Vietnamese women who were not associated with the Amerasian resettlement programme. Many resettlement workers predicted dire consequences from such groupings. They felt that the 'prostitute prejudice' would make it impossible for the two groups to study together. In fact, however, teachers report no such problem (beyond the occasional interpersonal conflict). Rather, the women seem to find mutual support natural. The ordinary Vietnamese refugee woman apparently finds little difficulty offering consolation to the mother of an Amerasian child. Whether such mutual support can continue after resettlement is yet to be seen.

The wave of Amerasian migration is now virtually over at the PRPC, though it continues to concern resettlement workers in the United States. The ESL teachers at the PRPC, particularly those who specialised in these women's classes, have benefitted from the experience as much as their students. They have come to respect, love and often admire a unique population. They have had to recognise and deal with their own prejudices. They have seen that ESL literacy classes that are based on the student's experiences can be successful, not just for privileged students, but also for these so-called 'at risk' students. And they have come to appreciate in a new way the importance of the ESL class and the ESL teacher in the psychological support of their students. The women in these classes have taught their teachers some important lessons.[3]

Notes

1. This is the text of one of a series of illustrated books for refugee learners of English produced by the International Catholic Migration Commission and available from the Center for Applied Linguistics, 1118 22nd Street NW, Washington, DC, USA.
2. The Refugee Forum issue of *Cross Currents* (Language Institute of Japan, Vol XVIII, No. 1, Summer 1991: Odawara, Japan) includes a number of articles describing in further detail the refugee population and the educational approach at the PRPC (Chas J. Algaier; Francisca Pao Moredo and Wu Zhaoyi; Donald Ronk). Several deal specifically with Amerasian women. The Forum also includes an article by James W. Tollefson, a well-known critic of current refugee education policies (See Bibliography: Classroom Processes.)
3. The Center for Applied Linguistics (see Note 1) can provide regularly updated information on the educational programmes offered at overseas sites for refugees bound for the United States. A video series on refugee education including such topics as the use of narrative, community libraries and story telling is also available. Specific information on Vietnamese Amerasians in the PRPC is regularly provided in *Amerasian Update*, published by InterAction and Lutheran Immigration and Refugee Service, 122 C Street NW, Suite 300, Washington, DC 20001, USA.

MY Love STORY

Story by: THOA THI TRAN
Edited by: LAURIE KUNTZ
Illustrated by: NORMA MARCAYDA
JACKIE BACAL-TORRES

I'm from Bac Lieu City.
It's a small city in Vietnam.

1

I quit school when I was
16, because my family was
poor.

2

I went to live with my
sister in Saigon. I got a
good job making clothes.

3

My friend, Lan, had an
American husband. He
introduced me to his friend,
Jay. Jay was in the
American military.

4

He was very nice. We began dating.

5

We fell in love and lived together for a year.

6

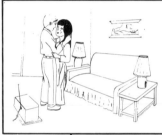

He left in 1973.

7

After he left, I found out I was pregnant.

8

Now, I have a daughter. She looks like her father. When I look at my daughter, I miss her father.

9

Soon, my daughter and I will be in America. I hope I can find my American boyfriend.

10

Comment

The different processes exemplified in Rebecca Oxford's, my own and Janet Holmes' contributions to this Quadrant – learning styles and strategies, the way teachers treat and speak to male and female learners, and learner–learner discourse, respectively – underline the complexity of the whole learning–teaching process. The sets of processes explored are dynamic and continually interacting with each other. They may further interact with considerations of English, as the target language, and with the teaching materials used. This happens within a sociocultural, political, linguistic and educational (system, school and classroom) context. This complex, organic situation within which language acquisition is shaped makes it impossible to formulate neat prescriptions for syllabuses, methods or materials that will automatically facilitate language learning – for learners of either sex.

Fran Byrnes' and William Burns' contributions underline the fact that since teaching and learning processes usually happen in relation to materials, it is impossible to separate the two. Materials have no life without a teacher or learner to interact with or interpret them. As discussed in the Introduction to Quadrant II, whether a textbook is sexist in the teaching/learning process (as opposed to when it is lying on a desk unopened) depends as much on the teacher and learners as on the book itself. This 'materials/processes interface' often pertains to gender, giving the teacher of a mixed-sex class decisions to make. For example: mixed-sex groups are doing a role play from the textbook, for which the roles are not specified by sex. Or: in each mixed-sex dialogue in the textbook, the male speaks first. In both cases the teacher has one or more decisions to make: in the first, whether to discourage distribution of learners' roles on traditional lines; in the second, whether to recast some of the first speakers as female.

Rebecca Oxford's contribution on learning styles and strategies raises the question of sex as well as gender differences, since some aspects of style or strategy use may be innate and sex-related. The question of the origin of differences in (language) learning styles and strategies is thus a thorny and potentially controversial one. The origin question is, however, important for its implications for change in styles and strategies, and for how teachable they are. It is also important in a wider sense: the sex/gender distinction is often fudged. The question of exactly what is innate and what is learned is unlikely ever to be fully resolved, so teachers and learners need to keep an open mind if they are to avoid stereotyping people of one sex as users of this style or that strategy. Such stereotyping would bring with it the risk of gender-biased evaluation associated with male-dominated society: that if, for example, males were shown to deploy learning strategy X better than females, females to deploy strategy Y better than males, strategy X would then become more highly valued as a strategy. If strategy X were seen as better simply because of its masculine association, females would gain nothing from trying to deploy it more efficiently – yet this is what they might aim for or be encouraged to do.[1]

As I suggested in the Introduction to this Quadrant, learning styles and strategies are crucial to the notion of proficiency, since proficiency in the classroom (at least) is presumably related to the effective (though possibly unconscious) deployment of styles and strategies. Their relationship with the notion of aptitude is less clear, but could be explored. The relationship between styles and strategies and gender also needs further investigation. Are those styles and strategies which appear to be gendered classroom specific, or could they also transfer to learning a new language in the target language community? How does the gendered nature of styles and strategies relate to the four skills of reading, writing, speaking and listening? And, if those teachers who claim that girls are, on the whole, more proficient than boys are in some sense right, is this a matter of aptitude, or is it because girls' styles and strategies are more appropriate, more effectively deployed?

No studies have illustrated ways in which learner–learner discourse in foreign language classrooms may differ from that in other subject classrooms. Holmes' findings on learner–learner discourse in the ESL classroom are in fact comparable with those in other subject classrooms. Her work is interesting in that the gendered patterns of discourse she identifies are operating not in the learners' first language but in the target language. If girls and women are indeed better language learners, it might be predicted that they would speak more than boys and men in the target language, though less in the first language – but this was not what Holmes (or Susan Gass and Evangeline Varonis, 1986; or Fran Munro, 1987) found. The students in these studies were all adults. It would be interesting to establish whether younger language learners, in whom these patterns may be less developed, behave similarly. Second-year learners of French and German, both boys and girls, have been shown to prefer oral work to any other aspect of language learning (Robert Powell and Julia Batters, 1985), but this may change as pupils get older, and may depend on whether boys, girls or both are in the class. Clare Burstall *et al.* identified speaking French in class as a particularly acute problem for 15- and 16-year-old girls in mixed schools, several of whom made comments such as 'If you get a question wrong or make a mistake the boys laugh at you' (1974: 230). The comments Burstall *et al.* collected refer to whole class discourse, but could apply too to pair- and groupwork, and could be an unfortunate effect of puberty.

The gendered nature of learner–learner discourse is unlikely to be primarily a matter of sex, resonating as it does with contemporary and historical beliefs and social practices. But whatever the origins of gender differences in classroom discourse, Holmes' contribution raises questions for future practice. One direction might be single-sex foreign language classes. These could be argued to benefit both female and male language learners (see, for example, Chris Beswick, 1976; also Jennifer Shaw, 1980; Peter Carpenter, 1985; Burstall *et al.*, 1974; R.R. Dale, 1974). A variation would be to encourage single-sex groups within mixed-sex language classes (in addition to those which exist as a result of boys' and girls' own preference for single-sex groups!). Jane Gilbert (1992) found that in science classes these worked better for girls in helping them develop their ideas than did mixed-sex groups. (The boys in Gilbert's study, however, benefited more from mixed-sex groups. . . .)

Teachers' classroom discourse may in recent years have been shaped by Equal Opportunities policies of (British) Local Education Authorities, schools and Language Departments and Faculties. Such policies, however, may have had less effect on students, and indeed the effect of any 'top-down' initiative on students may be limited. Gilbert (1992), for example, attempted to improve equal participation in groupwork by giving her male and female science students 'rules'. These had no effect; Gilbert suggests they were simply overridden by (among other things), existing gendered discoursal practices. Equal participation can only be achieved, she claims, by 'each group tak[ing] collective responsibility for setting up its own forms of organisation . . . . [and] all the participants develop[ing] an increased awareness of the underlying reasons for the changes, and . . . accept[ing] these reasons' (1992: 70). Challenging and changing male-dominated groupwork, then, may require similar measures to challenging and writers changing sexist textbooks.[2]

More work is needed on differential teacher treatment-by-gender specific to the foreign/second language classroom. How might differential treatment relate to topic, skill, activity, classroom organisation, the linguistic item(s) being learned and/ or L1 *vis à vis* target language use? Further, how does it vary with learner variables of age, level, academic ability, class, ethnicity and culture? It may be that few aspects of differential treatment are particularly characteristic of the language classroom. In my own study of learners' perceptions (this Quadrant), each of the manifestations of differential treatment indicated by the Greek, Austrian and Japanese respondents (with the exception of 'encouragement about studying the foreign language') could have occurred in most subject classrooms, and the two questionnaire items relating most closely to language classrooms – correction of spoken errors and demonstration of a dialogue – were ticked by only one or two respondents from each group. But participants' perceptions are only one way of investigating classroom learning and teaching processes, and other methods may provide other insights. For those teachers who claim that girls are the better language learners, at least, it might be predicted that their differential treatment is different from that of teachers who do not believe this. This would certainly be a research question worth investigating.

The list of interesting research questions can of course be extended almost indefinitely. Other areas of investigation as regards teacher treatment are the likelihood and relative frequency of occurrence of different manifestations of differential treatment in language classrooms; the mechanisms which enable it to occur (the 'how?'); what 'beyond the classroom' social practices shape it (the 'why?'); and its potential significance for language learning opportunities and by implication for language acquisition. Teachers will not all see boys getting more attention, for example, or female learners providing more feedback to male learners than they receive, as problematic, unless they see such tendencies as having the potential to hinder language acquisition.

When researching gender in language classrooms, observation can and often should complement questionnaire and interview studies of learners' and teachers' perceptions. Observation can take the form of fieldnotes, accompanied by, if possible, audiorecordings which can later be transcribed, and questions asked of them (for example: Did the teacher give lengthier feedback to female or male students' answers to her questions?). Observation schemes can also be used. Schemes already exist which are designed for the purpose of looking at differential teacher treatment, and at boys' and girls' different classroom behaviours (Myra Sadker and David Sadker, 1982; Judith Whyte, 1984; Richard Martini, Kate Myers and Sue Warner, 1984; Kate Myers, 1992), but these do not allow for gendered events which may be characteristic of the language classroom. It should be possible to incorporate the concepts of learner gender and differential teacher treatment into the more sophisticated observation schemes developed for use with language classrooms which employ contemporary teaching methods, schemes such as COLT, devised by Maria Frölich, Nina Spada and Patrick Allen (1985), and that developed by Rosamond Mitchell, Brian Parkinson and Richard Johnstone (1984).

To include a plea and/or identify implications for teacher education is commonplace when writing on classroom processes. William Burns and Fran Byrnes have in this Quadrant both focussed on language teacher education. Burns reminds us of the *de facto* role teaching a particular group of learners – in this case Vietnamese mothers of Amerasian children – plays in the on-going professional education of a teacher. In doing so, he also demonstrates how associated formal language teacher education may have to be highly context-specific, and how, in order to succeed, may have to encompass concerns beyond the target language, the syllabus, methodology, materials and psycholinguistics.

Byrnes demonstrates that English language teacher education has a role to play in all gender-related areas of ELT. She thus provides one answer to the question of whether gender should be dealt with in one or more special sessions, or throughout the teacher education curriculum. She shows that the latter is feasible and that there is plenty to say about it. (This is not to say that special sessions are undesirable. On a practical level, in many courses not all teacher educators would feel willing or able to deal with gender issues in the area for which they are responsible.)

In putting dealing with sexist teaching materials on the agenda of teacher education courses, Byrnes usefully progresses beyond the 'Isn't it awful!' response to textbook sexism. This may well be a more realistic use of time and energy than identifying sexist representations and discussing ideal alternatives. Also important is materials design by trainee teachers themselves: how can they best develop ways of avoiding stereotyping and bias, and how can they create opportunities for all their students to express their particular concerns? To achieve the latter for female students, Effie Cochran (1992: 31) suggests 'open-ended dramatic scenarios', which she claims improve students' self-image and help them 'to vocalise problems of discrimination': 'Students are asked to read and comprehend an open-ended dialogue, for which they are then required to provide their own written ending before they even begin to speak the dialogue's lines. . . . '

Discussions of teacher training beg the question of learner training, and whether differential teacher treatment and gender differences in learner–learner discourse would make good Action Research mini-project topics for the language classroom. Such projects may not, of course, achieve what they set out to. Jenny Pugsley asks:

> . . . when conditions of inequality are brought about by habit and by circumstance rather than by formal regulation or law, are they best tackled implicitly and without direct verbal reference, on an individual basis, or is there advantage in promoting group discussion and the taking of sides, on the assumption that an outcome of 'fairness' (as perceived by the disadvantaged party) will be almost certain? (1992: 10)

Pugsley suggests that an explicit, 'project' approach would make the situation tenser rather than easing it.

We are left with an apparent paradox. Girls and women in the language classroom get on the whole less help from the teacher than their male classmates, in terms of both quantity and quality of attention. Male students tend to speak more than female students in whole class work, and mixed-sex group and pairwork. Female characters are numerically fewer in textbooks and have more limited occupational and discoursal roles than males, which may impact on classroom practices and restrict female students' language learning opportunities and hinder their language acquisition. (Male-dominated mixed-sex dialogues, if the teacher follows the gendered discourse patterns laid down, are probably the best case in point.) Yet girls continue worldwide to take languages more than boys, and may even be in some sense the better language learners. Are the apparent disadvantages identified in this Quadrant irrelevant, or is it the case that, if they were removed, girls' performance in the language classroom would be even better? Could it even be that, in some bizarre way, girls respond positively to disadvantage?

Notes

1. This would be comparable to women attempting to adopt male speech styles in an attempt to be treated with a greater degree of seriousness, only to find that such treatment is given to males, not to their actual speech styles.

   Dale Spender points out one way in which masculine styles have been valued more favourably, at least linguistically. When in 1962 H.A. Witkin and colleagues were investigating sex differences in separating an embedded figure from the surrounding field, and found that females were more likely to see the figure and field as a whole, males to separate them, he 'named the behaviour of males as field independence, thereby perpetuating and strengthening the image of male supremacy; he named the female behaviour field dependence and thereby perpetuated and strengthened the image of female inferiority' (Spender, 1980a: 164). Spender notes what would have been possible alternatives: 'I could well have described the female response as context awareness and the male response as context blindness.' She comments: 'There is nothing inherently dependent or independent in seeing something as a whole, or dividing it into parts. Witkin has coined names which are consistent with the patriarchal order and in the process he has extended and reinforced that order' (1980a: 165).
2. It is worth considering to what extent Equal Opportunities in language teaching equate with a rejection of stereotypes; whether, say, the women in the class should ever be asked to discuss childcare while the men discuss car maintenance (Beverley Shaw, 1989). Readers will also hold different opinions on the extent to which girls in mixed schools should be encouraged not to drop foreign languages or encouraged to enter the socially more difficult world of science, and on whether boys should be actively encouraged to continue with languages.

Quadrant IV

BEYOND THE ENGLISH LANGUAGE CLASSROOM

Introduction

That English as a Foreign Language, English as a Second Language and English for Specific Purposes (ESP) extend beyond the classroom is evident. It is evident from donor countries' interest in directing overseas aid towards English language projects and recipient countries' interest in having funded ELT projects. It is evident in those learners' attitudes to English which relate to the historico-political role English has played in their country (if it has) and the sociocultural one it does now, attitudes which inevitably comprise contradictions. English may have been unwelcome as the language of colonisation but it may now be welcome in the language of pop music (cultural colonisation?). It is evident in the fact that language teaching is often a form of culture teaching – culture teaching which is highlighted, perhaps, when teaching about changing language.[1]

It is also evident that what goes on in the classroom is not shaped only by pedagogic principles stemming from classroom practice, but also by associated professions, such as examining, publishing and accreditation.

Experience tells English language teachers that this 'beyond the classroom' world has a lot to do with gender. At secondary school, for example, languages may be taken at higher levels mainly by girls – this is, of course, if girls get to secondary school in the first place. Girls in some developing countries rarely do, or indeed do not get to *school*, this being a privilege reserved, for different reasons, for their brothers.

The 'beyond the classroom' world of ELT is also highly gendered in the number and position of female and male practitioners. Most language teachers are women, hence the occasional 'generic' *she* to refer to the teacher in some recent educational texts. But though there are notable exceptions, in many countries most administrators, heads of teaching teams and Language Departments, Principals, Directors of Studies, curriculum designers, inspectors, testers, materials writers, and academic staff in Applied Linguistics Departments are male[2] (see also Rosemary Deem, 1991). It is not difficult to find a country where those people who study English in higher education (with a view to becoming English teachers) are mostly female, but where, several levels up the ladder, the English teachers chosen by the Ministry of Education to attend a prestigious INSET course at a university overseas are mostly male. International conferences such as TESOL and, to a lesser extent, IATEFL, may suggest that more women teachers than men are able to get the funding and time to attend, but the ratio of female to male conference participants does not necessarily reflect the proportions of women and men in the profession, and at many ELT conferences the ratio of female and male presenters reflects it even less. Male conference participants seem more willing to adopt what Jenny Pugsley calls a 'public persona' – a phenomenon which may be related to their holding on the whole higher positions.

There is certainly a gender differential in professional qualifications: whereas most people on PGCE/RSA courses in Britain, for example, are women, an equal number of males and females take relevant MA courses, and far fewer females than males study for PhDs in relevant areas.[3] It would be interesting to ascertain to what extent men get higher jobs because of these higher qualifications, or whether they get the jobs first and then seek qualifications (and, accordingly, whether women forego the qualifications or the jobs).

The gender differential in positions and qualifications does not stem from a patriarchal conspiracy to keep women at low levels of the ELT profession. Part of the problem is to do with the career structure (or lack of one), which Gillian Brown describes as a 'flat structure' (1989: 171). Most people in EFL are at the bottom; most people in EFL are women . . . complete the syllogism. This is, of course, a chicken and egg situation: the 'flat structure' may not have come about without so many women entering the profession in the first place. Not a conspiracy, then, but certainly a situation in which men, rather than women, seem to thrive.

Many women, though not all, lead complicated lives, and choose not to look for a way up the career ladder because it would make their lives still more complicated and add to their heavy domestic responsibilities. Many women teachers are (or want to be) mothers; child-bearing tends to carry in its wake child-rearing and a host of other domestic duties – which most men do not shoulder, or for which they at least do not take primary responsibility. Women with partners but without children may also shoulder a full domestic load, and may be expected to do more in looking after parents, in-laws and sick relations. Unless other women in the family help out, this leaves male but not female teachers with relative freedom and opportunity to rise in the profession and gain qualifications – and leaves women holding the babies. Childcare and child-rearing practices vary enormously; Katie Plumb describes her own western experience in her contribution 'A Guide to Working Mothers in TEFL'.

Although the present position of women in the ELT profession may then to some extent be shaped by our own 'wishes', these wishes are formed and articulated within a context of conditions of employment and other social practices. A further factor in women's position may be colleagues' attitudes: paraphrasing Virginia Valian in *The Cornell Lectures: Women in the Linguistics Profession*, Johnnie Johnson Hafernik writes: 'Women's performance is evaluated more negatively than men's, and women's successes tend to be attributed to luck and hard work, whereas men's successes tend to be attributed to ability and effort' (1992: 376). This claim would be hard, though not impossible, to verify empirically; it could perhaps be adapted and added to Jenny Pugsley's 'Checklist' of 'What do you know about your institution?' If found to be true, it would be an obvious candidate for Staff Development.

The fact that the profession is a very 'feminine' one, however, does not universally act to the disadvantage of women in it. In some countries, perhaps those where sex segregation is the rule rather than the exception, and where there are many single-sex establishments, there is room for women to move upwards. For those women who wish to rise, a feminine profession may provide the opportunity.

There are of course a large number of part-time English language teaching positions – at least in the developed world. This is a double-edged sword. On the one hand it means that women (or men) who wish to work part-time and parent part-time can do so; on the other hand it very often means low hourly rates of pay, unsocial working hours, few rights, little access to Unions, and minimal job security. Further, a profession in which many women do work part-time has continually to confront age-old prejudices about women not being bread-winners, hence not in need of real salaries.

What about those women teachers who do move into areas of the ELT profession beyond the classroom – test design, curriculum work, accreditation, publishing, consultancy, paid research? It would be interesting to know how many women in high positions shared Gillian Brown's experience. Asked 'Have you personally felt any sense of restriction or limitation?' she replied:

> On the contrary. There is a sense in which once you get past a certain level, people are so pleased to see a woman – because they need to have a token one around – that you keep on being put on every committee in sight. And you do become quite powerful. . . . It goes from being in a black hole to – well, it's like sitting on a rocket! (1989: 172)

Gillian Brown is a Professor of English as an International Language and Director of a Research Centre in English and Applied Linguistics. Her comment about being a token woman raises the question of the extent to which token women are better than no women, and of the value for other women of having a woman at the top. The originally token woman may be willing and able to use her position to make things better for other women, and may even achieve radical action – but if she accepts her tokenism uncritically, token is what she will remain. But there are also women who are neither Professors nor Directors who find outside the classroom an uncomfortable and distinctly more masculine world and culture to that which they are accustomed – a world of meetings, management and masculine discourses, which Pugsley in her contribution touches on.

At this stage in the book, it is possible to summarise (albeit crudely and selectively) what we have so far: the English language is characterised by masculine bias and English language use by a fair measure of male dominance in many contexts (Quadrant I); textbooks and other materials demonstrate a similar bias (Quadrant II); male students in mixed-sex classes tend to demand the lion's share of the teacher's attention and get it, in terms of quantity and probably quality, and tend themselves to speak more than female students (Quadrant III). If we add to this what happens beyond the classroom, it is not surprising to find an organisation entitled 'Women in TEFL'. In their Case Study, 'Why "Women in TEFL"?', the final contribution in the book, Ingrid Freebairn, Madeleine du Vivier and Judy

Garton-Sprenger explain the organisation's role (and that of its offshoot, 'Women in EFL Materials'), and tease out some of its apparent contradictions.

Notes

1. See also John Rogers' claims in 'The world for sick proper' (1982) that much English language teaching is a waste of time and damaging to learners, and Luke Prodromou's oppositional response (1988) to this; also Cem Alptekin and Margaret Alptekin (1984), Alastair Pennycook (1989, 1990), and James Tollefson (1991b).
2. According to the 1993 ARELS brochure, sixteen DOSs of schools belonging to the London Directors of Studies Association are women, eleven are men (with one unknown). One hundred and thirty-five of the owners/Principals, however, are men; fifty-nine are women (with three unknown). It is an interesting question why so many women enter the language teaching profession in the first place. Those in, or from, Anglophone developed countries at least may not have had (English language) teaching in mind when entering and going through higher education – often quite the reverse. But in these countries young women starting higher education perhaps consider the interest value of a subject rather than its likelihood to lead to a lucrative, high-status career. Certainly women in the UK tend to study languages and social sciences rather than engineering, technology, mathematical sciences or physical sciences; further, around twice as many females as males study languages (EOC, 1991). As a result, language teaching – where jobs, though often poorly paid jobs, do exist – is where many, eventually, find themselves.
3. In 1982 70–80 per cent of PGCE/RSA, 50 per cent of MA students and 20–30 per cent of PhD students (in relevant areas) were women (poster by 'Women in TEFL', 1992 IATEFL Conference, Lille).

Women and Management Structures

JENNY PUGSLEY

Introduction: who's pulling the strings?

The working environment is conditioned by many self-evident factors: geography, physical space, resources and facilities, conditions of employment, formal and informal relationships between colleagues. It is also conditioned by formal structures established between the school or college, for example, and those other institutions that bring to bear on the daily activities of the school's employees: examinations boards, accrediting bodies, sponsors of student grants, trade unions, etc.

It is important to know your own institution and the ways in which it works. This would seem to be stating the obvious. Yet, perhaps because women are less often in positions of acknowledged status, they may be unaware of the ways in which power, and influence (the covert side of power), operate in the working situation. It is commonplace to speak of the policy of institutions, their intentions and effects, as though a large institution functioned as single-mindedly as an individual (if indeed individuals do). But I would suggest that this perception is, just that: a perception, a construct, or the imposing of a uniform image and set of characteristics on what is an intricate structure of individuals. Like some of those wonderful impressionist pictures, if you look closely, the integral image disintegrates into a maze of dots.

Re-evaluating the structures

The awesome nature of authority

It is a cliché to say that knowledge is power. There is the knowledge that is information: the hard facts, so-called. There is the knowledge that is wisdom, or the ability to relate the facts and apply them to the common good, assuming such a concept has a realistic basis. In addition there is something we might call political awareness and skill or, in another register, street wisdom, i.e. the ability to use the facts, so-called, and their known context to achieve a specific aim, usually in one's own interest, but not necessarily to the exclusion of others'.

Authority – the perceived combination of power, knowledge and wisdom – is achieved in many ways. Most of us have known the experience of starting at the bottom of the organisation and looking 'up' (metaphorically) to authority with awe, respect or, at best, patient condescension. This is not only because authority pays us our salary and has the hiring/firing capacity. It is because one not uncommon characteristic of authority, or management, is the withholding (safeguarding?) of certain information, sometimes consciously, sometimes unconsciously. Questioning the *status quo* is difficult from a position of ignorance. How well do *you* know your own workplace?

Action plan

Ask yourself the following questions, on your own; write down the answers and compare them with a colleague's afterwards:

How many people work here?

Do they all have job titles?

If so, what are they?   If not, why not?

Do I know what their responsibilities   If not, am I worried?
are?

How many staff are permanent, how many temporary – long-term, short-term?

If I know, how do I know?   If not, why not? Do I need to know?
                                           Do I want to know?

Is the management a simple linear hierarchy?

Or a co-operative?

How equal is equal? How was my salary fixed? Do I know what other people earn? Do I need to know?

How are decisions taken? For example, allocation of teachers on the timetable? Selection of new books? Arrangement of staff meetings? Moving of students to an alternative class? Promotion of staff to senior positions?

Do I know how decisions are taken? Is it clear from job descriptions? Is it flexible? Is it done by whoever has the energy and initiative to do it?

Do I know what decisions I can take? How many decisions have I taken in the last month? Alone or in consultation? How many decisions were taken that affect me but without consultation with me?

What is the forum for participating in these decisions? For questioning them? What are my criteria for feeling I need to be included in the decision-making process? Have I ever challenged a decision? Or asked to be included in the making of a decision? Why did I do that? How did I go about it? Was I successful? If so, why? If not, why not?

In conclusion, who is in charge of whom, and what? And how do we know: through formal means – job descriptions, contracts, the school 'handbook'; being told verbally; simply through getting to 'know the ropes' and thereafter intuition?

Most groups of people rely on unwritten assumptions about who does what and when; this sometimes depends heavily on stereotypical views (Kate will wash the coffee cups, Keith will move the typewriters), sometimes on practical factors (Kate really isn't strong enough to carry a typewriter, Keith always drops the cups), sometimes on habit (Kate would be quite happy to carry a typewriter but never has, and doesn't want to become the albeit brief focus of attention by suddenly starting now; ditto for Keith and the cups).

What I am getting at is: are you unconsciously making assumptions about authority in *your* workplace or is your assessment based on a realistic and careful appraisal of the evidence?

Women and men

Fray and play

What is there here that applies particularly to women? Women often feel (rightly) that they are denied positions of authority, or the right to make decisions even when they find themselves in a position of authority. Many feminists claim that most structures in society are (literally) man-made and therefore conform to a particularly male concept of 'how things work'.

If knowledge is power, language and the ability to use it in the manner of those with designated authority is no less a form of power. I need not remind any woman reader of the prevalence of the military and sporting metaphor in working life. 'Let's all pull together; We'll dip our (?) toe in the water; I've got them on my side; Don't lay all your cards on the table right from the start; Always give the defeated opposition a face-saving device.' In other words, it's them or us and, if it's not us, it's them. Life (and work) is a battle, and the sporting metaphor merely amplifies the military one.

This is only one of the basic principles that seem to underline many of women's relationships with men, and men's relationships with men, and hence working life. Many feminists believe that any change in the *status quo*, in social life, in work and in creative activity, must be preceded by a very radical change in society to allow what they see as the female concept of 'how things work' to . . . find its feet!

I shall not argue the validity of this view. For many centuries the condition of women was largely determined by their child-bearing capacity and limited ability to control it. Many of us live in a material and social environment still strongly influenced by the social legacy of that biological difference.

Yet the radical view expressed in the previous paragraph at the practical level leaves the woman-in-the-street little by way of guidelines for what to do today. Radical change does occur, in politics, in the law and in education, but is frequently the outcome of lengthy and patient work by individuals whose names rarely see the limelight. A single event may appear to trigger (sorry) the revolution but revolutions also need an incubation period (better?).

Meanwhile, most working women – whatever their job, or its formal status – need to find a means of establishing (or reaffirming) themselves as figures of authority and responsibility within the existing framework – and preferably within the next twenty-four hours. A common dilemma may be articulated thus: 'Do I operate in my own mode, as it were, according to my own principles, or do I learn the ways of men? Do I have to join 'em in order to beat 'em, and if I join 'em, will I forget I ever wanted to beat 'em?'

For, make no mistake, you cannot *not* compete. You may compete quietly, sensitively and with due regard for the achievements of others. But you need not, generally speaking, expect your talents to be rewarded unless, firstly, you draw attention to yourself by asking questions and demonstrating your intellectual awareness and, secondly, you make some claim for your superiority – in one or two areas, at least. This often comes hard. As Dale Spender points out for another gender-related context:

> For boys who demand attention and explanations there is *not even a term in the language* to label their undesirable behaviour, but there is for girls – they are unladylike! . . . It is expected that boys should stand up for themselves, that they should assert themselves, and even if and when this may be inconvenient for a teacher, it is behaviour from boys that is still likely to be viewed positively! It is not expected that girls should act in an independent manner . . . (1982: 60)

Language and education

Whether life under matriarchal rule would be less (or perceived as less) of a battlefield, I dare not say. The military and sporting metaphors I find alienating not least because I neither sport nor soldier. But whatever the truth of the analogy behind the metaphor – life is a battle, and/or a game – metaphorical expressions are also frequently used to mask a vacuum. If you have no particular plan of action, or justification for an action, one way to argue your way out – defend your position? – is to employ metaphor. My intuition, based on unmethodical observation, tells me women do this rather less than men. This observation is based on experience in a middle-class, white-collar, educational, semi-academic, management-oriented work environment. And you, dear reader, would not be reading this if you did not share it with me.

It may be argued that all non-manual activity, and management of such activity, lends itself to this by-passing of detail. It is often argued that one of the strengths of the good manager is the ability not to become stranded in the minutiae of planning. Here is not the place to argue the degree to which attitudes to management in any one country have been conditioned by traditional attitudes to life in general, and to education in particular. However, I would suggest that the development of critical without creative or constructive ability is a somewhat morbid skill. It may be that the English teaching profession and related organisations in Britain have attracted rather more general arts graduates than is good for them. It could be that the profession would benefit from some students of engineering, some sheet metal workers, a trained hotelier or two. It may be that the metaphor-laden discourse of some managers in the EFL profession in Britain is not merely a masculine characteristic but a characteristic of a very particular stratum of the British educational system.

Femina britannica take hope: in order to effect the slow and painstaking transition from male-dominated to female–male shared management, you may not after all have to restructure the male psyche: you may merely have to counteract a few decades of traditional British education!

Women, language and power

Women and language

It is commonly claimed by researchers of discourse that women tend, *inter alia*, to oil the wheels (?) of discourse rather more than men, to ask open-ended questions and invite their partner, in sympathetic tones, to amplify a point. They are reputed to encourage and enhance their partner's argument, whether or not they wish to demolish it (see, for example, Daniel Maltz and Ruth Borker, 1982).

Maltz and Borker quote Pamela Fishman (1978) as proposing a power differential basis for the linguistic differences between men and women:

> . . . that norms of appropriate behaviour for women and men serve to give power and interactional control to men while keeping it from women. To be socially acceptable as women, women cannot exert control and must actually support men in their control. (Maltz and Borker, 1982: 199)

However, Maltz and Borker themselves seem to favour what they describe as a cultural basis for these differences: 'We argue that American men and women come from different sociolinguistic subcultures, having learned to do different things with words . . . The different social needs of men and women . . . have led them to sexually differentiated communicative cultures' (1982: 200).

A cultural basis for linguistic difference also appears in Deborah Tannen (1990: 77) who seems to view the differences in female and male speech as being rooted in (inherent?/biological?) differences in women's and men's psychological requirements:

> For most men, talk is primarily a means to preserve independence and negotiate and maintain status in a hierarchical social order . . . Girls and women feel it is crucial that they be liked by their peers . . . Boys and men feel it is crucial that they be respected by their peers . . .

She concludes:

> How are we [i.e. women and men] to open lines of communication? The answer is for both men and women to try to take each other on their own terms rather than applying the standards of one group to the behaviour of the other. (1990: 120)

With respect, this is not, in my view, the answer. 'Taking each other on their own terms' will perpetuate the perception, in what is still surely a male-dominated working world where masculine discourse is the norm, that women don't quite mean what they say.

It is easy to see why differences between male and female discourse affect our communication so forcefully. Witness the difficulty of women entering the field of verbal humour (of the joke variety). It's not just what you say, but who you are when you're saying it. But in normal busy, competitive working life, how far can we, and do we, make the necessary psychological adjustment to accommodate the 'who' as well as the 'what' in the verbal negotiation that constitutes discourse? As a working woman, I would prefer not to have to reply on the ability or willingness of male colleagues to translate my feminine discourse into their own masculine one: nor do I expect to make a counter adjustment. For the purpose of working life at least, I would like us to reach a reasonably common ground in terms of our discoursal features. But what would constitute reasonably common ground? Can you change the language people use by example and persuasion?

Language and power

Clear and expressive use of language is a powerful tool in the control of one's own life and the influencing of others' lives. Basic communication skills, productive and receptive, are indeed essential for daily life, and, since one's own language skills are to some extent in one's own control, are worth working on. In response to my question 'Can you change the language people use by example and persuasion?' – clearly the answer is 'yes'. Otherwise schools and companies would not go to so much trouble and expense to train their protegé(e)s in articulate expression; nor would the use of non-sexist and non-racist language have become reasonably well established in certain areas of public life.

Public speaking – whether at a staff meeting or a conference – makes considerable demands on one's verbal skills: are women disadvantaged here? If so, do they need to be?

Public speaking is also formal, so that what I say to you, or to you two, is not necessarily what I will say in front of the whole group. What I say at a meeting, for example, will indicate, or be perceived to indicate (a) my thought processes, actual or rehearsed; and (b) my definitive and published views on x and y.

Behind this perception of public speaking is an assumption about the public and private persona. This 'I' is not simply the private persona I, but I in my job: I as a representative of the organisation, even if I am not in sympathy with the sum total of its policies. It is unrealistic to expect to be given a position of responsibility in a group – the school, the college, the examinations board – and not in some way be seen to represent that group. Someone who wants to be a complete outsider must go freelance to retain verbal integrity and even freelancers will tell you it is not that easy.

There is often a perception that men talk about the public domain, women about the private. Men seek respect in showing their awareness of the wider implications of issues, women seek confirmation and reassurance of their views and authenticate them by relating them to personal anecdote.

I have, alas, no research to draw on to demonstrate how far men in their discussion of the public domain are actually consciously foregoing the luxury, or banality, of relating it to a personal experience. If men have traditionally held far more such positions of responsibility, it is perhaps not surprising that many express themselves as though addressing public issues, perhaps in fulfilment (real or imaginary) of the need to relate to the many rather than the few. If women have, on balance, held fewer such positions, it is perhaps unsurprising that they should generally refrain from speculating on the wider issues. Women have not in general been trained to see themselves as publicly important, in spite of the fact that, as (often) mothers, and this usually in the social as well as the biological sense, they are frequently the earliest and among the most influential of those who mould society.

Women whose job it is to participate in public speaking at whatever level might give some thought to this concept of the public persona. But it would help if our male colleagues would recognise that the breeding-ground of constructive views is not only or even principally the perception of public good, or the ability to express oneself in abstract terms, but also the perfectly reasonable value placed on personal experience. One anecdote doesn't make a case, but an anecdote based on common experiences reassures listeners that the speaker's views are based on first-hand knowledge and not merely on hearsay or the latest management tract.

We *can* change people's language by example and persuasion. Women in authority – and this includes all women known simply as 'teachers' – can help other women including their female successors by taking on board the responsibilities of 'public speaking'. Teachers of language are superbly placed to realise, in both senses, the potential for power and/or authority through language use, in their own interests, and in those of their (women) students.

Conclusion

An issue cutting across the 'women and men at work' debate is that of commitment to working life in general. This commitment may be motivated by a variety of factors. Whether a woman in management finds herself at the workaholic end of the spectrum or closer to '9 till 5', she will need to be aware of her own assumptions on this point and to consider others' assumptions. Any manager will need to accommodate a variety of attitudes to work.

A woman may approach the issue of women in management from two angles. Firstly, how does she handle her own job in the immediate term? My personal view is that thinking of herself specifically as a woman will be unproductive. She will inevitably think of herself as having the stereotypical strengths and weaknesses of women and will be no farther forward in the solution of everyday working problems. It seems to me indisputable that in many, if not most spheres, the averagely competent man will stand more chance of being heard, acknowledged and rewarded than the averagely competent women. This is unfair. But it is rarely useful to raise this as an issue in the workplace unless it really is *the* issue. Better to concentrate your efforts on doing the job well, and with confidence.

However, a woman in a position of some influence can take a more positive role by making a point of ensuring that the women in her sphere are well informed and assured of a sufficiently sympathetic hearing to feel confident enough to express their views. This means starting from the assumption that a woman may be less well informed, less confident, i.e. making the stereotypical assumption, but then acting on it positively. It also means helping men to recognise that they are not solely guided by intellect but are influenced also by 'emotions', i.e. personal feelings and interests that may run counter to 'objective' assessment.

Either way, a woman will risk disappointment, embarrassment and the jealousy of male *and* female colleagues. She will also risk the incomparable pleasure of being her own woman rather than someone else's: and having once taken the initiative on her own life, love and pursuit of happiness, she will probably find it impossible to relinquish. For better or worse. Well, I didn't say it would be easy, did I?

A Guide to Working Mothers in TEFL

KATIE PLUMB

Extracts from a diary

Aug. '90. I'M PREGNANT! I'm on a two-year contract! I wonder what I'm entitled to. I wish I'd found out before. Will I get maternity leave, job security and holiday pay? I've read my contract and there's nothing in it. The country I'm working in provides some basic benefits, but it doesn't look good. I wonder if the company has any other policies. How shall I approach my employer? Am I assertive enough to negotiate a deal? Will I end up without a job or financial backing?

Oct. '90. I've been given a booklet. I have to add up so many weeks, decide on the date leave begins, produce a special certificate and calculate how long I can work so that I can tag on holiday pay as well. I haven't been told if my job or the post I hold will be secured or whether I have to promise to return to work by a certain date.

Nov. '90. Well, I've done all the adding up and presented my claim. There seems to be a problem in my employer's perception of what I'm entitled to and what I think. Start counting and negotiating again.

Jan. '91. The company is checking on their policy after the union made a few noises. It's taking months and I still don't know what my position will be. In the meantime a teacher training post has come up. I wonder if I will be considered. I don't think I stand much chance as I'll be away for a couple of months. There's a single man applying for the post, he's ambitious and prepared to put in a lot of extra time so would be much more useful to the organisation.

Feb. '91. I didn't get the training post. I was told the students would need continuity and my having to take a few months off on maternity leave would be disruptive. I've got to ask for time off for my ante-natal appointments. I know it's my basic right but I'm sure it will cause a fuss especially at this time of the year with exams and registration.

March '91. There was no problem about taking time for appointments, but I've been asked to make up the time by teaching lessons I don't normally teach when I get back after the appointment. My colleagues have been complaining about all the time I'm taking off and the number of lessons they have to cover.

March '91. I've been talking to the accountant about getting Statutory Maternity Pay and holiday pay in the same month. There seems to be some disagreement. I shall have to approach the Director. She'll try her best but in the end she'll stick to company policy. Perhaps the union can help out again.

March '91. I feel really sick again today. I'll have to phone in ill. Last week I had to stay home to look after the two-year-old because the childminder was ill. Some of my colleagues won't even look at me because of the amount of cover they've had to do on my behalf.

March '91. We just had our appraisals again this year. Mine was brilliant apart from that one statement about being a little overdirect in dealings with management. As the only discussions we've had have been about maternity leave, I now realise I've had to pay for those benefits. I have also been told that when I return to work I will have the worst possible timetable with one of the heaviest loads. Great!

April '91. The final hour is getting closer. What if the baby is premature, will I lose the weeks I'm entitled to? If the baby's late, will I still have to come back to work on the same date?

May '91. The baby's been born and now it's time to go back to work. Can I juggle my lunch hour to rush home to check on the new childminder and breastfeed the baby?

Oct. '91. I'm teaching twenty-five hours a week. There really isn't any way that I can teach properly. I'm still getting up every two to three hours at night. I'm exhausted. I can't cope with housework, let alone lesson planning. Well, perhaps the students will be tolerant.

Dec. '91. I've been told I'm not entitled to full holiday pay because I haven't worked the correct number of accruing weeks since I got back. It's Xmas and money is short, what on earth am I going to do? I guess I'll have to ask the bank for another loan.

April '92. The annual TEFL conference is coming up and I'd like to give a paper. Apparently it will have a crèche but not for young babies. Perhaps my partner or a friend wouldn't mind holding the baby whilst I give my talk. That still leaves finding someone to look after the toddler.

May '92. I've been asked to write an article. The deadline is approaching and I've had months to do it in. How will I explain that I have two children who take turns not to sleep? I shall attempt to get it done even if it means carrying the baby on my hip and playing football with the other whilst I type.

Women tend to be in the majority in most EFL staff rooms, yet it is surprising to find that many workplaces still do not have very clear working terms and conditions for mothers. Trying to establish what one's statutory rights are is often a lengthy, complicated and stressful business. In EFL in the UK there are approximately 2,000 permanent jobs; there are many more posts that are seasonal or part-time and this affects maternity rights. Many employers or those in charge of timetabling are men, who, through lack of direct experience, may not be aware of all the problems working women have to cope with.

The following is a list of some of the problems and issues working mothers in EFL may have to consider in order to avoid having to cope with the difficulties described previously in the diary. Some of these problems are common to all working mothers, but the conditions in EFL lead to some specific problems. The observations come from direct experience and through talking to other working mothers in various countries. Future working mothers can perhaps be forewarned of possible obstacles they may come up against.

Contracts: When a woman becomes pregnant the wording in her contract becomes vitally important. If the job is permanent, temporary, part-time or full-time, the exact hours, length of service and holiday entitlement all have to be calculated carefully when claiming statutory rights. In the UK, for example, at the time of writing, you have to be in full-time employment for two years before being able to qualify for full statutory maternity pay and leave. Part-time workers are entitled to much less. A few organisations offer maternity benefits which are superior to the statutory ones. Careful reading of contracts is necessary as employees and employers often interpret the wording differently, which can lead to endless discussions and negotiations.

Job security: Most countries offer job security to women who want to take time off to have a child. Again the length of service and number of hours will affect this entitlement. If the work is seasonal or termly, then the period of leave is often dictated by the employer rather than the employee. Some organisations offer the opportunity for mothers to return to work on a part-time or job-share basis, but this is rare. The question of returning to the same post is also a little doubtful in EFL, as employers often argue that certain courses have to be organised by the same person for the sake of continuity.

Working load: Although most mothers would like to work throughout their pregnancy, it is not always possible in the last few months. In most EFL institutions they are expected to teach their full load (up to thirty hours a week) plus additional duties. This can also be the case if the mother has to return to work soon after the birth of her child. Negotiation of timetables is therefore advisable well beforehand.

Illness: Illness during and after pregnancy can affect entitlements and should be mentioned in contracts. Similarly, taking time off to look after a sick child can cause problems with some employers and resentment from colleagues who may be forced to provide cover.

Breastfeeding: Few workplaces make it easy for mothers to breastfeed. Negotiation with employers about working hours has generally to be done on an individual basis.

Pension, national insurance and holiday: What is often very straightforward in statutory maternity booklets is not always considered to be so by the accountant in a workplace. It is therefore advisable to check that payments are being made while on leave. All financial calculations depend on when the employer believes the year to begin and how much has been accrued over that period.

Childcare: Teaching timetables affect arrangements for childcare and these vary from institution to institution and country to country. The worst possible scenario is shift work: working early mornings and evenings and not returning home until half-past ten at night. These timetables tend to change from one term to the next and the employer is unable to give out the new timetables until the students have registered. Single parents who have no-one to share childcare with are sometimes faced with an impossible situation. In many workplaces one is expected to carry out 'extra' duties such as attending meetings. Trying to juggle the logistics of childcare is a nerve-wracking experience.

Paternity leave and support: Some countries offer this benefit as a statutory right. However, in order to find out if one qualifies, one must read the small print in the contract. Few workplaces have become accustomed to fathers taking time off to look after children during illness or otherwise.

Support: There are three directions one can take to get action and advice:
(a) Unions: In the UK, APEX (formerly MATSA)[1] is always prepared to read contracts, provide legal advice and send representatives to argue cases. Internationally, if you are unable to join a local union, then OCTAB[2] is also available but harder to contact. The NASU-WT[3] is very useful and helpful. Staff representations have little or no influence and are usually created by employers to show that they are willing to listen to their staff, but no more.
(b) Colleagues: It is essential in any situation to have the backing and support of one's colleagues. Employers sometimes argue the case that not all the staff are parents and therefore might be resentful of any privileges given to parents. Creating an awareness amongst colleagues of the difficulties of parenthood is important in improving conditions. When properly informed, colleagues tend to be supportive.
(c) Direct action by the parent: Voicing opinions, negotiating and asking for one's rights is often viewed by employers and others as leftist trouble making. Nevertheless, assertiveness does help and if more people participated in this direct approach it would seem less unusual and help to improve the prestige and respectability of EFL.

Applying for jobs: The difficulties involved when applying for new jobs or posts increase when one has children or is expecting a baby. Having to ask basic questions about timetables, duties and conditions at the interview makes some employers feel a little uneasy. If the job is in a different country, then the questions seem almost endless. Perhaps the best source of information is other parents working for the organisation. (The organisation might be desperate to fill a post and gloss over some of the difficulties one might face.)

The basic message to working mothers is to be prepared for any possible problems by:

1. Reading the contract carefully and getting the employer to spell out terms and conditions well beforehand.
2. Checking and double-checking all calculations, payments, dates and interpretations.
3. Being assertive in claiming, asking for clarification and negotiating.
4. Helping to raise the awareness of problems amongst colleagues, employers, unions and the EFL world.

Notes

1. MATSA: Managerial and Technical Staff Association. APEX: Association of Professional and Executive Staff. Thorne House, 152 Brent St., London NW4 2DP, UK.
2. OCTAB: Overseas Contract Teachers' and Advisers' Branch of IPMS (Institution of Professionals, Managers and Specialists). 9 Circular Rd., Manchester, UK.
3. NASU-WT: National Association of Schoolmasters' Union – Women Teachers. The Hillscourt Education Centre, Rose Hill, Rednal, Birmingham B45 8RS, UK.

Case Study: Why 'Women in TEFL'?

MADELINE DU VIVIER, INGRID FREEBAIRN AND JUDY
GARTON-SPRENGER

What is 'Women in TEFL'?

'Women in TEFL' is a British professional organisation run by women for women. It addresses itself exclusively to the interests and needs of women who work in ELT: teachers, teacher trainers, publishers, writers, administrators, and to a lesser extent students. Its main purpose is to provide a network and a forum for the exchange of ideas and expertise, and to campaign for women's rights within the profession. The founding conference of 'Women in TEFL' was held in 1986 and, since then, conferences have been held twice a year in various centres around Britain.

How is it organised?

At the Thirteenth National Conference in May 1993, 'Women in TEFL' decided to become a formal association with rules of membership and subscription fees on a sliding scale. Funds also come from participants' conference fees and donations from individuals and professional associations. The organisation of the bi-annual conferences and the day-to-day running of 'Women in TEFL' is carried out on a voluntary basis by a committee with rotating duties.

Why is an organisation like 'Women in TEFL' necessary?

From our own research it seems that women in ELT still do not make it more than two-thirds of the way up the career ladders. While the majority of teachers in Britain are female, women account for only 26 per cent of private language school principals[1] (though this compares relatively favourably with 16 per cent of university professors[2]). This bottom-heavy imbalance is mirrored in the UK publishing industry where women account for 60 per cent of all employees but only 22 per cent of company board directors.[3] There is little doubt that a glass ceiling exists.

An additional problem is that women often underplay their professional talents and skills. It is suspected that women inadvertently operate so as to underachieve in areas where they are competing with men, however competent they may be. They are often reticent about identifying professional goals because they are prone to underestimate themselves and the value of their needs. A survey report by Women in Publishing (1989) cites the case of a woman who spent ten years as an editor, before being promoted to senior editor: 'Feeling when I was there that I was very lucky to be an editor, I had to be pushed and cajoled into a senior editor's job.'

Women also face the problem of not being taken as seriously as their male counterparts in their field of expertise. Again, according to Women in Publishing, some women experienced difficulties at meetings. For example: 'I would notice that there would be someone who could only hear what I was saying after it had been repeated by one of my male colleagues.' And although attitudes towards women in the profession have changed, many women still feel they are only accepted 'as long as they conform to the "male" career norm'.

What are the aims and objectives of 'Women in TEFL'?

The specific aims for 'Women in TEFL' were formally established at the Fourth National Conference in 1987. These were:

1. To raise consciousness and provide professional expertise in order to encourage women to fulfil their potential;
2. to improve working conditions and maximise opportunities for women in ELT;
3. to provide personal and professional support within the workplace;
4. to guard against sexism in materials and to help women cope with sexism at work;
5. to increase contact among women in different institutions concerned with ELT.

Why are men excluded?

Like many other women's networks, 'Women in TEFL' is regarded with suspicion by members of both sexes. Questions range from 'Aren't women already equal to men?' and 'Doesn't it actually disadvantage women if we're hived off in this way?' to 'Doesn't the exclusion of men further bolster gender divisions and sexism?' Our experience suggests that women are more confident in the public arena with no men present and there is much evidence to show that men talk more than women in many contexts (see Shân Wareing, Quadrant I). For these reasons, 'Women in TEFL' believes that it is essential for its own conferences to be women-only events. If women are to remain the primary focus, a single-sex group is the only way to provide the right support and encouragement. Men are, however, very welcome to attend talks and workshops given at other conferences.

What does 'Women in TEFL' do and what has it achieved?

The range of activities divides into three broad categories.

Organising conferences

These provide the opportunity for women from all sectors of ELT to meet and exchange ideas and expertise. The wide range of workshops and talks reflects this broad spectrum of attendance and interests. The main areas so far covered are:

(a) Management skills, e.g. 'Team building', 'Time management'.
(b) Professional skills, e.g. 'Running and chairing meetings', 'Speaking with confidence', 'Dealing with job interviews'.
(c) Career opportunities, e.g. 'Breaking into print and publishing', 'The freelance option'.
(d) Classroom research, e.g. 'The role of learner gender in the classroom'.
(e) Interpersonal skills, e.g. 'Dealing with confrontation', 'Managing stress through assertiveness'.
(f) Teacher training, e.g. 'Making observation schedules for teacher development', 'Dealing with feedback'.
(g) ELT materials, e.g. 'Sexism in ELT materials'.

These topics arise from specific requests by members and it reflects the reputation of the conferences that many speakers (both experienced and inexperienced) now approach 'Women in TEFL' with offers to give talks or run workshops. Feedback has been very positive. This trend is a fulfilment of one of the initial aims of 'Women in TEFL', which was to offer inexperienced speakers the chance to participate in an unthreatening and supportive atmosphere. After gaining this experience, they have then gone on to give sessions at major conferences such as IATEFL (International Association of Teachers of English as a Foreign Language). This is particularly important in order to avoid the situation of 'preaching to the converted' and to encourage 'the unconvinced' – both men and women – to think about the concerns raised by 'Women in TEFL'.

Campaigning

Campaigns have so far focussed on two areas. The first is the representation of women on committees as well as at conferences. In 1990 'Women in TEFL' approached the English Language Committee of the ESU (English Speaking Union) to inquire why there was only one woman on the committee of over twenty. This prestigious committee, chaired by the Duke of Edinburgh, is responsible for awards for the best ELT materials published during the year. Considering the number of women in ELT, the committee was in no way representative of the profession as a whole. By 1992 the number of female committee members had risen to the impressive number of three!

The second area is the inclusion of information about cultural and gender appropriacy on both pre-service and in-service ELT training courses, particularly the Royal Society of Arts/Cambridge Certificate and Diploma in Teaching English as a Foreign Language to Adults (CTEFLA and DTEFLA) courses. Inappropriate lesson content may cause greater problems than lack of competence in teaching techniques. For example, the choice of contexts for presentation and practice of language may rely upon sexist stereotypes: a woman goes to her ex-boyfriend's wedding and the teacher elicits: 'She's going to have her legs waxed/nails manicured/ ears pierced . . . '; or a man chooses his fiancée from his repertoire of girlfriends on the basis of height, weight, age and sex appeal, and the teacher elicits sentences such as: 'She's too fat/old/unattractive for him.'

Teachers may also have insufficient training in how to deal with problematic interaction patterns in the classroom. For example, male students may dominate the lesson or try to monopolise the teacher's attention, or may ask inappropriate questions of female students such as: 'Do women have sex before marriage in your country?' A series of workshops on these issues has resulted in the adjustment of the CTEFLA and DTEFLA syllabuses to include the areas of cultural and gender appropriacy.

Consciousness-raising

Over the years, 'Women in TEFL' has come to be seen as an organisation which raises important issues within the ELT profession and is prepared to take decisive action. A particular area for concern is that of stereotypical attitudes towards women – and men – in classroom materials. As teachers, writers and publishers, it is important to ensure that ELT materials should not perpetuate patriarchal myths such as 'male-as-norm'. Out of the second conference was formed the 'Women in EFL Materials' group, which has been responsible for the publication of 'On Balance', guidelines for the representation of women and men in ELT materials, now endorsed by the British ELT Publishers Association (see Quadrant II).

It is achievements and activities like these which reflect the success of the group and help to answer the question: Why 'Women in TEFL'?

Quo vadis?

'Women in TEFL' is determined to raise the profile of the organisation through more prominent advertising, more frequent presentations at conferences, wider-ranging mailing lists, and more campaigning for women's rights and issues within TEFL. We are equally concerned to tighten our aims, ideals and procedures, and to consolidate our achievements. We hope that the newly formed association will not only ensure funds for continued activities, but will also provide a structured basis and a dynamic focus for the future development of 'Women in TEFL'.

Notes

1. ARELS-FELCO 1992 brochure, 2 Pontypool Place, Valentine Place, London SE1 8QF.
2. Universities' 'Statistical Record, 1992. *University Statistics 1990–91*, vol. 1: Students and Staff. Cheltenham: USR.
3. *Twice as Many, Half as Powerful?*, Polytechnic of North London/Women in Publishing, 1989.

'Women in TEFL' welcomes new members, and suggestions for speakers/sessions; interested people should write to:
'WOMEN IN TEFL', c/o Flat 4, 6 Clifton Crescent, Folkestone, Kent CT20 2EW.

Comment

The three contributions in this Quadrant underline the pervasiveness of gender – a pervasiveness which is glaringly obvious to some, unrecognised by others, seen but rarely acknowledged by a third group. Teachers in this group do not like to pay gender too much attention. They feel gender is not very important, or that discrimination did exist but does no longer, or that paying attention to gender would make them unpopular with colleagues, or would itself be sexist. In some circumstances focussing on gender may of course be counterproductive, as Jenny Pugsley suggests in her conclusion. In others, avowed 'gender blindness' may be little more than a smokescreen for a willingness to ignore gendered realities which could be adversely affecting the progress of a learner in the English classroom or a teacher in the school.

In many countries – USA, Canada, UK, Australia – ESL is politicised in a way that EFL is not. This is evidenced in the debates surrounding bilingualism and the label and concept of 'English as a second language' (a term now rarely used in British secondary education), and in teaching materials. Jeanette Redding, Jacquie Thomas and Sue Tomlinson observe that in ESL materials 'anti-racism and anti-sexism are pro-active positions and involve the creators of materials in challenging the "usual" representation of gender, class, race and culture' (1992: 2). This greater politicisation presumably stems in part from the nature of learners of ESL, many of whom are refugees or migrants, and from how they see themselves in relation to English and the country in which they are learning it. Gender is then a concern in ESL (see Amrit Wilson, 1978; Jean Guyot et al., 1978; Julia Naish, 1979; Barrie Wade and Pam Souter, 1992), but no more so than ethnicity, race and racism.

EFL, on the other hand, has for years consistently demonstrated more concern for issues of gender than of race or class: witness 'Women in TEFL', 'Women in EFL Materials' and an early group of feminist EFL teachers working in Italy in the early 1980s called 'ETHEL' (not an acronym!). The very existence and names of these groups indicate their members' refusal to be gender blind, and the fact that membership of 'Women in TEFL' and 'Women in EFL Materials' are all-female drives the point home further. Being 'women only' does not go unchallenged, by either women or men in the profession, and not all women working in EFL see a need for such organisations. However, as Madeline du Vivier, Ingrid Freebairn and Judy Garton-Sprenger observe, and as many contributions to this book illustrate, though there may not be a perceived need for such an organisation in the future, there is now.

In much of this book, gender may appear to have been conceptualised as operating independently of other social factors. Clearly, it does not. A woman or girl, a man or boy, in the English language teaching world also has a colour, an ethnic and racial background, a class background, an age, and may have some form of physical disability; these factors must be in constant interplay. In one rather crude sense, as suggested earlier, gender can be a metaphor for these different social divisions – although since gender by definition is socially constructed rather than 'given', it is arguably a better metaphor for ethnicity or class than colour, race, age or disability. However, by virtue of the fact that gender is not simply a factor of any of these other social divisions, it has to be examined as if it operated independently, in order to help us understand the meanings of gender. This does not mean that gender is more important, more formative, than ethnicity or class.

One group of women English language teachers with a special combination of circumstances, and for whom there is now documentation, is lesbian (or gay women) teachers, who have much in common with gay male teachers. For these teachers the 'beyond/inside the classroom' relationship is particularly problematic. If they have not come out, how do they best survive friendly questions about, say, their personal or domestic life and leisure activities? What of staffroom conversations with other women teachers about, for example, attractive men, or weekend activities – what do they say if they have been attending a workshop on 'Adopting as a Gay Woman'? What happens if they do decide to come out to their students? If they have already come out, does that mean they then talk openly with their students, who may be from cultures where homosexuality is severely frowned on or even deemed not to exist? For many years lesbian and gay issues have not been discussed by the mainstream English language teaching profession; the situation seems to be changing with the huge colloquium, 'We are your colleagues: lesbians and gays in ESL' (Lisa Carscadden, Cynthia Nelson and Jim Ward, 1992) at the 1992 TESOL Convention in Vancouver, and a session on 'Confronting heterosexism in the classroom' in the same year at the IATEFL Conference in Lille (Jackie Neff, 1992).

As suggested in the Introduction to this Quadrant, the male–female teacher imbalance in ELT may be more than a result of working conditions, attitudes within the profession, pressures on women to take primary responsibility for domestic chores and childcare, and women's desire to spend time with their children. These factors are true of many subject areas and indeed many professions. The imbalance may also be a creation of the profession itself, and as such self-perpetuating. Alastair Pennycook sees the preoccupation with 'method' in second language education ('method' in the sense of a way of teaching that is likely to bring about desired results) as a 'prescriptivist concept' that 'articulates a . . . patriarchal understanding of teaching' (1989: 589). He argues that classroom teachers, i.e. women, gradually become deskilled by 'teacher-proof' materials and prespecified teaching procedures, and that the method concept has 'played a major role in maintaining the gendered division of the workforce, a hierarchically organised division between male conceptualisers and female practitioners' (1989: 610).

Certainly more male conceptualisers than female conceptualisers come to mind when reflecting on the world of Applied Linguistics – conceptualisers who benefit financially through publications as well as in terms of influence and reputation. The method concept, however, is unlikely to go away, teaching more effectively being of interest to most language teachers. And method can empower women teachers: there is a value in feeling more certain of what you are doing, with some idea of why. It would, however, be refreshing to see the practitioner/conceptualiser gender division become less apparent.

As Katie Plumb's contribution illustrates, what is perhaps a more straightforward site of struggle is employment structures. Employing institutions need to recognise and meet the requirements of the largely female workforce. To penalise a teacher before her baby's birth and afterwards is unfair on more than an individual level: having babies is not just something many women wish to do; most societies want women to have babies. Penalising mothers is also unproductive in terms of loss of expertise for the profession. This is not letting men off the child-rearing hook, but pregnancy and breastfeeding are processes men cannot, unfortunately, take responsibility for.[2]

The position could be considerably alleviated by improved working conditions, in all types of jobs, for both women and men, so that childcare could be more equitably shared. If women then still preferred to devote a large part of their time and energy in their child-bearing years to their children, their return to the profession in a full-time capacity would be within a more progressive social system which would hopefully recognise the value of their years 'off'.

There is also an argument for affirmative action in employment practices, to help those women who would like to work full-time, and those whose experience and abilities have equipped them well for higher positions. Affirmative action does not have to mean favouring a female candidate over a better-qualified or equally well-qualified male.[1] It can mean creating conditions under which women are more likely to want to move on to full-time or higher positions. This includes advertising positions in publications aimed at women; flexible working hours; professional development sessions in the area of, say, public speaking for those women who want them; and a well-run crèche (though some partners who are parents may be able to share childcare between them, there are also many – female – single parents in the profession). It would also require active encouragement of line managers not to be gender blind (and similar encouragement of those with no line to manage). Needless to say, any affirmative action requires time, careful organisation and commitment on the part of all employees concerned; a 'top-down' approach is unlikely to succeed.

In all staff development sessions, it is important to make use of small group forums as well as large meetings, so that all employees get a chance to express their ideas. Many women do speak less in public contexts (see, for example, Janet Holmes, 1992); these contexts can often be made less public. It is very easy for a professional with thirty years' experience to see a group of twelve people as informal enough for everyone to talk together, but this perception may not be shared by, for example, the younger women round the table.

The effects of gender roles, relations and identities are everywhere. Ironically, because of this, in much writing and thinking on English language teaching, gender appears nowhere. Raised awareness may mean people 'seeing' gender when in fact something else is operating, or where gender is a very minor factor. Given our very gendered profession, however, raised awareness is more likely to mean recognising gender – rather than something that is 'common sense', 'natural' or 'normal' – for the first time. I hope that *Exploring Gender: Questions and Implications for English Language Education* will contribute to this.

Note

1. There are, however, arguments for (as well as against) this. Favouring a female candidate can be seen as a redressing of the balance in a 'race' in which women tend to encounter more obstacles than men (to use a sporting metaphor redolent of those seen as unhelpful and alienating by Pugsley). A further argument is that women teachers, and female students, need more women in high positions as role models.
2. National provision for maternity leave is also crucial: Britain at present lags behind many other European countries in this area.

Bibliography

I The English Language

AAUP Taskforce on Gender-free Language. 1988 (June, September). *Bias-free Communication: a Select Bibliography*. University of California Press.

Abbott, Gerry. 1984. 'Unisex "they".' *ELT Journal* 38/1: 45–8.

Adamsky, Cathryn. 1981, 'Changes in pronominal usage in a classroom situation.' *Psychology of Women Quarterly* 5: 773–9.

Aries, Elizabeth. 1982. 'Verbal and non-verbal behaviour in single-sex and mixed-sex groups: are traditional sex roles changing?' *Psychological Reports* 51: 127–34.

Aries, Elizabeth and Fern Johnson. 1983. 'Close friendship in adulthood: conversational contact between same-sex friends.' *Sex Roles* 9/12: 1183–96.

Barnes, Julian. 1991. *Talking It Over*. London: Jonathan Cape.

Baron, Dennis. 1981. 'The epicene pronoun: the word that failed.' *American Speech* 56: 83–97.

Baron, Dennis. 1986. *Grammar and Gender*. New Haven: Yale University Press.

Bate, Barbara. 1978. 'Non-sexist language use in transition.' *Journal of Communication* 28: 139–49.

Baxter, Leslie. 1984. 'An investigation of compliance-gaining as politeness.' *Human Communication Research* 10/3: 427–56.

Beattie, Geoffrey W. 1981. 'Interruption in conversational interaction, and its relation to the sex and status of the interactants.' *Linguistics* 19: 15–35.

Black, Maria and Rosalind Coward. 1990. 'Linguistic, social and sexual relations: a review of Dale Spender's *Man Made Language*.' In Deborah Cameron (ed.) *The Feminist Critique of Language: a Reader*. London: Routledge.

Blaubergs, Maija S. 1978. 'Changing the sexist language: the theory behind the practice.' *Psychology of Women Quarterly* 2: 244–61.

Blaubergs, Maija S. 1980. 'An analysis of classic arguments against changing sexist language.' In Cheris Kramarae (ed.) *The Voices and Words of Women and Men*. Oxford: Pergamon Press. (Also in *Women's Studies International Quarterly* 3/2–3 (1980).)

Bodine, Ann. 1990. 'Androcentrism in prescriptive grammar.' In Deborah Cameron (ed.) *The Feminist Critique of Language: a Reader*. London: Routledge.

Bolinger, Dwight. 1977. *Meaning and Form*. London: Longman.

Bradley, Patricia. 1981. 'The folk-linguistics of women's speech: an empirical examination.' *Communication Monographs* 48: 73–90.

Breakwell, Glynis. 1990. 'Social beliefs about gender differences.' In C. Fraser and G. Gaskell (eds.) *The Social Psychological Study of Widespread Beliefs*. Oxford: Clarendon Press.

Brend, Ruth. 1983. 'Male–female intonation patterns in American English.' In Barrie Thorne, Cheris Kramarae and Nancy Henley (eds.) *Language, Gender and Society*. Rowley, Mass.: Newbury House.

Brinberg, David and Joseph McGrath. 1985. *Validity and the Research Process*. Beverly Hills: Sage.

Brown, Penelope. 1980. 'How and why women are more polite: some evidence from a Mayan community.' In Sally McConnell-Ginet, Ruth Borker and Nelly Furman (eds.) *Women and Language in Literature and Society*. New York: Praeger.

Cameron, Deborah. 1985. 'What has gender got to do with sex?' *Language and Communication* 5/1: 19–27.

Cameron, Deborah (ed.) 1990. *The Feminist Critique of Language*. London: Routledge.

Cameron, Deborah. 1992a. *Feminism and Linguistic Theory* (2nd edition). London: Macmillan. (1st edition 1985.)

Cameron, Deborah. 1992b. 'Review: Deborah Tannen: *You Just Don't Understand: Women and Men in Conversation.*' *Feminism and Psychology* 2/3: 465–89.

Cameron, Deborah, 1993. 'Rethinking language and gender studies.' Plenary paper, 10th AILA Congress, Amsterdam.

Canale, Michael. 1983. 'From communicative competence to communicative language pedagogy.' In J.C. Richards and R.W. Schmidt (eds.) *Language and Communication*. London: Longman.

Canale, Michael and Merrill Swain. 1980. 'Theoretical bases of communicative approaches to language teaching and testing.' *Applied Linguistics* 1/1: 1–47.

Cancian, Francesca and Steven Gordon. 1988. 'Changing emotion norms in marriage: love and anger in US women's magazines since 1900.' *Gender and Society* 2/3: 308–42.

Cannon, Garland and Susan Roberson. 1985. 'Sexism in present-day English: is it diminishing?' *Word* 36/1: 23–35.

Chaudron, Craig, Graham Crookes and Michael Long. 1988. *Reliability and Validity in Second Language Classroom Research*. (Technical Report No. 8.) Honolulu: University of Hawaii, Centre for Second Language Classroom Research, Social Science Research Institute.

Chesebro, James W. (ed.) 1981. *Gayspeak: Gay Male and Lesbian Communication*. New York: Pilgrim Press.

Cheshire, Jenny. 1982. *Variation in an English Dialect*. Cambridge: Cambridge University Press.

Cheshire, Jenny. 1985. 'A question of masculine bias.' *English Today* 1: 22–6.

Cheshire, Jenny and Nancy Jenkins. 1991. 'Gender issues in the GCSE oral English examination: Part II,' *Language and Education* 5/1: 19–40.

Coates, Jennifer. 1987. 'Epistemic modality and spoken discourse.' In *Transactions of the Philological Society*: 110–31.

Coates, Jennifer. 1989a. 'Gossip revisited: language in all-female groups.' In Jennifer Coates and Deborah Cameron (eds.) *Women in their Speech Communities*. London: Longman.

Coates, Jennifer. 1989b. 'Women's speech, women's strength?' *York Papers in Linguistics* 13: 65–76.

Coates, Jennifer. 1989c. 'Some problems in the sociolinguistic explanation of sex differences.' In Jennifer Coates and Deborah Cameron (eds.) *Women in their Speech Communities*. London: Longman.

Coates, Jennifer. 1991. 'Women's co-operative talk: a new kind of co-operative duet?' In Claus Uhlig and Rudiger Zimmerman (eds.) *Anlistentag 1990 Marburg Proceedings*. Max Niemeyer Verlag, Tubingen: 296–311.

Coates, Jennifer. 1993 (revised edition). *Women, Men and Language*. London: Longman. (1st edition 1986.)

Coates, Jennifer and Deborah Cameron (eds.) 1989. *Women in their Speech Communities*. London: Longman.

Cooper, Robert. 1984. 'The avoidance of androcentric generics.' *International Journal of Social Language* 50: 5–20.

Corbett, Greville. 1991. *Gender*. Cambridge: Cambridge University Press.

Daly, Mary. 1973. *Beyond God the Father: Toward a Philosophy of Women's Liberation*. Boston: Beacon Press.

Daly, Mary. 1978. *Gyn/Ecology: the Metaethics of Radical Feminism*. London: The Women's Press.

Daly, Mary with Jane Caputi. 1988. *Webster's First Intergalactic Wickedary of the English Language*. London: The Women's Press.

Dubois, Betty Lou and Isobel Crouch. 1976. 'The question of tag questions in women's speech: they don't really use more of them, do they?' *Language in Society* 4: 289–94.

Dubois, Betty Lou and Isobel Crouch. 1979. '*Man* and its compounds in recent prefeminist American English.' *Papers in Linguistics* 12: 261–9.

Eckert, Penelope and Sally McConnell-Ginet. 1992. 'Communities of practice: where language, gender and power all live.' Paper, Berkeley Women and Language Conference, University of California, Berkeley.

Edelsky, Carole. 1977. 'Acquisition of an aspect of communicative competence: learning what it means to talk like a lady.' In Susan Ervin-Tripp and Claudia Mitchell-Kernan (eds.) *Child Discourse*. New York: Academic Press.

Edelsky, Carole. 1981. 'Who's got the floor?' *Language in Society* 10: 383–421.

Ehrlich, Susan and Ruth King. 1992a. 'Feminist meanings and sexist speech communities.' Paper, Berkeley Women and Language Conference, University of California, Berkeley.

Ehrlich, Susan and Ruth King. 1992b. 'Gender-based language reform and the social construction of meaning.' *Discourse and Society* 3/2: 151–66.

Eisenberg, Nancy, Richard Fabes, Mark Schaller and Paul Miller. 1989. 'Sympathy and personal distress: development, gender differences, and interrelations of indexes.' *New Directions for Child Development* 44: 107–26.

Fairclough, Norman (ed.) 1992. *Critical Language Awareness*. Harlow: Longman.

Fairclough, Norman and Marilyn Martin-Jones. 1993. 'Reclaiming the language: containment and struggle.' Lecture handout, Linguistics Department, Lancaster University.

Fasold, R. 1988. 'Language policy and change: sexist language in the periodical news media.' In P. Lowenberg (ed.) *Language Spread and Language Policy*. Washington, DC: Georgetown University Press.

Fishman, Pamela. 1978. 'What do couples talk about when they're alone?' In Douglas Butturf and Edmund Epstein (eds.) *Women's Language and Style*. Akron, OH: University of Akron.

Fishman, Pamela. 1980. 'Conversational insecurity.' In Howard Giles and W.P. Robinson (eds.) *Language: Social Psychological Perspectives*. Oxford: Pergamon Press.

Fishman, Pamela. 1983. 'Interaction: the work women do.' In Barrie Thorne, Cheris Kramarae and Nancy Henley (eds.) *Language, Gender and Society*. Rowley, Mass.: Newbury House.

Frank, Francine and Frank Anshen. 1983. *Language and the Sexes*. Albany: State University of New York.

Frank, Francine and Paula A. Treichler. 1989. *Language, Gender and Professional Writing*. New York: Modern Language Association.

Freed, Alice and Alice Greenwood. 1992. 'Why do you ask?: an analysis of questions between friends.' Paper presented at the meeting of the American Association of Applied Linguistics, Seattle.

Gershuny, H. Lee. 1977. 'Sexism in dictionaries and texts: omissions and commissions.' In Alleen Pace Nilsen, Haig Bosmajian, H. Lee Gershuny and Julia P. Stanley (eds.) *Sexism and Language*. Urbana, Ill.: National Council for Teachers of English.

Giles, Howard, Philip Smith, Caroline Browne, Sarah Whiteman and Jennifer Williams. 1980. 'Women's speech: the voice of feminism.' In Sally McConnell-Ginet, Ruth Borker and Nelly Furman (eds.) *Women and Language in Literature and Society*. New York: Praeger.

Graddol, David and Joan Swann. 1989. *Gender Voices*. Oxford: Basil Blackwell.

Graham, Alma. 1974. 'The making of a non-sexist dictionary.' *ETC: A Review of General Semantics* XXXI/1: 57–64. Also in Barrie Thorne and Nancy Henley (eds.) 1975. *Language and Sex: Difference and Dominance*. Rowley, Mass.: Newbury House.

Greer, Germaine. 1971. *The Female Eunuch*. London: Paladin.

Gumperz, John (ed.) 1982. *Language and Social Identity*. Cambridge: Cambridge University Press.

Gumperz, John. 1982. *Discourse Strategies*. Cambridge: Cambridge University Press.

Hamilton, Heidi. 1992. 'Bringing ageing into the language/gender equation.' Paper, Berkeley Women and Language Conference, University of California, Berkeley.

Hellinger, Marlis. 1989. 'Revising the patriarchal paradigm. Language change and feminist language politics.' In Ruth Wodak (ed.) *Language, Power and Ideology*. Amsterdam: John Benjamins.

Hellinger, Marlis. 1991. 'Feminist linguistics and linguistic relativity.' *Working Papers on Language, Gender and Sexism* 1/1: 25–37.

Hellinger, Marlis. 1993. 'A comparison of English and German guidelines for the equal treatment of women and men.' Paper, 10th AILA Congress, Amsterdam.

Henley, Nancy. 1987. 'This new species that seeks a new language: on sexism in language and language change.' In Joyce Penfield (ed.) *Women and Language in Transition*. Albany, NY: Suny Press.

Herbert, Robert K. 1986. 'Say "thank you" – or something'. *American Speech* 61: 76–88.

Herbert, Robert K. 1989. 'The ethnography of English compliment and compliment responses: a contrastive sketch.' In Wieslaw Olesky (ed.) *Contrastive Pragmatics*. Amsterdam: John Benjamins.

Herbert, Robert K. 1990. 'Sex-based differences in compliment behaviour.' *Language in Society* 19: 201–24.

Herbert, Robert K. and H.S. Straight. 1989. 'Compliment rejection vs compliment avoidance.' *Language and Communication* 9: 35–47.

Holmes, Janet. 1986. 'Compliments and compliment responses in New Zealand English.' *Anthropological Linguistics* 28/4: 485–508.

Holmes, Janet. 1988. 'Paying compliments: a sex-preferential positive politeness strategy.' *Journal of Pragmatics* 12/3: 445–65.

Holmes, Janet. 1990. 'Politeness strategies in New Zealand women's speech.' In Allan Bell and Janet Holmes (eds.) *New Zealand Ways of Speaking English*. Clevedon, Avon: Multilingual Matters.

Holmes, Janet. 1992a. 'Language and gender: a state-of-the-art survey article.' *Language Teaching* 24/4: 207–20.

Holmes, Janet. 1992b. 'Women's talk in public contexts.' *Discourse and Society* 3/2: 131–50.

Hymes, Dell. 1971. 'On communicative competence.' In J.B. Pride and Janet Holmes (eds.) *Sociolinguistics*. Harmondsworth: Penguin.

James, Deborah. 1992. 'Interruptions, gender and power: a critical review of the literature.' Paper, Berkeley Women and Language Conference, University of California, Berkeley.

Jenkins, Nancy and Jenny Cheshire. 1990. 'Gender issues in the GCSE oral English examination. Part I.' *Language and Education* 4/4: 261–91.

Jesperson, Otto. 1922. *Language: Its Nature, Development and Origin*. London: Allen and Unwin.

Johnson, Donna M. and Duane H. Roen. 1992. 'Complimenting and involvement in peer reviews: gender variation.' *Language in Society* 21/1: 27–56.

Kerekes, Julie. 1992a. 'Perception of gender-related assertiveness and supportiveness in English.' Paper presented at the meeting of the American Association of Applied Linguistics, Seattle.

Kerekes, Julie. 1992b. 'Gender-related miscommunication: the ESL teacher's role.' Paper presented at the TESOL Conference, Vancouver.

Kerekes, Julie. 1992c. 'Development in nonnative speakers' use and perceptions of assertiveness in mixed-sex conversations.' *Occasional Paper 21*. Department of ESL, University of Hawaii.

Knight, H. Merle. 1992. 'Gender interference in transsexuals' speech.' Paper, Berkeley Women and Language Conference, University of California, Berkeley.

Kramarae, Cheris (ed.) 1980. *The Voices and Words of Women and Men*. Oxford: Pergamon.

Kramarae, Cheris. 1981. *Women and Men Speaking*. Rowley, Mass.: Newbury House.

Kramarae, Cheris and Paula Treichler. 1985. *A Feminist Dictionary*. London: Pandora.

Kristeva, Julia. 1986. *The Kristeva Reader* (ed. Toril Moi). Oxford: Basil Blackwell.

Labov, William. 1990. 'The intersection of sex and social class in the course of linguistic change.' *Language Variation and Change* 2: 205–54.

Lakoff, Robin. 1973. 'Language and woman's place.' *Language in Society* 2: 45–80.

Lakoff, Robin. 1975. *Language and Woman's Place*. New York: Harper and Row.

Leech, Geoffrey. 1983. *Principles of Pragmatics*. London: Longman.

Leet-Pellegrini, Helena M. 1980. 'Conversational dominance as a function of gender and expertise.' In Howard Giles *et al.* (eds.) *Language: Social Psychological Perspectives*. Oxford: Pergamon.

Lewandowska-Tomaszczyk, Barbara. 1989. 'Praising and complimenting.' In Wieslaw Olesky (ed.) *Contrastive Pragmatics*. Amsterdam: John Benjamins.

Lott, Bernice. 1987. 'Sexist discrimination as distancing behaviour: 1. A laboratory demonstration.' *Psychology of Women Quarterly* 11/1: 47–58.

Maccoby, Eleanor and Carol Jacklin. 1974. *The Psychology of Sex Differences*. Stanford, CA: Stanford University Press.

MacKay, Donald G. 1983. 'Prescriptive grammar and the pronoun problem.' In Barrie Thorne, Cheris Kramarae and Nancy Henley (eds.) *Language, Gender and Society*. Rowley, Mass.: Newbury House.

Maggio, Rosalie. 1988. *The Nonsexist Word Finder – a Dictionary of Gender-free Usage*. Boston: Beacon Press.

Maltz, Daniel and Ruth Borker. 1982. 'A cultural approach to male–female miscommunication.' In John Gumperz (ed.) *Language and Social Identity*. Cambridge: Cambridge University Press.

Manes, Joan. 1983. 'Compliments: a mirror of cultural values.' In Nessa Wolfson and Elliot Judd (eds.) *Sociolinguistics and Second Language Acquisition*. Rowley, Mass.: Newbury House.

Martin, Samuel. 1964. 'Speech levels in Japanese and Korean.' In Dell Hymes (ed.) *Language in Culture and Society*. New York: Harper and Row.

Martyna, Wendy. 1978. 'What does "he" mean?' *Journal of Communication* 28: 131–8.

Martyna, Wendy. 1980. 'The psychology of the generic masculine.' In Sally McConnell-Ginet, Ruth Borker and Nelly Furman (eds.) *Women and Language in Literature and Society*. New York: Praeger.

Martyna, Wendy. 1983. 'Beyond the he/man approach: the case for non-sexist language.' In Barrie Thorne, Cheris Kramarae and Nancy Henley (eds.) *Language, Gender and Society*. Rowley, Mass.: Newbury House.

McConnell-Ginet, Sally, Ruth Borker and Nelly Furman (eds.) 1980. *Women and Language in Literature and Society*. New York: Praeger.

Mey, Jacob. 1984. 'Sex and language revisited: can women's language change the world?' *Journal of*

Pragmatics 8: 261–83. (Review of Senta Troemel-Ploetz. 1982. *Frauensprache – Sprache der Veranderung* (*Women's Language – Language of Change*). Frankfurt am Main: Fischer.)

Millard, Elaine. 1989. 'French feminisms.' In Sara Mills, Lynne Pearce, Sue Spaull and Elaine Millard (eds.) *Feminist Readings, Feminists Reading*. Hemel Hempstead: Harvester Wheatsheaf.

Miller, Casey and Kate Swift. 1989 (2nd edition). *The Handbook of Non-sexist Writing for Writers, Editors and Speakers*. London: The Women's Press. (1st edition 1981.)

Mills, Jane. 1990. *Womanwords*. London: Virago.

Milroy, Lesley. 1980. *Language and Social Networks*. Oxford: Basil Blackwell.

Moi, Toril (ed.) 1986. *The Kristeva Reader*. Oxford: Basil Blackwell.

Niedwelski, Nancy Anne. 1992. 'Masculine pronouns as generic: A view from the child'. Paper, Berkeley Women and Language Conference, University of California, Berkeley.

Nilan, Pam. 1991. 'Having fun and thinking deeply.' *Working Papers on Language, Gender and Sexism* 1/1: 88–104.

Notarius, Clifford and Lisa Herrick. 1988. 'Listener response strategies to a distressed other.' *Journal of Social and Personal Relationships* 5/1: 97–108.

NUJ Book Branch. 1982. *Non-sexist Code of Practice for Book Publishing*.

O'Barr, William and Bowman Atkins. 1980. 'Women's language or powerless language?' In Sally McConnell-Ginet, Ruth Borker and Nelly Furman (eds.) *Women and Language in Literature and Society*. New York: Praeger.

Olshtain, Elite and Liora Weinbach. 1987. 'Complaints: a study of speech act behaviour among native and nonnative speakers of Hebrew.' In J. Verschueren and M.B. Papi (eds.) *The Pragmatic Perspective*. Amsterdam: John Benjamins.

Pauwels, Anne. 1989a. 'Some thoughts on gender, inequality and language reform.' *VOX* 3: 78–84.

Pauwels, Anne. 1989b. 'Feminist language change in Australia: changes in generic pronoun use.' Paper given at the Annual Conference of the German Linguistic Society, Osnabruck.

Pauwels, Anne. 1991a. *Non-Discriminatory Language*. Canberra: Australian Government Publishing Service.

Pauwels, Anne. 1991b. 'Sexism and language planning in English-speaking countries: some issues and problems.' *Working Papers on Language, Gender and Sexism* 1/2: 17–30.

Pauwels, Anne. 1993. 'The role of women and men in language shift: Evidence from Australia,' Paper, 10th AILA Congress, Amsterdam.

Pauwels, Anne and Joanne Winter. 1991. 'Language and gender research in the 1990s: a new forum for ideas.' *Working Papers on Language, Gender and Sexism* 1/1: 5–10.

Pearson, Bethyl A. and K. Samuel Lee. 1992. 'Discourse structure of direction-giving: effects of native/ nonnative speaker status and gender.' *TESOL Quarterly* 26/1: 113–27.

Penelope, Julia. 1978. 'Two essays on language and change: I. Power and the opposition to feminist proposals for language change.' *College English* 44/8: 840–8.

Penfield, Joyce (ed.) 1987. *Women and Language in Transition*. Albany, NY: Suny Press.

Philips, Susan U., Susan Steele and Christine Tanz (eds.) 1987. *Language, Gender and Sex in Comparative Perspective*. Cambridge: Cambridge University Press.

Poynton, Cate. 1989. *Language and Gender: Making the Difference*. Oxford: Oxford University Press.

Purnell, Sandra. 1978. 'Politically speaking, do women exist?' *Journal of Communication*, Winter: 150–5.

Pusch, Luise. 1980. 'Das Deutsche als Mannersprache – Diagnose und Therapievorschlage.' *Linguistische Berichte* 69: 59–74.

Quirk, Randolph, Sydney Greenbaum, Geoffrey Leech and Jan Svartvik. 1985. *A Comprehensive Grammar of the English Language*. London: Longman.

Ricks, Christopher and Leonard Michaels. 1990. *The State of the Language*. London: Faber and Faber.

Robertson, Sally and Sara Mills. n.d. 'Gender-free language: guidelines for the use of staff and students.' University of Strathclyde.

Romaine, Suzanne. 1978. 'Postvocalic /r/ in Scottish English: sound change in progress?' In Peter Trudgill (ed.) *Sociolinguistic Patterns in British English*. London: Edward Arnold.

Russ, Joanna. 1983. *How To Suppress Women's Writing*. London: The Women's Press.

Schneider, Joseph and Sally Hacker. 1973. 'Sex role imagery and use of the generic "man" in introductory texts.' *American Sociologist* 8: 12–18.

Schulz, Muriel. 1975. 'The semantic derogation of women.' In Barrie Thorne and Nancy Henley (eds.) *Language and Sex: Difference and Dominance*. Rowley, Mass.: Newbury House. (Also in Deborah Cameron (ed.) 1990. *The Feminist Critique of Language*. London: Routledge.)

Sheldon, Amy. 1990. 'Pickle fights: gendered talk in pre-school disputes.' *Discourse Processes* 13: 5–31.

Sheldon, Amy. 1992. 'Conflict talk: sociolinguistic challenges to self-assertion and how young girls meet them.' *Merrill-Palmer Quarterly* 38/1: 95–117.

Silveira, Jeanette. 1980. 'Generic masculine words and thinking.' *Women's Studies International Quarterly* 3: 165–78.

Sklar, Elizabeth S. 1983. 'Sexist grammar revisited.' *College English* 45/4: 348–58.

Smith, Philip. 1985. *Language, the Sexes and Society*. Oxford: Basil Blackwell.

Sommers, Elizabeth and Sandra Lawrence. 1992. 'Women's ways of talking in teacher-directed and student-directed peer response groups.' *Linguistics and Education* 4: 1–36.

Spender, Dale. 1980. *Man Made Language*. London: Routledge and Kegan Paul.

Stanley, Julia. 1978. 'Sexist grammar.' *College English* 39/7: 800–11.

Sunderland, Jane. 1990. 'Vocabulary and gender.' *English Studies* 4: 8–10. London: British Council.

Sunderland, Jane. 1991. 'The decline of *man*.' *Journal of Pragmatics* 16: 505–22.

Sunderland, Jane. 1992. 'Gender in the EFL classroom.' *ELT Journal* 46/1: 81–91.

Sunderland, Jane. 1993. 'Teacher-differentiation-of-learners-by-gender: What about the modern foreign language classroom?' Paper, 10th AILA Congress, Amsterdam.

Swacker, Marjorie. 1975. 'The sex of the speaker as a sociolinguistic variable.' In Barrie Thorne and Nancy Henley (eds.) *Language and Sex: Difference and Dominance*. Rowley, Mass.: Newbury House.

Talbot, Mary. 1990. ' "I wish you'd stop interrupting me!": interruptions and asymmetries in speaker-rights in "equal encounters".' *Lancaster University Centre for Language in Social Life Working Papers* 21. (Also in (1992) *Journal of Pragmatics* 18/5: 451–66.)

Talbot, Mary. 1992. 'The construction of gender in a teenage magazine.' In Norman Fairclough (ed.) *Critical Language Awareness*. London: Longman.

Tannen, Deborah. 1991. *You Just Don't Understand*. London: Virago. (Also 1990, New York: William Morrow.)

Thomas, Beth. 1989. 'Differences of sex and sects: linguistic variation and social networks in a Welsh mining village.' In Jennifer Coates and Deborah Cameron (eds.) *Women in their Speech Communities*. London: Longman.

Thorne, Barrie and Nancy Henley (eds.) 1975. *Language and Sex: Difference and Dominance*. Rowley, Mass.: Newbury House.

Thorne, Barrie, Cheris Kramarae and Nancy Henley (eds.) 1983. *Language, Gender and Society*. Rowley, Mass.: Newbury House.

Thwaite, A. 1993. 'Gender differences in Australian English.' Paper, 10th AILA Congress, Amsterdam.

Toth, Emily. 1970. 'How can a woman "man" the barricades?' *Women: a Journal of Liberation* 2/1: 57.

Treichler, Paula A. 1989. 'From discourse to dictionary: how sexist meanings are authorised.' In Francine Frank and Paula A. Treichler (eds.) *Language, Gender and Professional Writing*. New York: Modern Language Association.

Troemel-Ploetz, Senta. 1991. 'Review essay [of Deborah Tannen's *You Just Don't Understand*]: selling the apolitical.' *Discourse and Society* 2/4: 489–502.

Trudgill, Peter. 1975. 'Sex, covert prestige, and linguistic change in the urban British English of Norwich.' In Barrie Thorne and Nancy Henley (eds.) *Language and Sex: Difference and Dominance*. Rowley, Mass.: Newbury House.

Vetterlin-Braggin, Mary (ed.) *Sexist Language: a Modern Philosophical Analysis*. Totowa, NJ: Littlefield Adams.

Wardhaugh, Ronald. 1986. *An Introduction to Sociolinguistics*. Oxford: Basil Blackwell.

Weedon, Chris. 1987. *Feminist Practice and Poststructural Theory*. Oxford: Basil Blackwell.

West, Candace and Don Zimmerman. 1983. 'Small insults: a study of interruptions in cross-sex conversations between unacquainted persons.' In Barrie Thorne, Cheris Kramarae and Nancy Henley (eds.) *Language, Gender and Society*. Rowley, Mass.: Newbury House.

Willis, Jane. 1992. 'Grammar or idiom? Working out from the word.' Paper, IATEFL Conference, Lille.

Wilson, Lavisa Cam. 1978. 'Teachers' inclusion of males and females in generic nouns.' *Research in the Teaching of English* 12: 155–61.

Winter, Joanne. 1992. 'The semantics and pragmatics of difference.' *Working Papers on Language, Gender and Sexism* 2/1: 99–115.

Wolfson, Nessa. 1981. 'Compliments in cross-cultural perspective.' *TESOL Quarterly* 15/2: 117–24.

Wolfson, Nessa. 1983. 'An empirically based analysis of complimenting in American English.' In Nessa Wolfson and Elliot Judd (eds.) *Sociolinguistics and Second Language Acquisition*. Rowley, Mass.: Newbury House.

Wolfson, Nessa. 1984. 'Pretty is as pretty does.' *Applied Linguistics* 5/3: 236–44.
Woods, Nicola. 1989. 'Talking shop: sex and status as determinants of floor apportionment in a work setting.' In Jennifer Coates and Deborah Cameron (eds.) *Women in their Speech Communities*. London: Longman.
Woolf, Virginia. 1979. *Women and Writing*. London: The Women's Press.
Zuber, Sharon. 1990. 'Rules are meant to be broken' (unpubl.). College of William and Mary, Virginia, USA.

II Materials

Abbott, Gerry. 1984. 'Unisex "they".' *ELT Journal* 38/1: 45–48.
Abraham, John. 1989. 'Teacher ideology and sex roles in curriculum texts.' *British Journal of Sociology of Education* 10/1: 33–51.
Adamsky, Cathryn. 1981. 'Changes in pronominal usage in a classroom situation.' *Psychology of Women Quarterly* 5: 773–9.
Alexander, Louis. 1985. *Excel in English. Students' Book 1*. Harlow: Longman.
Alexander, Louis. 1986. *Excel in English. Students' Book 2*. Harlow: Longman.
Alexander, Louis. 1987. *Excel in English. Students' Book 3*. Harlow: Longman.
Alexander, Louis. 1988. *Longman English Grammar*. Harlow: Longman.
Baron, Dennis. 1986. *Grammar and Gender*. New Haven: Yale University Press.
Bate, Barbara. 1978. 'Non-sexist language use in transition.' *Journal of Communication* 28: 139–49.
Bates, Martin. 1988. *Welcome to English – Students' Book 1*. Cairo: Egyptian International Publishing Co./Longman.
Bates, Martin and Jonathon Higgens. 1986. *Welcome to English – Students' Book 1*. Cairo: Egyptian Intrernational Publishing Co./Longman.
Bates, Martin and Jonathon Higgens. 1987. *Welcome to English – Students' Book 1 and 2*. Cairo: Egyptian International Publishing Co./Longman.
Blankenship, Glen. 1984. 'How to test a textbook for sexism.' *Social Education* 48/4: 282–3.
Bodine, Ann. 1990. 'Androcentrism in prescriptive grammar.' In Deborah Cameron (ed.) *The Feminist Critique of Language*. London: Routledge.
Bradley, John and Lidio Presutti. 1990. *Tact – Users' Guide Version 1, 2*. Toronto: University of Toronto.
Brend, Ruth. 1975. 'Male–female patterns in American English.' In Barrie Thorne and Nancy Henley (eds.) *Language and Sex: Difference and Dominance*. Rowley, Mass.: Newbury House.
Bressan, Dino. 1978. '*Italiano Vivo* and Its Women.' In Reinhold Freudenstein (ed.) *The Role of Women in Foreign Language Textbooks: a Collection of Essays*. Collection d'Etudes Linguistiques, No 24. Ghent: Fédération Internationale des Professeurs de Langues Vivantes.
Britton, Gwyneth and Margaret Lumpkin. 1983. 'Basal readers: paltry progress pervades.' *Interracial Books for Children Bulletin* 14/6: 4–7.
Broverman, Inge, Susan R. Vogel, Donald M. Broverman, Frank E. Clarkson and Paul S. Rosenkrantz. 1972. 'Sex role stereotypes: a current appraisal.' *Journal of Social Issues* 28: 59–78.
Bruce, Kay. 1986. 'Sex stereotyping in English language coursebooks: is it still an issue?' *TESOL France News* 6/1: 46–8.
Cameron, Deborah. 1985. *Feminism and Linguistic Theory*. London: Macmillan. (See also 2nd edition, 1992.)
Cannon, Garland and Susan Roberson. 1985. 'Sexism in present-day English: is it diminishing?' *Word* 36/1: 23–35.
Carroll, David and Johanna Kowitz. 1989. 'Text concordancing – what it is and what it can do for you.' Paper presented at 23rd IATEFL Annual Conference, Warwick. (ERIC Accession Number: ED309649.)
Carroll, David and Johanna Kowitz. 1990. 'An objective tool for textbook evaluation and selection.' Paper presented at 1990 IATEFL Conference, Dublin.
Carroll, Fairlee Winfield. 1978. 'The limits of my language are the limits of my world.' In Reinhold Freudenstein (ed.) *The Role of Women in Foreign Language Textbooks: a Collection of Essays*. Collection d'Etudes Linguistiques, No 24. Ghent: Fédération Internationale des Professeurs de Langues Vivantes.
Cerezal, Fernando. 1991. 'Gender discrimination and ELT textbooks.' Paper presented at 25th IATEFL Conference, Exeter.

Chalker, Sylvia. 1984. 'Why can't someone write a nice, simple grammar?' *ELT Journal* 32/2: 79–85.

Cincotta, Madeleine S. 1978. 'Textbooks and their influence on sex role stereotype formation.' *Babel: Journal of the Australian Federation of MLTS Association* 14/3: 24–9.

Coles, Michael and Basil Lord. 1976. *Turning Point*. Oxford: Oxford University Press.

Collins COBUILD English Dictionary. 1987. London: Collins.

Cooper, Robert. 1984. 'The avoidance of androcentric generics.' *International Journal of Social Language* 50: 5–20.

Dendrinos, Bessie. 1992. *The EFL Textbook and Ideology*. Athens: N.C. Grivas Publications.

Dendrinos, Bessie, Sophia Marmaridou, Triantafillos Triantafillou, Cleanthis Vicas and Apostolos Ouzounis. 1988. *Task Way English* 1, 2, 3. Athens: Publishing Organisation of Educational Books.

Dirven, René. 1990. 'Pedagogical grammar.' (State of the art article). *Language Teaching* 23/1: 1–18.

Equal Opportunities Commission (EOC). 1991. 'Some facts about women 1991.' Manchester: EOC.

ETHEL. 1980. 'Ethel in Genderland.' *ETHEL* 5. [A newsletter for feminist teachers of EFL: no longer in publication.]

Florent, Jill and Catherine Walter. 1989. 'A better role for women in TEFL.' *ELT Journal* 43/3: 180–4.

Freudenstein, Reinhold (ed.) 1978. *The Role of Women in Foreign Language Textbooks: a Collection of Essays*. Collection d'Etudes Linguistiques, No. 24. Ghent: Fédération Internationale⁻ des Professeurs de Langues Vivantes.

Gaff, Robin. 1982. 'Sex stereotyping in modern language teaching – an aspect of the hidden curriculum.' *British Journal of Language Teaching* 20/3: 71–8.

Garrity, Kathleen. 1987. 'Sexism in two editions of a primary reading series.' MA thesis. Kean College of New Jersey. (ERIC Accession Number ED284191).

Gershuny, H. Lee. 1974. 'Sexist semantics in the dictionary.' *ETC: A Review of General Semantics* XXXI/2: 159–69.

Gershuny, H. Lee. 1977. 'Sexism in dictionaries and texts: omissions and commissions.' In Alleen Pace Nilsen, Haig Bosmajian, H. Lee Gershuny and Julia P. Stanley (eds.) *Sexism and Language*. Urbana, Ill.; National Council for Teachers of English.

Goldberg, P. 1976. 'Are women prejudiced against men?' In J. Stacey *et al.* (eds.) *And Jill Came Tumbling After: Sexism in American Education*. New York: Dell Publishing.

Gower, Roger. 1981. 'Grammar books for teachers of English as a foreign language.' *ELT Journal* 36/1: 52–6.

Graci, Joseph. 1989. 'Are foreign language textbooks sexist? An exploration of modes of evaluation.' *Foreign Language Annals* 22/5: 477–86.

Graham, Alma. 1974. 'The making of a non-sexist dictionary.' *ETC: A Review of General Semantics* XXXI/1: 57–64. Also in Barrie Thorne and Nancy Henley (eds.) 1975. *Language and Sex: Difference and Dominance*. Rowley, Mass.: Newbury House.

Greenbaum, Sydney. 1987. 'Reference grammars and pedagogical grammars.' *World Englishes* 6/3: 191–7.

Greer, Germaine. 1971. *The Female Eunuch*. London: Paladin.

Gupta, Anthea Fraser and Ameline Lee Su Yin. 1990. 'Gender representation in English language textbooks used in the Singapore primary classroom: an interactional account.' *Language and Education* 4/1: 29–50.

Hadfield, Charles and Jill Hadfield. 1990. *Writing Games*. Walton-on-Thames: Nelson.

Hartman, Pat and Elliot Judd. 1978. 'Sexism and TESOL materials.' *TESOL Quarterly* 12/4: 383–92.

Hellinger, Marlis. 1980. ' "For men must work, and women must weep": sexism in English language textbooks used in German schools.' *Women's Studies International Quarterly* 3: 267– 75.

Hill, P. 1980. 'Women in the world of ELT textbooks.' *EFL Gazette*, June/July.

Hingley, Phil. 1983. 'Modern languages.' In J. Whyld (ed.) *Sexism in the Secondary Curriculum*. London: Harper and Row.

Ittzes, Kata. 1978. 'Hungarian women in reality.' In Reinhold Freudenstein (ed.) *The Role of Women in Foreign Language Textbooks: a Collection of Essays*. Collection d'Etudes Linguistiques, No. 24. Ghent: Fédération Internationale des Professeurs de Langues Vivantes.

Jaworski, Adam. 1983. 'Sexism in textbooks.' *British Journal of Language and Teaching* 21/2: 109–13.

Jones, Leo. 1977. *Functions of English*. Cambridge: Cambridge University Press.

Judd, Elliot. 1983. 'The problem of applying sociolinguistic findings to TESOL: the case of male/female language.' In Nessa Wolfson and Elliot Judd (eds.) *Sociolinguistics and Second Language Acquisition*. Rowley, Mass.: Newbury House.

Kaye, Patricia. 1989. ' "Women are alcoholics and drug addicts", says dictionary.' *ELT Journal* 43/3: 192–5.

Keise, Celestine. 1992. 'Languages.' In Kate Myers (ed.) *Genderwatch! After the Education Reform Act.* Cambridge: Cambridge University Press.

Kingston, Albert and Terry Lovelace. 1977–78. 'Sexism and reading: a critical review of the literature.' *Reading Research Quarterly* 13: 133–61.

Kjellmer, Goran. 1986. ' "The lesser man": observations on the role of women in modern English writings.' In J. Aarts and W. Meijs (eds.) *Corpus Linguistics II – New Studies in the Analysis and Exploitation of Computer Corpora.* Amsterdam: Rodopi.

Kowitz, Johanna and David Carroll. 1990. 'ELT textbooks – the hidden gender curriculum.' Paper presented at 1990 IATEFL Conference, Dublin.

Kramarae, Cheris, Paula A. Treichler and Ann Russo. 1985. *A Feminist Dictionary.* London and Boston: Pandora.

MacKay, Donald G. 1983. 'Prescriptive grammar and the pronoun problem.' In Barrie Thorne, Cheris Kramarae and Nancy Henley (eds.) *Language, Gender and Society.* Rowley, Mass.: Newbury House.

Makri-Tsilipakou, Marianthi. 1987. 'Language, the sexes and the teacher of English.' *Journal of Applied Linguistics* 3: 66–87.

Maltz, Daniel and Ruth Borker. 1982. 'A cultural approach to male–female miscommunication.' In John Gumperz (ed.) *Language and Social Identity.* Cambridge: Cambridge University Press.

Morine-Dershima, Greta. 1985. 'Gender, classroom organisation and grade level as factors in pupil perceptions of peer interaction.' In Louise Cherry Wilkinson and Cora Marrett (eds.) *Gender Influences in Classroom Interaction.* New York: Academic Press.

Naish, Julia. 1979. ' "The chance to say what they think." Teaching English as a second language.' *Feminist Review* 3: 1–11.

Narisawa, Yoshio and Tsutomi Yokotu. 1991. 'Portrayal of women in English textbooks in Japan.' Paper presented at TESOL Annual Convention 1991, New York.

Neff, Jackie. 1992. 'Confronting heterosexism in the classroom.' Workshop given at 1992 IATEFL Conference, Lille.

Nilsen, Alleen Pace. 1977. 'Sexism in children's books and elementary classroom materials.' In Alleen Pace Nilsen, Haig Bosmajian, H. Lee Gershuny and Julia P. Stanley (eds.) *Sexism and Language.* Urbana, Ill.: National Council for Teachers of English.

Ogren, Sandra L. 1985. *The Problem of Evaluating Sex Bias in Textbooks and an Analysis and Evaluation of Sex Bias in Selected Editions of 'Rise of the American Nation'.* (ERIC Accession Number ED 268028.)

One, Varda. 1971. 'Manglish.' (Reprint available from KNOW Inc., P.O. Box 86031, Pittsburgh, Penn., USA.)

Osugi, Kyoko, Kumi Sadakane, Yuko Shimogouchi and K. Takhashi. 1990. 'Sex bias in Japan-published mono-lingual dictionaries.' *JALT Journal* 12/2: 219–35.

Oxford Advanced Learner's Dictionary of Current English. Oxford: Oxford University Press.

Pascoe, Joy. 1989. 'The invisibility of women in language and TEFL materials.' Long essay, Diploma in TEFL, Christchurch College, Kent.

Pascoe, Joy. 1993. 'Women in international EFL examinations: visibility and representation.' MA Dissertation, University of Kent, Canterbury.

Pauwels, Anne. 1989. 'Feminist language change in Australia: changes in generic pronoun use.' Paper given at the Annual Conference of the German Linguistics Society, Osnabruck.

Pauwels, Anne. 1991. *Non-discriminatory Language.* Canberra: Australian Government Publishing Service.

Porecca, Karen. 1984. 'Sexism in current ESL textbooks.' *TESOL Quarterly* 18/4: 705–24.

Pugsley, Jenny. 1988. 'Teaching English as a foreign language; the female protagonist in EFL literature.' Second Prize Winning Entry for the English-Speaking Union English Language Competition, 1988.

Pugsley, Jenny. 1989. 'Sexism in EFL materials.' *IATEFL Newsletter* 105, October: 22.

Pugsley, Jenny. 1992. 'Sexist language and stereotyping in ELT materials: language, bureaucracy and the teacher.' *Working Papers on Language, Gender and Sexism* 2/2: 5–13.

Purnell, Sandra. 1978. 'Politically speaking, do women exist?' *Journal of Communication*, Winter: 150–5.

Redding, Jeanette, Jacquie Thomas and Sue Tomlinson. 1992. 'Stereotyping in EFL textbooks.' Unpublished essay, MA in Linguistics for ELT, Lancaster University.

Rees-Parnell, Hilary. 1976. 'Women in the world of *Kernel Lessons Intermediate.*' *ARELS Journal* 2/2: 29–31.

Rinvolucri, Mario and Marge Berer. 1981. *Mazes.* London: Heinemann.

Rodriguez-Nieto, Catherine. 1980. 'Review of *American Kernel Lessons.*' *TESOL Newsletter* XIV/6: 21.

Salter-Duke, Linden. 1983. 'Woman–machine interaction.' MA thesis (unpublished), Lancaster University.

Schmitz, Betty. 1975. 'Sexism in French language textbooks.' In Robert Lafayette (ed.) *The Cultural Revolution in Foreign Language Teaching.* Skokie, Ill.: National Textbook Company.

Schulz, Muriel. 1990. 'The semantic derogation of women.' In Deborah Cameron (ed.) *The Feminist Critique of Language.* London: Routledge. (Also in Barrie Thorne and Nancy Henley (eds.) 1975. *Language and Sex: Difference and Dominance.* Rowley, Mass.: Newbury House.)

Sklar, Elizabeth S. 1983. 'Sexist grammar revisited.' *College English* 45/4: 348–58.

Spurling, Susan and Donna Ilyin. 1985. 'The impact of learner variables on test performance.' *TESOL Quarterly* 19/2: 283–301.

Stanley, Julia. 1978. 'Sexist grammar.' *College English* 39/7: 800–11.

Stern, Rhoda. 1976. 'Review article: sexism in foreign language textbooks.' *Foreign Language Annals* 9: 294–9.

Stephens, Kate. 1990. 'The world of John and Mary Smith: a study of Quirk and Greenbaum's *University Grammar of English.*' *CLE Working Papers* 1: 91–107.

Sunderland, Jane. 1986. 'The grammar book and the invisible woman.' Dissertation for MA in Linguistics for English Language Teaching, Linguistics Department, Lancaster University (unpublished).

Sunderland, Jane. 1991. 'The decline of *man.*' *Journal of Pragmatics* 16: 505–22.

Sunderland, Jane. 1992a. 'Gender in the EFL classroom.' *ELT Journal* 46/1: 81–91.

Sunderland, Jane. 1992b. 'Teaching materials and teaching/learning processes: gender in the language classroom.' *Working Papers on Language, Gender and Sexism* 2/2: 15–26.

Swan, James. 1981. 'Characterisation: an ignored aspect of the social dimension of ESOL materials.' Thesis, Graduate Division, University of Hawaii.

Swan, Michael. 1992. 'From Michael Swan' (in 'Correspondence'). *ELT Journal* 46/3: 325.

Swann, Joan. 1992. *Girls, Boys and Language.* Oxford: Basil Blackwell.

Talansky, Sandra B. 1986. 'Sex role stereotyping in TEFL teaching materials.' *Perspectives* XI/3: 32–41.

Toth, Emily. 1970. 'How can a woman "man" the barricades?' *Women: a Journal of Liberation* 2/1: 57.

Treichler, Paula A. 1989. 'From discourse to dictionary: how sexist meanings are authorised.' In Francine Frank and Paula A. Treichler (eds.) *Language, Gender and Professional Writing.* New York: Modern Language Association.

Walford, Geoffrey. 1981. 'Tracking down sexism in physics textbooks.' *Physics Education* 16/5: 261–5.

Walter, Catherine. 1986. 'Writing non-sexist EFL materials: the nuts and bolts.' *TESOL France News* 6/1: 71–2.

Willeke, Audrone and Ruth Sanders. 1978. 'Walter ist intelligent und Brigitte ist blond; dealing with sex bias in language texts.' *Unterrichtspraxis* 11: 60–5.

Woods, Edward G. and Nicole McLeod. 1992. *Using Basic English Grammar.* Hemel Hempstead: Prentice Hall.

Writers and Readers Publishing Co-operative. 1976. *Sexism in Children's Books.* London: WRPC.

Zografou, Anastasia. 1990. 'Explore the way language supports and generates sexist values, concepts and models in the ELT textbook *Turning Point.*' Essay (unpublished), MA in Language Studies, Lancaster University.

III Classroom Processes

Adamson, H.D. and Vera M. Regan. 1991. 'The acquisition of community speech norms by Asian immigrants learning English as a second language.' *Studies in Second Language Acquisition* 13: 1–22.

Alcon, E. and J.R. Guzman. 1993. 'The role of participation and gender in NNS-NNS classroom interaction.' Paper, 10th AILA Congress, Amsterdam.

Algaier, Chas J. 1991. 'A method for teaching literacy to the orally proficient.' *Cross Currents* XVIII/1: 71–3.

Almlov, Cecilia and Britt-Louise Gunnarsson. 1993. 'Gender and the academic seminar.' Paper, AILA 10th Congress, Amsterdam.

Altani, Cleopatra. 1992. 'Gender construction in classroom interaction: primary schools in Greece.' PhD thesis, Linguistic Department, Lancaster University (unpublished).

Aries, Elizabeth J. 1982. 'Verbal and non-verbal behaviour in single-sex and mixed-sex groups: are traditional sex roles changing?' *Psychological Reports* 51: 127–34.

Arnot, Madeleine (ed.) 1985. *Race and Gender: Equal Opportunities Policies in Education.* Oxford: Pergamon Press/The Open University.

Arnot, Madeleine and Gaby Weiner. 1987. *Gender and the Politics of Schooling.* London: The Open University.

Bacon, Susan M. 1992. 'The relationship between gender, comprehension, processing strategies, and cognitive and affective response in foreign language listening.' *The Modern Language Journal* 76/2: 160–78.

Bacon, Susan M. and Michael D. Finnemann. 1992. 'Sex differences in self-reported beliefs about foreign-language learning and authentic oral and written input.' *Language Learning* 42/4: 471–95.

Barnes, Douglas. 1976. *From Communication to Curriculum.* Harmondsworth: Penguin.

Barnes, Douglas, James Britton and Harold Rosen. 1969. (revised version 1971). *Language, the Learner and the School.* Harmondsworth: Penguin.

Bashiruddin, Ayesha, Julian Edge and Elizabeth Hughes-Pelegrin. 1990. 'Who speaks in seminars? Status, culture and gender at Durham University.' In Romy Clark, Norman Fairclough, Roz Ivanic, Nicki McCleod, Jenny Thomas and Paul Meara (eds.) *Language and Power.* London: Centre for Information on Language Teaching (CILT).

Batters, Julia. 1986. 'Do boys really think languages are just girl-talk?' *Modern Languages* 67/2: 75–9.

Batters, Julia. 1987. 'Pupil and teacher perceptions of foreign language learning.' PhD thesis, University of Bath.

Belenky, Mary F., Blythe N. Clinchy, Nancy R. Goldberger and Jill M. Tarule. 1986. *Women's Ways of Knowing: the Development of Self, Voice and Mind.* New York: Basic Books.

Beswick, Chris. 1976. 'Mixed or single-sex for French?' *Audio-Visual Language Journal* 14: 34–8.

Birckbichler, Diane W. 1984. 'The challenge of proficiency: student characteristics.' In G.A. Jarvis (ed.) *The Challenge for Excellence in Foreign Language Education.* Middlebury, VT: Northeast Conference.

Boersma, P. Dee, Debora Gay, Ruth Jones, Lynn Morrison and Helen Remick. 1981. 'Sex differences in college student–teacher interactions: fact or fantasy?' *Sex Roles* 7/8: 775–84.

Boyle, J.P. 1987. 'Sex differences in listening vocabulary.' *Language Learning* 37/2: 273–84.

Bradford Gender Trainers' Group. 1986–7. *Gender Issues Training for Teachers and Lecturers.* Bradford: Directorate of Educational Services.

Briere, E.J. 1978. 'Variables affecting native Mexican children's learning Spanish as a second language.' *Language Learning* 28: 159–74.

Brooks, Virginia R. 1982. 'Sex difference in student dominance behavior in female and male professors' classrooms.' *Sex Roles* 8: 683–90.

Brophy, Jere. 1985. 'Interactions of male and female students with male and female teachers.' In Cora Marrett and Louise Cherry Wilkinson (eds.) *Gender Influences in Classroom Interaction.* Orlando: Academic Press.

Burstall, Clare. 1975. 'Factors affecting foreign language learning: a consideration of some recent research findings.' *Language Teaching and Linguistic Abstracts* 8: 5–25.

Burstall, Clare, Monika Jamieson, Susan Cohen and Margaret Hargreaves. 1974. *Primary French in the Balance.* Windsor, Berks: NFER Publishing Company.

Busch, Deborah. 1982. 'Introversion–extraversion and the EFL proficiency of Japanese students.' *Language Learning* 32/1: 109–32.

Carpenter, Peter. 1985. 'Single sex schooling and girls' academic achievements.' *Australian and New Zealand Journal of Sociology* 21/3: 456–72.

Carroll, Brendan. 1991. 'Response to Don Porter's paper: "Affective Factors in Language Testing".' In Charles Alderson and Brian North (eds.) *Language Testing in the Nineties* 1/1: 41–5. London: Macmillan/British Council.

Carscadden, Lisa, Cynthia Nelson and Jim Ward. 1992. 'We are your colleagues: lesbians and gays in ESL.' Presentation at TESOL 1992, Vancouver.

Case, Susan Schick. 1988. 'Cultural differences, not deficiencies: an analysis of managerial women's language.' In Suzanna Rose and Laurie Larwood (eds.) *Women's Careers: Pathways and Pitfalls.* New York: Praeger.

Cheshire, Jenny and Nancy Jenkins. 1991. 'Gender issues in the GCSE oral English examination: Part II.' *Language and Education* 5/1: 19–40.

Christensen, Carol A. and David Massey. 1989. 'Perpetuating gender inequity: attitudes of teacher education students.' *Australian Journal of Education* 33/3: 256–66.

Claire, Hilary. 1992. 'Classroom organisation, interaction and observation.' In Kate Myers (ed.) *Genderwatch!* Cambridge: Cambridge University Press.

Clark, Dianne. 1992. 'Cultural diversity: lesbians and gays in ESL.' *TESOL Matters*, August/September: 15.

Clarricoates, Katherine. 1980. 'The importance of being Ernest . . . Emma . . . Tom . . . Jane: the perception and categorisation of gender conformity and gender deviation in primary schools.' In Rosemary Deem (ed.) *Schooling for Women's Work*. London: Routledge and Kegan Paul.

Clarricoates, Katherine. 1981. 'The experience of patriarchal schooling.' *Interchange* 12/2–3: 185–205.

Clarricoates, Katherine. 1983. 'Classroom interaction.' In Janie Whyld (ed.) *Sexism in the Secondary Curriculum*. New York: Harper and Row.

Coates, Jennifer. (1st edition 1986.) 1993. *Women, Men and Language*. London: Longman.

Cochran, Effie Papatzikou. 1992. 'Towards degendered English in the ESL classroom: the Medusa syndrome.' *Working Papers on Language, Gender and Sexism* 2/2: 27–35.

Cohen, Andrew D. 1990. *Language Learning: Insights for Learners, Teachers and Researchers*. New York: Newbury House.

Cornett, Claudia E. 1983. *What You Should Know About Teaching and Learning Styles*. Bloomington, IN.: Phi Delta Kappa Educational Foundation.

Craig, D. and M.K. Pitts. 1990. 'The dynamics of dominance in tutorial discussions.' *Linguistics* 28: 125–38.

Croll, Paul. 1985. 'Teacher interaction with individual male and female pupils in junior age classrooms.' *Educational Research* 27/3: 220–3.

Cross, David. 1983. 'Sex differences in achievement [in modern foreign language learning].' *System* 11/2: 159–62.

Crouch, Isobel and Betty Lou Dubois. 1977. 'Interpersonal communication in the classroom: which sex's speech is inferior?' *Journal of the Linguistics Association of the Southwest* 2: 129–41.

Dale, R.R. 1974. *Mixed or Single-sex School? Vol. 3: Attainment, Attitudes and Overview*. London: Routledge and Kegan Paul.

Dart, Barry and John Clarke. 1988. 'Sexism in schools: a new look.' *Educational Review* 40/1: 41–9.

de Bie, Marloes L.W. 1987. 'Classroom interaction: survival of the fittest.' In Dede Brouwer and Dorian de Haan (eds.) *Women's Language, Socialisation and Self-Image*. Dordrecht: Foris.

Deem, Rosemary. 1978. *Women and Schooling*. London: Routledge and Kegan Paul.

Deem, Rosemary (ed.) 1980. *Schooling for Women's Work*. London: Routledge and Kegan Paul.

Delamont, Sara. 1990. *Sex Roles and the School*. London: Methuen.

DES. 1985. 'Boys and modern languages: a DES report from HM Inspectors.' (Copies from DES Publications Despatch Centre, Honeypot Lane, Stanmore, Middlesex HA7 1AZ.) (See also Review in *Education*, 19 April 1985.)

Dunn, Rita, Kenneth Dunn and Gary E. Price. 1989. *Learning Style Inventory*. Lawrence, KS.: Price Systems.

Edelsky, Carole. 1981. 'Who's got the floor?' *Language in Society* 10: 383–421.

Ehrman, Madeline E. and Rebecca L. Oxford. 1988. 'Ants and grasshoppers, badgers and butterflies: qualitative and quantitative exploration of adult learning styles and strategies.' Paper presented at the Symposium on Research Perspectives on Adult Learning and Acquisition, Ohio State University, Columbus. OH.

Ehrman, Madeline E. and Rebecca L. Oxford. 1989. 'Effects of sex differences, career choice and psychological type on adults' language learning strategies.' *Modern Language Journal* 73: 1–13.

Ehrman, Madeline E. and Rebecca L. Oxford. 1990. 'Adult language learning styles and strategies in an intensive training setting.' *Modern Language Journal* 74: 311–27.

Ekstrand, Lars. 1980. 'Sex differences in second language learning? Empirical studies and a discussion of related findings.' *International Review of Applied Psychology* 29: 205–59.

Elliot, John. 1978. 'Sex role constraints on freedom of discussion: a neglected reality of the classroom.' *The New Era* 55: 147–55.

Ellis, Gail and Barbara Sinclair. 1989. *Learning to Learn English*. Cambridge: Cambridge University Press.

Evans, Terry. 1982. 'Being and becoming: teachers' perceptions of sex-roles and actions toward their male and female pupils.' *British Journal of Sociology of Education* 3/2: 127–43.

Fishman, Pamela M. 1983. 'Interaction: the work women do.' In Barrie Thorne, Cheris Kramarae and Nancy Henley (eds.) *Language, Gender and Society*. Rowley, Mass.: Newbury House.

French, Jane and Peter French. 1984. 'Gender imbalances in the primary classroom: an interactional account.' *Educational Research* 26/2: 127–36.

Frölich, Maria, Nina Spada and Patrick Allen. 1985. 'Differences in the communicative orientation of L2 classrooms.' *TESOL Quarterly* 19: 27–56.

Galloway, Vicki and Angela Labarca. 1991. 'From student to learner: style, process and strategy.' In Diane W. Birckbichler (ed.) *New Perspectives and New Directions in Foreign Language Education*. Lincolnwood, Ill.: National Textbook Co. and American Council on the Teaching of Foreign Languages.

Gass, Susan and Evangeline Varonis. 1986. 'Sex differences in nonnative speaker–nonnative speaker interactions.' In R. Day (ed.) *Talking to Learn: Conversation in Second Language Acquisition*. New York: Newbury House.

Gilbert, Jane. 1990. 'Secondary school students talking about science: language functions, gender and interactions in small group discussions.' MA thesis. Victoria University, Wellington.

Gilbert, Jane. 1992. 'Achieving equity in small group discussions.' *Working Papers on Language, Gender and Sexism* 2/2: 55–73.

Good, Thomas. 1970. 'Which pupils do teachers call on?' *Elementary School Journal* 70: 190–8.

Good, Thomas and Jere Brophy. 1986. *Educational Psychology* (3rd edition). New York: Longman.

Good, Thomas, Neville Sykes and Jere Brophy. 1973. 'Effects of teacher sex and student sex on classroom interaction.' *Journal of Educational Psychology* 65: 74–87.

Goodwin, Marjorie H. and Charles Goodwin. 1987. 'Co-operation and competition across girls' and boys' task activities.' In Alexandra D. Todd and Sue Fisher (eds.) *Gender and Discourse: the Power of Talk*. Norwood, NJ: Ablex.

Goodwin, Marjorie H. and Charles Goodwin. 1988. 'Children's arguing.' In Susan U. Phillips, Susan Steele and Christine Tanz (eds.) *Language, Gender and Sex in Comparative Perspective*. Cambridge: Cambridge University Press.

Gore, Dolores and Daniel Roumagoux. 1983. 'Wait time as a variable in sex-related differences during fourth grade mathematics instruction.' *Journal of Educational Research* 76/5: 273–5.

Graddol, David and Joan Swann. 1989. *Gender Voices*. Oxford: Basil Blackwell.

Graham, Janet. 1992. 'Bias-free teaching as a topic in a course for international teaching assistants.' *TESOL Quarterly* 26/3: 585–9.

Gubb, Jenny. 1980. 'Language and roles in mixed and single sex groups.' *Language for Learning* 2/1: 3–10.

Hammersley, Martin. 1990. 'An evaluation of two studies in gender imbalance in primary classrooms.' *British Educational Research Journal* 16/2: 125–43.

Hansen, Jacqueline and Charles W. Stansfield. 1981. 'The relationship of field dependent–independent cognitive styles to foreign language achievement.' *Language Learning* 31: 349–67.

Hansen, M.J. 1982. 'Spatial performance, activity preferences, and masculinity–femininity.' Paper presented at the annual meeting of the American Psychological Association, Washington, DC.

Heath, Shirley Brice. 1982. 'Questioning at home and at school: a comparative study.' In G. Spindler (ed.) *Doing the Ethnography of Schooling: Educational Anthropology in Action*. New York: Holt, Rinehart and Winston.

Hirst, Graeme. 1982. 'An evaluation of evidence for innate sex differences in linguistic ability.' *Journal of Psycholinguistic Research* 11/2: 95–113.

Ho, David Y.F. 1987. 'Prediction of foreign language skills: a canonical and part canonical correlation study.' *Contemporary Educational Psychology* 12: 119–30.

Holmes, Janet. 1986. 'Classroom interaction and the second language learner.' *Guidelines* 8/2: 19–31.

Holmes, Janet. 1988. 'Sex differences in seminar contributions.' *BAAL Newsletter* 31: 33–41.

Holmes, Janet. 1989a. 'Is sex relevant in the ESL classroom?' *Language Issues* 3/1: 14–18.

Holmes, Janet. 1989b. 'Stirring up the dust: the importance of sex as a variable in the ESL classroom.' *Proceedings of the ATESOL 6th Summer School, Sydney* 1/4: 4–39.

Holmes, Janet. 1990. 'Politeness strategies in New Zealand women's speech.' In Allan Bell and Janet Holmes (eds.) *New Zealand Ways of Speaking English*. Clevedon, Avon: Multilingual Matters.

Holmes, Janet. 1992. 'Women's talk in public contexts.' *Discourse and Society* 3/2: 131–50.

ILEA Working Party. n.d. *Equal Opportunities: Gender. Guidelines for Teachers of Languages*. London.

Jenkins, Nancy and Jenny Cheshire. 1990. 'Gender issues in the GCSE oral examination: Part I.' *Language and Education* 4/4: 261–91.

Johnson, Donna M. 1992. 'Consequences of native-like gendered language use in written discourse.' Paper given at 1992 TESOL Conference, Vancouver.

Keirsey, David and Marilyn Bates. 1984. 'Keirsey Temperament Sorter.' *Please Understand Me.* Del Mar, CA: Prometheus Nemesis Press.

Kelly, Alison. 1988. 'Gender differences in teacher–pupil interactions: a meta-analytic review.' *Research in Education* 39: 1–23.

Klann-Delius, Gisela. 1981. 'Sex and language acquisition–is there any influence?' *Journal of Pragmatics* 5: 1–25.

Knubb-Manninen, Gunnel. 1988. 'Cultural background and second language acquisition.' *Scandinavian Journal of Education* 32/2: 93–100.

Kuiper, Koenraad. 1991. 'Sporting formulae in New Zealand English: two models of male solidarity.' In Jenny Cheshire (ed.) *English Around the World: Sociolinguistic Perspectives.* Cambridge: Cambridge University Press.

Kunnan, Antony John. 1990. 'DIF in native language and gender groups in an ESL placement test.' *TESOL Quarterly* 24/4: 741–6.

Leder, Gilah. 1987. 'Teacher–student interaction: a case study.' *Education Studies in Mathematics* 18: 255–71.

Leech, Geoffrey. 1983. *Principles of Pragmatics.* London: Longman.

Leinhardt, Gaea, Andrea Mar Seewald and Mary Engel. 1979. 'Learning what's taught: sex differences in instruction.' *Journal of Educational Psychology* 71/4: 432–9.

Levy, Betty. 1972 (Summer). 'The school's role in the sex-role stereotyping of girls: a feminist review of the literature.' *Feminist Studies*: 5–23.

Lippitt, Ronald and Martin Gold. 1959. 'Classroom social structure as a mental health problem.' *Journal of Social Issues* 15: 40–9.

LoCastro, Virginia. 1991. 'Sex role stereotyping in behaviour.' *The Language Teacher* XV/7: 11–12.

Loulidi, Rafik. 1990. 'Is language learning really a female business?' *Language Learning Journal* 1: 40–3.

Ludwig, Jeanette. 1983. 'Attitudes and expectations: a profile of female and male students of college French, German and Spanish.' *The Modern Language Journal* 67/3: 216–27.

Maccoby, Eleanor and Carol Jacklin. 1974. *The Psychology of Sex Differences.* Stanford, CA: Stanford University Press.

Maltz, Daniel and Ruth Borker. 1982. 'A cultural approach to male–female miscommunication.' In John Gumperz (ed.) *Language and Social Identity.* Cambridge: Cambridge University Press.

Marsh, Herbert W. 1989. 'Sex differences in the development of verbal and mathematics constructs: the High School and Beyond study.' *American Eduational Research Journal* 26/2: 191–225.

Martini, Richard, Kate Myers and Sue Warner. 1984. *Is Your School Changing?* Research and Statistics Branch, Inner London Education Authority.

Merrett, Frank and Kevin Wheldall. 1992. 'Teachers' use of praise and reprimands to boys and girls.' *Education Review* 44/1: 73–9.

Meyer, William and George Thompson. 1956. 'Teacher interactions with boys as contrasted with girls.' *Journal of Educational Psychology* 47: 385–96.

Mitchell, Rosamond, Brian Parkinson and Richard Johnstone. 1984. 'The foreign language classroom: an observational study.' Stirling Educational Monographs No. 9, Department of Education, University of Stirling.

Moredo, Francisca Pao and Wu Zhaoyi. 1991. 'Literacy for mothers of Amerasians.' *Cross Currents* XVIII/1: 69–70.

Morine-Dershimer, Greta. 1985. 'Gender, classroom organisation and grade level as factors in pupil perceptions of peer interaction.' In Louise Cherry Wilkinson and Cora Marrett (eds.) *Gender Influences in Classroom Interaction.* New York: Academic Press.

Mulac, Anthony, John M. Wiemann, Sally J. Widenmann and Toni W. Gibson. 1988. 'Male/female language differences and effects in same sex and mixed-sex dyads: the gender-linked language effect.' *Communication Monographs* 55/4: 315–35.

Munro, Fran. 1986. 'Sex and language use in the ESL classroom.' Unpublished terms paper. Graduate Diploma in TESOL, Sydney College of Advanced Education.

Munro, Fran. 1987. 'Female and male participation in small-group interaction in the ESOL classroom.' Unpublished terms project. Graduate Diploma in TESOL, Sydney College of Advanced Education.

Murphy, Patricia. 1991. 'Assessment and gender.' *Cambridge Journal of Education* 21/2: 203–14.

Murphy, Patricia. 1992. 'Assessment.' In Kate Myers (ed.) *Genderwatch! After the Education Reform Act*. Cambridge: Cambridge University Press.

Murphy, Roger. 1980. 'Sex differences in GCE examination entry statistics and success rates.' *Educational Studies* 6/2: 169–78.

Myers, Isobel B. and Mary McCaulley. 1990. *Manual: a Guide to the Development and Use of the Myers-Briggs Type Indicator*. Palo Alto: Consulting Psychologists Press.

Myers, Kate (ed.) 1992. *Genderwatch! After the Education Reform Act*. Cambridge: Cambridge University Press.

Naiman, Neil, Maria Frölich and Angie Todesco. 1975. 'The good second language learner.' *TESL Talk* 6/1: 58–75.

Nyikos, Martha. 1987. 'The effect of color and imagery as mnemonic strategies on learning and retention of lexical items in German.' Dissertation, Purdoe University, W. Lafayette, IN.

Nyikos, Martha. 1990. 'Sex-related differences in adult language learning: socialisation and memory factors.' *Modern Language Journal* 74/3: 272–87.

O'Brien, Lynn. 1990. *Learning Channel Preference Checklist*. Rockville, MD: Specific Diagnostic Studies.

O'Malley, J. Michael and Anna U. Chamot. 1990. *Learning Strategies in Second Language Acquisition*. Cambridge: Cambridge University Press.

Oxford, Rebecca L. 1989. 'Use of language learning strategies: a synthesis of studies with implications for strategy training.' *System* 17: 235–47.

Oxford, Rebecca L. 1990a. 'Language learning strategies and beyond: a look at strategies in the context of styles.' In Sally S. Magnan (ed.) *Shifting the Instructional Focus to the Learner*. Middlebury, VT: Northeast Conference.

Oxford, Rebecca L. 1990b. *Language Learning Strategies: What Every Teacher Should Know*. New York: Newbury House/Harper and Row.

Oxford, Rebecca L. 1990c. 'Styles, strategies and aptitude: connections for language learning,' In Thomas S. Parry and Charles W. Stansfield (eds.) *Language Aptitude Reconsidered*. Englewood Cliffs, NJ: Prentice Hall.

Oxford, Rebecca L. 1993. *Style Analysis Survey*. Tuscaloosa, AL: University of Alabama.

Oxford, Rebecca L. and David Crookall. 1989. 'Language learning strategies: methods, findings and instructional implications.' *Modern Language Journal* 73: 404–19.

Oxford, Rebecca L. and Madeline E. Ehrman. 1988. 'Psychological type and adult language learning strategies; a pilot study.' *Journal of Psychological Type* 16: 23–32.

Oxford, Rebecca L. and Roberta Z. Lavine. 1991. 'Teacher–student "style wars" in the language classroom. Research insights and suggestions.' *Bulletin of the Association of Departments of Foreign Languages* 23/2: 38–45.

Oxford, Rebecca L. and Martha Nyikos. 1989. 'Variables affecting choice of language learning strategies by university students.' *Modern Language Journal* 73: 219–300.

Oxford, Rebecca L., Martha Nyikos and Madeline Ehrman. 1988. '*Vive la différence?* Reflections on sex differences in use of language learning strategies.' *Foreign Language Annals* 21/4: 321–9.

Oxford, Rebecca L., Young Park-Oh, Sukero Ito and Malenna Sumrall. 1993. 'Learning a language by satellite television: what influences student achievement?' *System* 21/1:31–45.

Parry, Thomas S. 1984. 'The relationship of selected dimensions of learner cognitive style, aptitude and general intelligence factors to selected foreign language proficiency tasks of second-year students of Spanish at the secondary level.' Dissertation, Ohio State University, Columbus, OH.

Pascoe, Joy. 1993. 'Women in international EFL examinations: visibility and representation.' MA Dissertation, University of Kent, Canterbury.

Phillips, Angela. 1993. *The Trouble with Boys*. London: Pandora.

Pica, Teresa, Lloyd Holliday, Nora Lewis, Dom Berducci and Jeanne Newman. 1992. 'Language learning through interaction: what role does gender play?' *Studies in Second Language Acquisition* 13: 343–76.

Pica, Teresa, Lloyd Holliday, Nora Lewis and Lynelle Morgenthaler. 1989. 'Comprehensible output as an outcome of linguistic demands on the learner.' *Studies in Second Language Acquisition* 11: 63–90.

Politzer, Robert. 1983. 'An exploratory study of self-reported language learning behaviors and their relation to achievement.' *Studies in Second Language Acquisition* 6: 54–68.

Porter, Don. 1991. 'Affective factors in language testing.' In Charles Alderson and Brian North (eds.) *Language Testing in the Nineties* 1/1: 32–40. London: Macmillan/British Council.

Powell, Robert. 1979. 'Sex differences and language learning: a review of the evidence.' *Audio-Visual Language Journal* 17/1: 19–24.

Powell, Robert and Julia Batters. 1985. 'Pupils' perceptions of foreign language learning at 12+: some gender differences.' *Educational Studies* 2/1: 11–23.

Powell, Robert and Julia Batters. 1986. 'Sex of teacher and the image of foreign languages in schools.' *Educational Studies* 12/3: 245–54.

Poynton, Cate. 1989. *Language and Gender: Making the Difference*. Oxford: Oxford University Press.

Provo, John. 1991. 'Sex differences in nonnative speaker interaction.' *The Language Teacher* XV/7: 25–8.

Pugsley, Jenny. 1991. 'Language and gender in the EFL classroom.' *The Teacher Trainer* 5/1: 27–9.

Pugsley, Jenny. 1992. 'Sexist language and stereotyping in ELT materials: language, bureaucracy and the teacher.' *Working Papers on Language, Gender and Sexism* 2/2: 5–13.

Ramsay, Eleanor. 1983. 'Language, politics and sexism in the classroom.' *Education News* 18: 20–2.

Rees, Felicity. 1986. 'The wrong gender? (Boys and modern languages – a new light on the statistics).' *Times Educational Supplement*, 31/10/86.

Rich, Adrienne. 1980. *On Lies, Secrets, Silence*. London: Virago. (Essay: 'Toward a woman-centred university.')

Ricks, Francis and Sandra Pyke. 1973. 'Teacher perceptions and attitudes that foster or maintain sex role differences.' *Interchange* 4/1: 26–33.

Riddell, Sheila. 1989. 'Pupils, resistance and gender codes: a study of classroom encounters.' *Gender and Education* 1/2: 183–97.

Roberts, T. 1979. 'Reflection–impulsivity and reading ability in seven-year-old children.' *British Journal of Educational Psychology* 49/3: 311–15.

Ronk, Donald. 1991. 'Vietnam's Amerasian families: The face of jeopardy in resettlement.' *Cross Currents* XVIII/1: 67–9.

Rubin, Joan. 1975. 'What the "good language learner" can teach us.' *TESOL Quarterly* 9/1: 41–51.

Ryckman, David B. and Percy Peckham. 1987. 'Gender differences in attributions for success and failure situations across subject areas.' *Journal of Educational Research* 81/2: 120–25.

Sadker, Myra and David Sadker. 1982. *Sex Equity Handbook for Schools*. New York: Longman.

Sadker, Myra and David Sadker. 1985. 'Sexism in the schoolroom of the '80s.' *Psychology Today*, March: 54–7.

Sandra, Maggie. 1992. 'Language.' In Kate Myers (ed.) *Genderwatch! After the Education Reform Act*. Cambridge: Cambridge University Press.

Sarah, Elizabeth. 1980. 'Teachers and students in the classroom: an examination of classroom interaction.' In Dale Spender and Elizabeth Sarah (eds.) *Learning to Lose*. London: The Women's Press.

Schmeck, Ronald R. 1983. 'Learning styles of college students.' In R. F. Dillon and Ronald R. Schmeck (eds.) *Individual Differences in Cognition*, Vol. 1. New York: Academic Press.

Schools Commission, Australia. 1975. *Girls, School and Society*. Woden, ACT.

Sears, P. and D. Feldman. 1986. 'Teacher interactions with boys and girls.' *The National Elementary Principal* XLVI/2: 30–5.

Serbin, Lisa A., K. Daniel O'Leary, Ronald N. Kent and Illene J. Tonick. 1973. 'A comparison of teacher response to the pre-academic and problem behaviour of boys and girls.' *Child Development* 44: 796–804.

Shaw, Beverley. 1989. 'Sexual discrimination and the Equal Opportunities Commission: ought schools to eradicate sex stereotyping?' *Journal of Philosophy of Education* 23/2: 295–302.

Shaw, Jennifer. 1980. 'Education and the individual. School for girls, or mixed schooling – a mixed blessing?' In Rosemary Deem (ed.) *Schooling for Women's Work*. London: Routledge and Kegan Paul.

Sheir, Alcya A. and Mary Dupuis. 1987. 'Developing procedures for assessing the perception and production of English sentence patterns by prospective teachers of English.' *Journal of Educational Research* 81/2: 103–8.

Shipman, Stephanie and Virginia Shipman. 1985. 'Cognitive styles: some conceptual, methodological and applied issues.' In E. Gordon (ed.) *Review of Research in Education* 12. Washington, DC: American Educational Research Association.

Sinclair, John M. and Malcolm Coulthard. 1975. *Towards an Analysis of Discourse*. London: Oxford University Press.

Sommers, Elizabeth and Sandra Lawrence. 1992. 'Women's ways of talking in teacher-directed and student-directed peer response groups.' *Linguistics and Education* 4: 1–36.

Spaulding, Robert. 1963. *Achievement, Creativity and Self-concept Correlates of Teacher–Pupil Transactions in Elementary School*. Washington, DC: Department of Health, Education and Welfare.

Spear, Margaret Goddard. 1984. 'Sex bias in science teachers' ratings of work and pupil characteristics.' *European Journal of Science Education* 6/4: 369–77.

Spencer, Mary L. with Paula Gilbert Lewis. 1985. 'Sex equity in bilingual education, English as a second language and foreign language instruction.' *Theory into Practice* XXV/4: 257– 66.

Spender, Dale. 1980a. *Man Made Language*. London: Routledge and Kegan Paul.

Spender, Dale. 1980b. 'Talking in class.' In Dale Spender and Elizabeth Sarah (eds.) *Learning to Lose*. London: The Women's Press.

Spender, Dale. 1982. *Invisible Women: the Schooling Scandal*. London: The Women's Press. (Also London: Writers' and Readers' Publishing Co-operative Society.)

Spender, Dale and Elizabeth Sarah (eds.) 1980. *Learning to Lose*. London: The Women's Press.

Stanworth, Michelle. 1983. *Gender and Schooling*. London: Hutchinson.

Sternglanz, Sarah and Shirley Lyberger-Ficek. 1977. 'Sex differences in student–teacher interactions in the college classroom.' *Sex Roles* 3/4: 345–52.

Stubbe, Maria. 1991. 'Talking at cross purposes: the effect of gender on New Zealand primary schoolchildren's interaction strategies in pair discussions.' MA thesis. Victoria University, Wellington.

Sunderland, Jane. 1992a. 'Do teachers treat male and female students differently?' *Lancaster Lines* 5 (March): 18–19.

Sunderland, Jane. 1992b. 'Gender in the EFL classroom.' *ELT Journal* 46/1: 81–91.

Sunderland, Jane. 1992c. 'Teaching materials and teaching/learning processes: gender in the language classroom.' *Working Papers on Language, Gender and Sexism* 2/2: 15–26.

Sunderland, Jane. 1993a (forthcoming). ' "We're boys, miss!": getting learners to reflect on their own and their peers' classroom behaviour.' In Sara Mills (ed.) *Language and Gender*. London: Longman.

Sunderland, Jane. 1993b. 'Teacher-differentiation-of-learners-by-gender: what about the modern foreign language classroom?' Paper, 10th AILA Congress, Amsterdam.

Sunderland, Jane. 1994. 'Learner gender and language testing: any connections?' *IATEFL Testing SIG Newsletter*: 4–7. (Also in 1993. *Language Testing Update* 13: 46–56.)

Swann, Joan. 1989. 'Talk control: an illustration from the classroom of problems in analysing male dominance in conversation.' In Jennifer Coates and Deborah Cameron (eds.) *Women in their Speech Communities*. London: Longman.

Swann, Joan. 1992. *Girls, Boys and Language*. Oxford: Basil Blackwell.

Swann, Joan and David Graddol. 1988. 'Gender inequalities in classroom talk.' *English in Education* 22/1: 48–65.

Swann, Joan and David Graddol. 1990. 'Response to Hammersley's evaluation of two studies of gender imbalance in primary classrooms.' *British Educational Research Journal* 16/2: 145–7.

Talburt, Susan. 1991. 'Reinventing lives: the stories of three Soviet refugee women.' MA thesis, University of Maryland, Baltimore County.

Tannen, Deborah. 1990. *You Just Don't Understand: Women and Men in Conversation*. New York: Ballantine (also New York: William Morrow).

Thorne, Barrie, Cheris Kramarae and Nancy Henley (eds.) 1983. *Language, Gender and Society*. Rowley, Mass.: Newbury House.

Tollefson, James. 1991. 'Refugees: an integrated approach.' *Cross Currents* XVIII/1: 91–8.

Tran, Thanh V. 1988. 'Sex differences in English language acculturation and learning strategies among Vietnamese adults aged 40 and over in the United States.' *Sex Roles* 19/11–12: 747–58.

Vann, Roberta and Roberta Abraham. 1989. 'Strategies of unsuccessful language learners.' Paper presented at the annual meeting of Teachers of English to Speakers of Other Languages, San Francisco, CA.

Walker, Steven and Len Barton (eds.) 1983. *Gender, Class and Education*. Lewes: The Falmer Press.

Walkerdine, Valerie. 1981. 'Sex, power and pedagogy.' *Screen Education*, Spring: 14–24.

Walkerdine, Valerie. 1985. 'On the regulation of speaking and silence: subjectivity, class and gender in contemporary schooling.' In Carolyn Steadman, Cathy Urwin and Valerie Walkerdine (eds.) *Language, Gender and Childhood*. London: Routledge and Kegan Paul.

Webb, N.M. and C.M. Kenderski. 1985. 'Gender differences in small group interaction and achievement in high- and low-achieving classes.' In Louise Cherry Wilkinson and Cora Marrett (eds.) *Gender Influences in Classroom Interaction*. New York: Academic Press.

Weiler, Kathleen. 1988. *Women Teaching for Change*. Mass.: Bergin and Garvey.

Weinstein, Rhona S., Hermine S. Marshall, Karen A. Brattesani and Susan E. Middlestadt. 1982. 'Students' perceptions of differential teacher treatment in open and traditional classrooms.' *Journal of Educational Psychology* 74/5: 678–92.

Wenden, Anita and Joan Rubin (eds.) 1987. *Learner Strategies in Language Learning*. Englewood Cliffs, NJ: Prentice Hall.

West, Candace and Don Zimmerman. 1983. 'Small insults: a study of interruptions in cross-sex conversations between unacquainted persons.' In Barrie Thorne, Cheris Kramarae and Nancy Henley (eds.) *Language, Gender and Society*. Rowley, Mass.: Newbury House.

Whyte, Judith. 1984. 'Observing sex stereotypes and interactions in the school lab and workshop.' *Educational Review* 36/1: 75–86.

Wilkinson, Louise Cherry, J. Lindow and C-P. Chiang. 1985. 'Sex differences and sex segregation in students' small-group communication.' In Louise Cherry Wilkinson and Cora Marrett (eds.) *Gender Influences in Classroom Interaction*. New York: Academic Press.

Wilkinson, Louise Cherry and Cora Marrett (eds.) 1985. *Gender Influences in Classroom Interaction*. New York: Academic Press.

Willing, Kenneth. 1988. *Learning Styles in Adult Migrant Education*. Adelaide: National Curriculum Research Council.

Witkin, Herman A. *et al.* 1962. *Psychological Differentiation*. New York: Wiley

Witkin, Herman A. and J.W. Berry. 1975. 'Psychological differentiation in cross-cultural perspective.' *Journal of Cross-Cultural Psychology* 6: 4–87.

Wood, Robert. 1978. 'Sex differences in answers to English language comprehension items.' *Educational Studies* 4/2: 157–65.

Woods, Nicola. 1989. 'Talking shop: sex and status as determinants of floor apportionment in a work setting.' In Jennifer Coates and Deborah Cameron (eds.) *Women in their Speech Communities*. London: Longman.

Yepez, Mary. 1990. 'A case study of sex-differentiated treatment of ESL students.' Paper given at AILA Conference 1990, Thessaloniki.

Yepez, Mary. 1993. 'A case study of sex-differentiated treatment of ESL students.' Paper, AILA, Amsterdam.

Zammit, S.A. 1993. 'Gender differences, test results, motivation and foreign language: What is the association?' Paper, 10th AILA Congress, Amsterdam.

Zuengler, Jane and Hye-Sook Wang. 1993. 'Gender and communication strategy use.' Paper, 10th AILA Congress, Amsterdam.

IV Beyond the English Language Classroom

Adler, Sue, Jenny Laney and Mary Packer. 1993. *Managing Women*. Buckingham: Open University Press.

Alptekin, Cem and Margaret Alptekin. 1984. 'The question of culture: EFL teaching in non-English-speaking countries.' *ELT Journal* 38/1: 14–20.

ARELS. 1993. *English in Britain with ARELS*. London: ARELS.

Broverman, Inge, Susan Vogel, Donald Broverman, Frank Clarkson, Paul Rosenkrantz. 1972. 'Sex role stereotypes: a current appraisal.' *Journal of Social Issues* 28: 59–78.

Brown, Gillian. 1989. 'Sitting on a rocket: interview with Gillian Brown.' *ELT Journal* 43/3: 167–72.

Burton, Leone and Gaby Weiner. 1990. 'Social justice and the National Curriculum.' *Research Papers in Education* 5/3: 203–27.

Byrne, Eileen. 1987. 'Gender in education: educational policy in Australia and Europe, 1975–1985.' *Comparative Education* 23/1: 11–22.

Byrne, Eileen. 1989. 'Grounded theory and the snark syndrome: the role of the international organisations in research in gender in education.' *Evaluation and Research in Education* 3/3: 111–23.

Cameron, Deborah. 1992. *Feminism and Linguistic Theory* (2nd edition). London: Macmillan (1st edition 1985).

Carscadden, Lisa, Cynthia Nelson and Jim Ward. 1992. 'We are your colleagues: lesbians and gays in ESL.' Forum given at TESOL 1992, Vancouver.

Davies, Bronwyn. 1982. *Frogs and Snails and Feminist Tales: Preschool Children and Gender*. Sydney: Allen and Unwin.

Davison, Alice and Penelope Eckert (eds.) 1990. *The Cornell Lectures: Women in the Linguistic Professions*. Washington, DC: The Committee on the Status of Women in Linguistics of the Linguistics Society of America.

Deem, Rosemary. 1980. 'Women, work and schooling: the relevance of gender.' In Rosemary Deem (ed.) *Schooling for Women's Work*. London: Routledge and Kegan Paul.

Deem, Rosemary. 1991. 'Governing by gender? School governing bodies after the education reform act.' In P. Abbott and C. Wallace (eds.) *Gender, Sexuality and Power*. London: Macmillan.

Equal Opportunities Commission. 1989. 'Gender issues: the implications for schools of the Education Reform Act, 1988.' Manchester: EOC.

Equal Opportunities Commission. 1991. 'Some facts about women 1991.' Manchester: EOC.

Faludi, Susan. 1992. *Backlash: the Undeclared War Against Women*. London: Chatto and Windus.

Fishman, Pamela. 1978. 'What do couples talk about when they're alone?' In Douglas Butturf and Edmund Epstein (eds.) *Women's Language and Style*. Akron, OH: University of Akron.

Florent, Jill and Catherine Walter. 1989. 'A better role for women in EFL.' *ELT Journal* 43/3: 180–4.

Garton-Sprenger, Judy. 1990. 'Why "Women in TEFL"?' *BAAL Newsletter* 36: 9–11.

Goldstein, Tara. 1992. 'Language choice and women learners of ESL.' Paper, Berkeley Women and Language Conference, University of California, Berkeley.

Goodenough, Ruth G. 1987. 'Small group culture and the emergence of sexist behaviour: a comparative study of four children's groups.' In G. Spindler and L. Spindler (eds.) *Interpretive Ethnography of Education*. London: Lawrence Erlbaum Associates.

Guyot, Jean, Ruth Padrun, Evelyne Dauphinet, Yvonne Jospa, Elena Fischli, Marianne de Mestral, Doriana Gludici and Chantal Scheidecker. 1978. *Migrant Women Speak*. London: Community Relations Commission.

Hafernik, Johnnie Johnson. 1992. 'Review of Alice Davison and Penelope Eckert (eds.) *The Cornell Lectures: Women in the Linguistics Profession*.' *TESOL Quarterly* 26/2: 375–7.

Hearn, Jeff, Deborah L. Sheppard, Peta Tancred-Sheriff and Gibson Burrell (eds.) 1989. *The Sexuality of Organization*. London: Sage.

Holmes, Janet. 1992. 'Women's talk in public contexts.' *Discourse and Society* 3/2: 131–50.

Humm, Maggie. 1989. *The Dictionary of Feminist Theory*. Hemel Hempstead: Harvester Wheatsheaf.

Kelly, Rita Mae. 1991. *The Gendered Economy: Work, Careers and Success*. London: Sage.

Lewis, Susan, Dafna N. Izraeli and Helen H. Hootsmans. 1991. *Dual-Earner Families*. London: Sage.

Maccoby, Eleanor and Carol Jacklin. 1974. *The Psychology of Sex Differences*. Stanford, CA: Stanford University Press.

Maltz, Daniel and Ruth Borker. 1982. 'A cultural approach to male–female miscommunication.' In John Gumperz (ed.) *Language and Social Identity*. Cambridge: Cambridge University Press.

McIntosh, Sheila. 1990. 'Human rights and "Free and Fair Competition"; the significance of European education legislation for girls in the UK.' *Gender and Education* 2/1: 63–79.

Mills, Albert J. and Peta Tancred (eds.) 1992. *Gendering Organizational Analysis*. London: Sage.

Moody, Linda A. 1986. 'Women students in our institutions: a response to the U.N. Decade for Women (1976–1985).' *TESOL Quarterly* 20/1: 347–54.

Myers, Kate. 1992. *Genderwatch! After the Education Reform Act*. Cambridge: Cambridge University Press.

Naish, Julia. 1979. ' "The chance to say what they think." Teaching as a second language.' *Feminist Review* 3: 1–11.

Narasimhan, Sakuntala. 1993. 'The unwanted sex.' *New Internationalist* 240: 9–10.

Neff, Jackie. 1992. 'Confronting heterosexism in the classroom.' Workshop given at 1992 IATEFL Conference, Lille.

Nelson, Cynthia. 1993. 'Heterosexism in ESL: examining our attitudes.' *TESOL Quarterly* 27/1: 143–50.

Nilan, Pam. 1991. 'Having fun and thinking deeply.' *Working Papers on Language, Gender and Sexism* 1/1: 88–104.

Ozga, Jenny (ed.) 1993. *Women in Educational Management*. Buckingham: Open University Press.

Pennycook, Alastair. 1989. 'The concept of method, interested knowledge, and the politics of language teaching.' *TESOL Quarterly* 23/4: 589–618.

Pennycook, Alastair. 1990. 'Towards a critical applied linguistics for the 1990s.' *Issues in Applied Linguistics* 1/1: 8–28.

Prodromou, Luke. 1988. 'English as cultural action.' *ELT Journal* 42/2: 73–83.

Redding, Jeanette, Jacquie Thomas and Sue Tomlinson. 1992. 'Stereotyping in EFL textbooks.' Unpublished essay, MA in Linguistics for ELT, Lancaster University.

Rogers, John. 1982. 'The world for sick proper.' *ELT Journal* 36/3: 144–51.

Ruth, Sheila. 1980. *Issues in Feminism: a First Course in Women's Studies*. Boston: Houghton Mifflin Company.

Sampson, Shirley. 1989. 'Australian research on gender in education.' *Evaluation and Research in Education* 3/3: 133–41.

Sekaran, Uma and Frederick T.L. Leong. 1991. *Womanpower: Managing in Times of Democratic Turbulence*. London: Sage.

Shah, Sneh. 1990. 'Equal opportunity issues in the context of the National Curriculum: a black perspective.' *Gender and Education* 2/3: 309–18.

Shaw, B. 1979. 'Sex discrimination in education: theory and practice.' *Journal of Philosophy of Education* 13: 33–40.

Spender, Dale. 1982. *Invisible Women: the Schooling Scandal*. London: The Women's Press. (Also London: Writers and Readers Publishing Co-operative Society.)

Stivers, Camilla. 1992. *Gender Images in Public Administration*. London: Sage.

Summers, Anne. 1975. *Damned Whores and God's Police*. Ringwood, Victoria: Penguin Books Australia.

Sutherland, Margaret B. 1987. 'Sex differences in education: an overview.' *Comparative Education* 23/1: 5–9.

Talbot, Mary. 1992. 'The construction of gender in a teenage magazine.' In Norman Fairclough (ed.) *Critical Language Awareness*. London: Longman.

Tannen, Deborah. 1990. *You Just Don't Understand: Women and Men in Conversation*. New York: Ballantine (also New York: William Morrow).

Tollefson, James. 1991a. 'Refugees: an integrated approach.' *Cross Currents* XVIII/1: 91–8.

Tollefson, James. 1991b. *Planning Language, Planning Inequality*. London: Longman.

Universities' Statistical Record. 1992. *University Statistics 1990–91*, Vol. 1: Students and Staff. Cheltenham: USR.

Wade, Barrie and Pam Souter. 1992. *Continuing to Think: the British Asian Girl*. Clevedon, Avon: Multilingual Matters.

Wilson, Amrit. 1978. *Finding a Voice*. London: Virago.

Women in Publishing. 1989. *Twice as Many, Half as Powerful?* London: Polytechnic of North London/WIP.